THE
CROWN

THE
CROWN

THE OFFICIAL COMPANION
VOLUME 2

*Political Scandal, Personal Struggle, and
the Years That Defined Elizabeth II
(1956–1977)*

ROBERT LACEY

CROWN
NEW YORK

Published in the United States by Crown, an imprint of Random House,
a division of Penguin Random House LLC, New York.

Originally published in hardcover in Great Britain by
Blink Publishing, London, in 2019.

CROWN and the Crown colophon are registered trademarks of
Penguin Random House LLC.

Grateful acknowledgment is made to Aitken Alexander Associates Ltd. for permission
to reprint "Silver Jubilee Hymn," copyright © 1977 by John Betjeman. Reprinted by
permission of Aitken Alexander Associates Ltd.

Hardback ISBN 978-0-525-57337-1
Ebook ISBN 978-0-525-57339-5

Printed in the United States of America on acid-free paper.

randomhousebooks.com

Image credits appear on page 296.

2 4 6 8 9 7 5 3

First American Edition

Designed by EnvyDesign Ltd

CONTENTS

FOREWORD BY

Peter Morgan

THE CROWN IS A HISTORICAL DRAMA ABOUT AN ORDINARY WOMAN born into extraordinary circumstances. It is not a documentary or a docudrama. Everything from the scripts that I write to the costumes, production design and locations that add such richness on screen, as well as to the performances by our two stellar casts – headed initially by Claire Foy and now, in Season 3, by Olivia Colman – is underpinned by a vast and exhaustive amount of research, analysis, thought, care and consideration.

The relationship between history and narrative, fact and fiction, is much more fluid and unreliable, but also more interesting, than anyone might imagine. That is what makes *The Crown* so enjoyable to write – and, I hope, to watch.

I am delighted once again to invite the royal historian Robert Lacey to provide a deep-dive into some of the remarkable history upon which our drama is built. I hope that Robert's expert analysis into some of the events, people and wider cultural context will enrich viewers' appreciation of *The Crown* by providing fresh and often surprising insights.

So, let me hand you over to Robert to take you back to 1956, on the eve of the traumatic Suez Crisis, when there are grave problems brewing in Britain – and problems too inside the royal marriage…

SUEZ, SCANDAL, SOCIALISM – AND TRAGEDY AT ABERFAN

———

*T*HE CROWN MOVES ON ... IN THE FIRST VOLUME OF OUR *Inside History* we followed Queen Elizabeth II from her childhood through to love and marriage, savouring the hidden history of her coronation and her early years of apprenticeship with Winston Churchill – as based on the first ten episodes (101–110) of *The Crown* Season 1.

Now, in Seasons 2 and 3, the Queen must work with prime ministers who are shadows of the great man – the devious Anthony Eden and Harold 'Supermac' Macmillan, as well as with Alec Douglas-Home, whose mistakes paved the way for Harold Wilson, the most successful Labour Prime Minister of Elizabeth's reign. Twenty Netflix episodes (201–210 and 301–310) and 20 matching chapters (One to Twenty) of this book will transport us from the Suez Crisis of 1956 to the Silver Jubilee celebrations of 1977, a saga of intrigue, tragedy, more royal babies – and, this being the Cold War, a surprising amount of trouble with *spies*.

This book, volume 2, tracks the history of the still-maturing Elizabeth II through the second phase of her reign as she feels her way towards more confident regality, while her country stumbles quite dramatically, losing hold of the self-assurance – the smugness, indeed – that characterised the British Establishment after the victory of the Second World War. In 1956 the Suez adventure put paid to London's pretensions that it ruled the world, while the Profumo Scandal of 1963 discredited the elite who liked to think that *they* ruled London. But from these misadventures emerged a more populist identity under the Labour governments of Harold Wilson – for whom Elizabeth II developed something of a soft spot – with the Swinging Sixties, divorce and homosexual law reform, the Beatles, miniskirts, England winning The World Cup ...

In one sense, the monarchy rode serenely – and not a little superciliously – above all these social and political changes. Elizabeth II, her critics complained, occupied a completely different universe from the 'Women's Lib' movement that developed in the 1960s and 1970s – and so she did. On the other hand, the antiquated British system of hereditary monarchy delivered supreme national prestige and authority to a woman throughout these tumultuous years, with an open-mindedness and, yes, a modernity, that the contemporary United States still cannot bring itself to embrace. Every episode of *The Crown* (201–310) – and every chapter of our book (One to Twenty) – plays with this delicious paradox: the sight of powerful men having to bow and kneel to an unremarkable mother of two (of four by the end of Season 2).

This second volume follows the first in attempting to separate history from invention. How much of the drama that viewers so enjoy in *The Crown* is historically 'true'? And how much has series creator Peter Morgan invented? On several occasions we will follow Elizabeth II as she meets characters whom we are 99 per cent certain she cannot possibly have encountered in this way – the rebel peer Lord Altrincham, for example, visiting Buckingham Palace after his dramatic criticisms of the monarchy, or Eileen Parker, the wife of Philip's friend Mike Parker, whom Elizabeth seeks out to discuss her marriage problems. No, dear viewer and reader, these encounters did *not* happen. But, yes, these dramatic inventions have been devised to embody the central themes and messages of the plot. Drama, remember, is not the same as documentary.

Peter Morgan does not write a word of *The Crown* until he has worked out a documented historical template for each episode with the series' research team. Solid factual data – letters, documents, newsreels and first-hand interviews with surviving participants and witnesses – form the backbone and skeleton of every story. Then the writer and his fellow writers add dramatic flesh to the bones, creating a drama on screen that is a unique blend of real history and imagined truths – as exemplified by the famous 'Stag Scene' in *The Queen*, Peter Morgan's Oscar-winning movie of 2006.

Towards the climax of *The Queen*, which depicts the events following the death of Diana, Princess of Wales in August 1997, we see Elizabeth II, played by Helen Mirren, lost in the Highlands of Scotland in the course of a deer hunt. Suddenly she catches sight of the deer, a magnificent Imperial stag, standing proudly on the river bank in front of her – an embattled and harassed monarch just like her, pursued as she is at that moment by the media of the world who are condemning her for her apparent indifference to Diana's death. Elizabeth starts talking to the stag. She senses their common plight, and it pierces her to the quick. Stricken with anxiety as she hears the hunters approach, she then waves her arms and shoos the imperilled beast to run away to safety – which he does. One minute he is there – the next minute he is gone.

The 'Peter Morgan Stag Scene' is taught in film schools around the world as an illustration of how sheer invention, plucked out of the air, is essential to make history performable. No one imagines that Queen Elizabeth II has ever spoken to a wild stag in her life. But it is the scene that people remember as summing up the essential truth of *The Queen* and conveying the totally accurate and historical message of the movie – that if Diana was destroyed by the monarchy, her mother-in-law was another type of casualty.

Every episode of *The Crown* TV series has been imaginatively built in a similar fashion around a major historical event of the period – from the Anglo-French-Israeli conspiracy behind the invasion of Suez in 1956 to the tragic deaths of 116 children and 28 adults in the Welsh mining village of Aberfan in 1966. The corresponding chapter in this book will seek to explain the different layers of that episode, analysing how research and interpretation have worked together to create the final dramatic mix.

In 1956, for example, only a few inner, top-level government conspirators knew the details of the plot that Britain and France hatched with Israel to create an excuse for invading the Suez Canal Zone. Similarly, in 1966 it took months to lay bare the shameful culpability of the National Coal Board in failing to monitor the waste tip that fatally smothered Aberfan's Pantglas Junior School.

So should the dramatist depict such episodes by working solely with the surface, contemporary knowledge and ignorance of the participants at the time? Or is the writer permitted to 'enrich' the narrative with the benefit of hindsight? That debate provides a running tug-of-war through every chapter of this book – enhanced by two illustrated colour picture sections that display *The Crown*'s production stills – reflecting the key scenes from Seasons 2 and 3. Has the screen version improved on history, or corrupted it? The question is there for the reader to decide.

Hilary Mantel, the historical novelist, has offered a profound and illuminating description of the difference between history and the past – two very different horses, in her view, who are each of a contrasting colour. As she explained in her BBC Reith Lectures of 2017, the past is what *really existed* – all the lives and loves and hopes and dreams of the billions and trillions of people who have lived and died on earth since time began. Then along comes the historian – rather like a gardener, suggests Ms Mantel, who is holding out a sieve to try and capture any fragments of the past that might get caught in the mesh: the books and surviving documents, the monuments and artefacts that remain, along with the shards unearthed by the archaeologists.

These fragments make up 'history' – the comparatively few and often banal relics that survive in the sieve. But *most* of humanity's past, all those glorious personal dreams and loves, all the beautiful and creative emotions fizzing away inside people's heads and hearts for countless millennia – all *that* precious reality has escaped history's mesh.

Poor historians! You can sense Ms Mantel's pity for the paper-shufflers who have missed out on the real life of the past through sticking to their stolid, fact-based approach. What a glorious opportunity for the historical novelist and screen writer to pounce upon all those treasures that have passed *through* the sieve, deploying their imaginations to recreate a drama that is both fictitious and true.

'You got it all wrong and you got it all right,' declared one of the Queen's private secretaries a year or so back when Peter Morgan invited him to pass judgement on the early seasons of *The Crown* – and that is the theme examined in the pages that follow. History requires the magic of the dramatist's imagination in order to become performable – which means, in the most basic sense, that the drama you see on screen is 'all wrong'.

But when you take account of the human truths about the Queen and her family that have been confected and conveyed to you by *The Crown*, then the dazzling creation on the screen in front of you can certainly be judged to be 'all right'. That is the paradox which this book now invites you to explore.

Robert Lacey
September 2019

CHAPTER ONE

'MISADVENTURE'

JULY–NOVEMBER 1956

———

'I THINK WE BOTH AGREE,' SPITS OUT AN ANGRY AND WOUNDED Queen Elizabeth II, looking icily at her husband … 'It cannot go on like this.'[1]

Season 2 of *The Crown* opens on a stormy night aboard the Royal Yacht *Britannia*, anchored in the choppy waters of the North Atlantic off Setúbal, the Portuguese port and fishing harbour to the south-east of Lisbon. It is February 1957, and a crowd of British reporters and press photographers is gathering on the quay, their intrusive new telephoto lenses aiming out at the ship across the water.

The media's sniping targets are the 30-year-old Queen Elizabeth II, freshly landed from London, and her husband Philip, 35, who has just arrived in Portugal after a four-month tour of the British Commonwealth, largely in the southern hemisphere, where, among many other duties, he has opened the Olympic Games in Melbourne on his wife's behalf.

Philip's plan after that was to sail home serenely, stopping off in various isolated and seldom-visited British dependencies – the Falkland Islands, St Helena and Ascension Island, for example – while also enjoying a month or so of the cheery naval quarterdeck fellowship that he had had to surrender when he signed up for the royal family.

But now plans have changed. Suddenly the once-respectful British press has become focused on tales of trouble in the royal marriage – 'Intense speculation,' runs one newsflash of the time from Reuters, 'about relations between Her Majesty the Queen and the Duke of Edinburgh'[2] – with rumours of infidelity, and questions as to why Britain's 'model couple' should have chosen to spend more than a third of a year apart. So, to quieten the rumours, Buckingham Palace has decided to bring forward the timetable of the Queen's long-planned State Visit to Portugal, flying her out earlier to be reunited with her husband ahead of schedule in an assertive display of marital harmony.[3]

Behind the scenes, however, in their *Britannia* stateroom, we hear a private conversation that is confrontational. 'The events of the past week …' opens Elizabeth, referring to the leering and suggestive headlines. 'The revelations … have just been too upsetting. Too painful.'

Philip opens his mouth to protest, then looks out of the porthole towards the quay, where more reporters and photographers are arriving.

'So I thought,' says his wife, 'that we might take this opportunity where we have 24 hours alone, without children, without distraction … to put our cards on the table. And talk …'[4]

The tensions between Elizabeth II and her husband provide

the principal personal theme of *The Crown* Season 2. The Mountbatten–Windsor marriage was the world's most scrutinised until the 'Camelot' phenomenon of US President John F. Kennedy and his wife Jacqueline Bouvier in 1961 – which we shall visit briefly when the Kennedys come to London in Episode 208 (Chapter Eight). And alongside this private Windsor theme of marital trouble, we shall dig into the public drama of Britain in decline – the so-called Suez Crisis of late 1956. In a desperate, last-gasp reassertion of colonial authority, British and French paratroopers landed along the Suez Canal at the beginning of November 1956 to recapture the waterway that Egypt's President Gamal Abdel Nasser had dared to claim for his nation the previous July. But this old-time exercise in *force majeure* proved as fallible as the glitter of Britain's once-unchallenged monarchy. Welcome to a nation – and a marriage – in trouble …

'I have never felt more alone,' says Elizabeth, 'than I have in the past five months.'

'And why do you think that was?' responds Philip … 'Because you sent me away.'[5]

In the Preface we examined Peter Morgan's famous 'Stag Scene' in his Oscar-winning movie *The Queen*, when Elizabeth II is poignantly depicted talking to a hunted deer, an imaginary tableau that captures a critical truth. Now here, near the beginning of Episode 201, we encounter the first of the 'Stag Scenes' in *The Crown* Season 2 – when the Queen goes to slip a surprise travelling gift (a ciné camera) into her husband's briefcase before he leaves on his trip to Australia, only to discover the framed photograph of the Bolshoi Ballet star Galina Ulanova staring out at her. What is Elizabeth to make of that?

History tells us that Philip and Ulanova can never possibly have met, since the ballerina rarely left the Soviet Union – and then only briefly to destinations where Philip was not present. In the 1950s Ulanova's celebrity was comparable to that of Britain's Margot Fonteyn, and the Russian caused a sensation when she finally came to Covent Garden with the Bolshoi in October 1956.[6] But Philip was not in London at the time – he was already on the other side of the world, carrying out his Olympic and Commonwealth duties aboard the *Britannia*.[7]

So the framed photograph in this scene never existed. It is a dramatic device intended to acknowledge the idea that the young Queen's husband was popularly suspected of infidelity at the time, without providing conclusive evidence one way or the other – for how do we know? Ulanova acts as *The Crown's* symbol of the various women with whom the Duke's name was linked, accurately or not, in these years notably the Greek cabaret star Hélène Cordet, whom Philip had known since childhood, and with whom he reconnected in the mid-1940s, sparking rumours of romance when he became godfather to her son.[8]

As we shall see in the next chapter, the young Philip (26 years old in November 1947 when he married the 21-year-old Princess Elizabeth) might have encountered some racy ladies at the men-only Thursday Club whose luncheons he attended in Soho,[9] but no solid evidence of marital infidelity has ever been produced. The furore of February 1957 contained a major dose of post-coronation hangover, with the newspapers seizing on the troubles in the marriage of the Duke's private secretary, Mike Parker, whose separation from his wife Eileen became public on 3 February, while the royal yacht was in Portugal, leading Parker to resign 24 hours later.[10]

Then there is the central question as to how much the Queen herself may have shared the general suspicions – did she hear or give any credence to the rumours? We follow Elizabeth in this episode as she goes to Covent Garden, and looks down meaningfully from the royal box at the dancing Ulanova, who stares back up at her as she takes her curtain call. But again, this swapping of glances is surmised. It is known that the Queen did attend Ulanova's performance of *Giselle* at the Royal Opera House in October 1956 during her husband's absence in the Pacific, but no personal exchange was recorded.[11] The imagined sequence is intended to reflect the reality of what many people have wondered about the royal marriage, while leaving the truth in the drama as uncertain as it has always been in real life.

1956 – Galina Ulanova dancing with
the Bolshoi Ballet

While *The Crown* depicts Queen Elizabeth the Queen Mother as orchestrating Philip's World Tour – remarking that Philip needed to 'settle' – it was, in fact, very much Elizabeth II's own choice to accord her husband the honour of opening the Olympic Games in Melbourne. Then it was Philip who suggested that his Australasian adventure might be extended – with his wife heartily supporting this. Elizabeth loved the idea that her maritime husband should have the fun of taking the still newish Royal Yacht *Britannia* (in service 1954–97) on its first trip around the globe.

Mike Parker – Lieutenant Commander Michael Parker VCO AM (1920–2001) – was an old friend of Philip's, dating back to their naval service in the war, so the break-up of the Parkers' marriage was exploited by the British press as a pretext for casting doubt on the state of the royal marriage.

In October 1956, the central attention of Queen Elizabeth II – left alone at home, with her husband on the other side of the world – was focused on Egypt and Israel and on London's attempts to maintain its ancient imperial control of the Suez Canal. 'A squalid episode ends in a pitiable climb-down ...' complained the *Daily Herald* in those weeks, decrying Britain's hapless misadventures in the Middle East that were to bring about the fall of a prime minister and produced something close to a national nervous breakdown. 'Our moral authority in the world has been destroyed ...'[12]

One of the wonders of the pre-modern world, the Suez Canal was first opened in 1869, a visionary feat of engineering that linked the Mediterranean to the Red Sea, eliminating the long and hazardous voyage around the Cape of Good Hope, and shortening Britain's links to its prized Indian possessions by nearly 4,000 miles. The inspiration and execution of the enterprise came from the French entrepreneur Ferdinand de Lesseps, but Britain soon got in on the act. In 1875 Prime Minister Benjamin Disraeli bought up 44 per cent of the stock in the Suez Canal Company to make the British government the largest shareholder in the enterprise.

In 1882 Suez effectively became part of the Empire, when British troops occupied Alexandria, making Egypt a British possession for the best part of 70 years. Then the 20th-century discovery of oil in the Middle East made Suez even more of a jewel in the crown. By the early 1950s more than half of Europe's oil supplies travelled through the waterway with its surrounding Suez Canal Zone, a 120-mile strip garrisoned by some 40,000 British troops, many of them young men who were still serving their compulsory National Service.

The pilots who shepherded the laden oil tankers and cargo ships up and down the Canal made up an elite cadre of French and British mariners, and there was little role for the local population. Not surprisingly, the Anglo-French mastery of Suez was a festering grievance to the Egyptian nationalist movement, headed from 1954 by the charismatic figure of General Gamal Abdel Nasser. The son of a postal clerk, Nasser had risen to the head of the Free Officers' movement, which deposed the Egyptian King Farouk in 1952, and he became an eloquent inspiration to radicals across the Arab world – all of whom made British occupation of the Canal Zone a particular object of complaint.

Britain's post-war generation of politicians shrugged their shoulders. 'Tell them,' growled Winston Churchill to his Foreign Minister, Anthony Eden, in 1954, '[that] if we have any more of their cheek, we will set the Jews on them and drive them into the gutter from which they never should have emerged.'[13]

Churchill was referring to the recently formed State of Israel, which had carved out its existence eight years earlier from the former British Mandate of Palestine in a bloody war that confronted the massed Arab forces dispatched from across the Middle East, fighting them to a standstill in 1947. Britain saw Israel as a natural ally against Nasser and the forces of Arab nationalism that dared to threaten British hegemony in the Middle East, and Israel became one cornerstone of Anthony Eden's policy when he moved into 10 Downing Street as successor to Churchill in the spring of 1955.

In dramatic terms, *The Crown* inhabits Britain's two principal spheres of power and prestige – Buckingham Palace and No. 10 Downing Street. The series' title and its continuous running narrative focus obviously on the Queen, but each season of episodes is structured to portray a new set of political figures. Monarchy provides continuity, while democracy generates change – well, that's the theory, anyway. So, while Season 1 covered the Winston Churchill years of the early 1950s, Season 2 brings the story forward to Churchill's successors, starting with Sir Anthony Eden, whose misfortune it was to be especially burdened by his association with the great man.

As one of Britain's youngest ever foreign secretaries – he was just 38 when he first got the job in 1935 – Eden had been Churchill's helpmate through the difficult days of appeasement in the late 1930s, when he showed himself willing to sacrifice his political career by resigning over his opposition to Neville Chamberlain's accommodation with Mussolini in 1938, a prelude to the notorious Munich Agreement later that year.

Eden was subsequently rewarded by becoming Churchill's Secretary of State for War, then Foreign Secretary and Leader of the House of Commons during the years of the Second World War, sharing Churchill's glory and acting as his heir apparent as the old man plodded through his late seventies – finally, and reluctantly resigning in April 1955 at the age of 80.

No prime minister in modern times has entered Downing Street with a more impressive résumé than Anthony Eden. Promptly calling a general election, which handsomely increased the Conservative majority by 60 seats, and enjoying 70+ per cent ratings in the new Gallup opinion polls that were just taking hold in Britain, Eden seemed set fair for glory. Still relatively young at 57, he retained the aura of the young crusader-against-appeasement, his matinée idol looks now enhanced with a greying moustache and brilliantined hair.

But those who knew the private Eden were not so sure. 'I don't believe Anthony can do it,' confided Churchill to just about anyone who asked his opinion.[14] Highly strung and lacking close friends, the new Prime Minister was 'an exceptionally tense, lonely and shy man', in the words of his official biographer, David Thorpe.[15] R. A. Butler, Eden's feline colleague and Chancellor of the Exchequer, who had been Eden's only possible rival for Downing Street, put it less kindly, describing his new boss as 'part mad baronet, part beautiful woman'.[16]

Eden's solitary and nervous disposition had been sabotaged in April 1953 by medical misfortune, when a surgeon's knife working to remove gallstones had slipped and cut into his bile duct. The accident nearly killed him, leaving Eden susceptible to migraines, liver failure, jaundice and a succession of abdominal infections requiring further surgery. To keep their patient going over these medical hurdles, Eden's doctors prescribed him Benzedrine, the wonder drug of the moment. But this only increased the PM's restlessness, as well as his sleepless nights. According to the photographer Cecil Beaton, Eden complained, rather strangely, about the noise made by the fashionable, small-wheeled Italian motor scooters that were just appearing on London's streets – he said they kept him awake in Downing Street.[17]

Restlessness, insomnia and mood swings – we now know these are the dangerous and routine consequences of taking Benzedrine. But in the 1950s amphetamines were casually dispensed by doctors as harmless stimulants, and their side effects were plaguing Britain's Prime Minister harshly in the summer of 1956 when Egypt's General Nasser dispatched Egyptian troops to occupy the Suez Canal Zone.

Nasser chose 26 July 1956, the anniversary of his ending of the Egyptian monarchy, to make his move, which he announced in code in a speech that opened with some apparently random reflections on history: 'I went back in my memory to what I used to read about the year 1854,' he declaimed to the crowds massed in Cairo. 'In that year, Ferdinand de Lesseps arrived in Egypt.'[18]

De Lesseps was the code word – the signal to Nasser's generals who were listening to the broadcast to order their troops into action – and the Egyptian leader repeated the Frenchman's name 14 more times in the course of his speech, just in case his officers missed the alert. They didn't. Taken by surprise, British troops surrendered the Canal Zone into Egyptian hands.

'Hitler of the Nile'[19] and 'Fuehrer Nasser'[20] were samples of the headlines in the newspapers the next day, and Anthony

Eden naturally made the same connection. 'Military action!' we see him declaring emphatically to his cabinet in Episode 201 making his own attempt at Churchillian resolution. 'There is only one proven way to deal with fascists!'[21]

Eden had encountered Nasser in his days as Foreign Secretary and had sniffed at the Egyptian with a disdain that Nasser detected and fully reciprocated. The Prime Minister looked back to his own glory days in the late 1930s: 'I was right about Mussolini. I was right about Hitler. And I am right about this fella …'[22] But the problem with Britain, or Britain and France, directly retaliating against Egypt, was that the United Nations had moved quickly to play its own role in the Suez situation. A fair number of nations – not least the Soviet Union, which had sent Russian pilots to help keep Canal traffic moving – were sympathetic to Nasser's anti-colonialist stance.

'There can be no military action,' argues Anthony Nutting, the young Minister of State whom Peter Morgan depicts as the voice of scepticism in Eden's cabinet, 'without support from the UN – support we do not have. We cannot go to war alone.'[23]

Eden had, in fact, already taken account of this – and his solution to the dilemma was one of the most barefaced deceptions in modern British history. On 22 October 1956 British and French representatives met secretly with David Ben-Gurion, the Israeli Prime Minister, his Defence Minister Shimon Perez and Chief of Staff Moshe Dayan, at a villa in Sèvres on the outskirts of Paris. Eden had adopted Churchill's advice to recruit 'the Jews', though not in an obvious or acknowledged fashion. In the following 48 hours the three nations cooked up a plot whereby Israeli forces would invade

Egypt to take control of the Suez Canal, thus allowing Britain and France, both ostensibly taken by surprise, to pose as the honest brokers and peacemakers – 'Shock! Horror!' – and intervene to separate the combatants.

'In the early hours of this morning', we hear Anthony Eden explaining in apparently surprised and alarmed terms to Elizabeth II at the end of October, 'the Israeli army launched an attack into Egyptian territory … The Egyptian army has mobilised a retaliatory force, and … Her Majesty's Government has now issued a deadline to both Israel and Egypt to halt all acts of war and to allow Anglo-French forces into the country.'[24] Six days later, on 5 November 1956, Britain and France landed paratroopers along the length of the Suez Canal, taking back possession of the waterway – but to little effect, since the Egyptians sank most of the shipping in the Canal before they withdrew, rendering the route impassable to navigation for the next six months.

It was nearly 20 years before the details of the secret Anglo-French-Israeli collusion at Sèvres were publicly revealed by Lord Mountbatten in an interview in the 1970s.[25] But Mountbatten himself, Chief of Naval Staff in 1956, said that he suspected the plot at the time. There was no way that massive British paratroop landings could have taken place without advance preparations that were widely known in military and intelligence circles. All through August tanks and armoured cars had been getting trucked down to Southampton and put on ships bound for the Middle East. So *The Crown* uses this military foreknowledge to create a fascinating confrontation between the Queen and Anthony Eden.

'When you mentioned that the Israelis had launched an

attack,' says the Queen, looking quizzically at her Prime Minister in their audience of early November 1956, and speaking with a sharpness which makes Eden sit up with a jolt, 'you didn't seem *surprised*.'[26]

This may be another 'Stag Scene' – we do not know the details. Apart from the Queen and Prime Minister themselves – along with their private secretaries who have prepared the briefs for their encounter – no one has the slightest idea what goes on in the weekly audiences between Britain's theoretically ceremonial Head of State and her hands-on, elected Head of Government. The meetings usually take place in Buckingham Palace on a weekday evening when Parliament is in session – pushed back from 6 to 6.30pm at the start of the reign so that Elizabeth could enjoy the bath-time of her children, Charles and Anne.

The primeministerial audience is supposed to cover the government's policy and priorities of the moment, at home and abroad, along with details of cabinet personnel changes – who's in and who's out of favour. According to a few indiscreet prime ministers, the Queen greatly enjoys hearing Westminster gossip and takes a particular interest in matters where she feels personally responsible – the welfare of the Armed Forces, for example.

But all these leaks have come from the political side of the fence. If Elizabeth II has ever discussed her audience conversations with her private secretaries, they have kept that information confidential. So this leaves a free hand for a writer to imagine what monarch and minister might have said to each other in this meeting – and addressing the height of the 1956 Suez Crisis, series creator Peter Morgan goes for the heart of the matter:

'Have we colluded with Israel? In any way?' Elizabeth asks Eden.

And so the story comes out. Eden confesses to his monarch the details of the Sèvres conspiracy and the subsequent British invasion of Egypt, while the background music plays a theme, 'Colluding with Israel' ...

'Six days ago,' admits Eden shamefacedly, 'this Government met with representatives of the French and Israeli Governments in a small village on the outskirts of Paris, where a document was signed – the Sèvres Protocol ...'[27]

This opening episode of *The Crown* Season 2 suggests that Britain's shrewd and still youthful constitutional monarch – aged just 30 that previous 21 April – saw through the prevarications of her duplicitous prime minister to make him confess the truth about his Suez deception. Half a century later, we still lack the evidence to be certain either way. We know that Elizabeth II had access in August, September and October 1956 to the intelligence documents which set out Britain's advance plans for paratroop landings in the Suez Canal Zone in alliance with the French – the joint invasion that did indeed occur.

So this does provide some historical basis for the Queen's confrontation with Eden in this episode, which must, for the moment be judged to be a blending of both invention and the truth. And we should never forget that even invention – shrewd imagination applied to a close reading of the facts – can always constitute a valid reflection of the truth.

CHAPTER TWO

'A COMPANY OF MEN'

NOVEMBER–DECEMBER 1956

O N THURSDAY 17 JANUARY 2019, BRITAIN'S EDITORS cleared their front pages to cover an everyday car accident on a rural road in Norfolk.[28] No one was killed, nor catastrophically injured. But the incident was reported on the scale of a national emergency, only to turn into a convulsive national debate when the 97-year-old driver of the upturned Land Rover took delivery of a replacement vehicle the next day and defiantly headed out onto the public roads again – without wearing a seatbelt.[29]

It was Prince Philip, Duke of Edinburgh, of course, up to his old tricks – the eternal curmudgeon and enduring enigma at the heart of the British royal family. How can a man who is blessed with the love of Britain's gracious Queen behave with such a bristling lack of graciousness? Does he really respect the institution she embodies? And what forces are at play when an apparently trivial issue like one old man's car crash can so disturb the composure of a nation?

The fascinating roots of Prince Philip's contrarian spirit will be examined in a few chapters' time, in Chapter Nine (Episode 209 on the screen) where we address the troubled childhood of the Queen's husband and the family traumas that shaped his psyche. But here we learn how these disturbing questions first tumbled into the forefront of public consciousness in the late 1950s – the focus of Episode 202 of *The Crown* by Peter Morgan, 'A Company of Men'.

The Duke of Edinburgh's world tour through the winter of 1956–7 was originally planned for a number of totally serious reasons – to give the Royal Yacht *Britannia* and its crew their first lengthy proving voyage; to allow Philip to open the Olympic Games in Melbourne on his wife's behalf; and, at Philip's particular suggestion, to visit a number of remote British island dependencies that were, in those days, only accessible by sea, so had never before been visited by any British royals. By the end of his great southern odyssey, Philip had set foot on more of the then-British Empire than any other member of the royal family – a record that stands to this day.[30]

But history has viewed the trip less kindly – as a dated exercise in empire repair that ignored the complexities of late colonial politics, and as a patronising lads' 'jolly'. As one critic put it, Philip and his raucous naval comrades appeared to treat the south sea islands 'as spaces of exotic sexual spectacle for the white male colonial gaze'.[31] We see the Duke splashing ashore to be greeted by bemedalled British governors in white ducks and pith helmets, then vanishing into crowds of clay-caked locals – and oodles of straw-skirted dancing girls. Little is left to the imagination as we watch *Britannia*'s crew succumb to their embraces, and we hear the encounters described in leering tones in the (fictional) letters that Philip's aide, Mike Parker, writes home to be read out to the cheering members of the Thursday Club.

'We've pipped the locals pretty much everywhere we've been,' writes Parker, describing the athletic contests and cricket matches organised by *Britannia*'s crew, 'mainly because cricket as a sport has never been seen before in New Guinea ... Philip, as you all know, is a work-hard-play-hard man who would never stand in the way of a bit of fun, and in New Guinea, as it turns out, there is no such thing as infidelity ... [cue Loud cheers from the Thursday Club members ...] By the end of this tour, I think we'll be able to make a qualitative assessment about where the finest women in the world come from.'[32]

The Thursday Club was 'the gang of cronies that the Duke of Edinburgh used to gather round him in the 1950s' in the words of the humourist Miles Kington, recalling his own time at the club some 40 years later. The basic purpose of the gathering, in Kington's opinion, was to provide the recently married – and hence, tied-down – Philip with 'a bit of fun away from his serious life at Buckingham Palace'.[33] Later feted as one of the developers of 'Franglais', Kington was then a young writer on the staff of the satirical magazine *Punch*. As such, he was rather impressed to find himself rubbing shoulders with the likes of Philip's uncle, Lord Louis 'Dickie' Mountbatten, as well as with Philip himself – along with such free-thinking figures of the time as the poet John Betjeman, actor David Niven and 'Little Larry Adler playing his mouth organ in the corner'.[34] The organiser and presiding spirit of these cosmopolitan Thursday gatherings at Wheeler's restaurant in Soho, was Stirling Henry 'Baron' Nahum, Philip's Jewish-Italian photographer friend who had taken the pictures at the royal wedding of 1947.

Kington recalled being puzzled by the number of ladies present at these supposedly all-male gatherings – 'Flo, Loulou, Beryl, Gertie, Simone, Pat and one or two others ...'

'You men are all distinguished people ...' he later remembered questioning 'Dickie' Mountbatten, 'all distinguished in action or thought or culture...but these girls?'

'Don't knock these girls,' said Lord Louis ...' [They] are all great ladies in their own right – the Duchess of Northumberland, the Percy, the Lady Devonshire.'

'These are their titles?' Kington asked, amazed.

'No,' replied Mountbatten, at that date the First Lord of the Admiralty. 'Those are the pubs they work at!'[35]

This was precisely why Philip enjoyed his 'Thursdaying'. The mildly louche atmosphere of the fish restaurant went some way, at least, to keeping him in touch with ordinary life – and it provides *The Crown* creator Peter Morgan with the ideal vehicle for Philip's Pacific adventures to be related in the letters that Mike Parker reads out to his fellow club members in London by 'Baron' Nahum.

These letters are, of course, imaginary, as are the night-time interactions depicted between the crew of HMY *Britannia* and various local populations. But the timetable and destination of *Britannia's* southern tour of 1956–7 are based on the official records of the voyage, and there are vivid newsreel reports of the royal yacht being welcomed with dancing and feasting at receptions during the day. The sequence of *Britannia* coming to the rescue of a Polynesian man was inspired by an incident when the royal yacht diverted to meet the SS *Mabel Ryan*, en route to St Helena, in order to pick up a naval engineer who was in need of surgery.

While some of the Thursday Club antics may have been exaggerated, what went on inside Wheeler's Restaurant did become more sinister as Parker's wife, Eileen, went digging for evidence to support her suspicions of her husband's infidelity. We do not, in fact, know precisely what evidence Eileen Parker gathered to sue her husband for divorce in 1957. But we do know that she suspected him of having affairs. She certainly went to meet Richard Colville, the Queen's press secretary, in the winter of 1956–7 to give notice of her intention to divorce.

Buckingham Palace's stance towards Eileen Parker's marital problems was politely sympathetic, making no attempt to impede or dissuade her from her course, though they did ask her to delay going public until Philip and Parker were safely back from the tour.[36] Eileen agreed, only for her lawyer to spill the beans at a press conference – held without her approval, Eileen later claimed[37] – and the press pounced delightedly, starting with a dramatic feature in the pages of the *Baltimore Sun*.

'A vague, unhappy discomfort is growing among Britons,' reported the *Sun's* London correspondent, Joan Graham, 'that all is not well with the royal family ...

'The whisper started last summer ... that the Duke of Edinburgh had more than a passing interest in an unnamed woman and was meeting her regularly in the private apartment of Baron, the court photographer ... When it was announced that Philip was to make a four-month round-the-world-tour (which is just ending) there were plenty of people ready to say, "I told you so – he is being got out of the country to cool down." When it further transpired that Baron had been invited to go along as a private guest and not in his official capacity as photographer, there were more wise nods ...'[38]

The *Baltimore Sun* had first discovered the attractions of British royal scandal in the 1930s – Baltimore, Maryland, was the home base of Bessie Wallis Warfield, better known later as Wallis Simpson, and in due course as Duchess of Windsor.[39] Now, 21 years later, the paper helped to whip up another media storm, bringing the press of Britain and the world to besiege the royal yacht in Lisbon in February 1957. Not a word might have been printed if 'Baron' Nahum had not died of a botched hip operation the previous September at the early age of 50. Thus he was not able to take up Philip's invitation to go on the trip – and his death removed the possibility of any libel action from the photographer. Now insinuating stories about Philip could be printed using the credibility of Baron's name, with the *Baltimore Sun*'s 'un-named woman' in the photographer's apartment remaining conveniently un-named and hypothetical, with sinister whispers becoming a matter of public discussion. It was the most severe crisis to face Elizabeth II's monarchy in the first decade of her reign.

The traditional Buckingham Palace response to such a media storm had always been to ignore it completely. But Elizabeth was not prepared to let the allegations go unchallenged. She was furious. She instructed Richard Colville to issue a flat denial – 'It is quite untrue,' Colville insisted, 'that there is any rift between the Queen and the Duke' – the first time that the Palace had deigned to address a personal rumour during her reign.[40]

Elizabeth then told her staff and the Foreign Office to accelerate her travel arrangements so she could arrive early in Lisbon, where she staged a private welcome ceremony to make her feelings clear to her husband and to her personal circle. Having heard that Philip and his *Britannia* companions had occupied their weeks at sea with a beard-growing contest, the Queen organised half a dozen theatrical ginger beards for herself and her ladies-in-waiting to be wearing when Philip bounded up the aircraft stairs and into the cabin.[41]

The story of the theatrical beards did not leak out for several years. But Elizabeth organised a very public gesture on the day after the couple arrived back in London. Ten years earlier, Prince Philip of Greece had had to forfeit both his nationality and his title in order to marry Princess Elizabeth as a naturalised British subject. King George VI had ennobled him on his wedding day, 20 November 1947, as Duke of Edinburgh (and also Baron Greenwich and Earl of Merioneth),[42] but he had offered his new son-in-law nothing grander. Philip remained an ex-prince.

Now seemed the moment to put that right, and on 22 February 1957 it was formally announced that His Royal Highness the Duke of Edinburgh would, henceforward, carry 'the style and dignity of a prince of the United Kingdom'. This was 'in recognition of the great services which His Royal Highness has provided to the country', read the citation – and, with a perceptible dig at the newspapers, it went on to praise the new Prince for 'his unique contribution to the life of the Commonwealth, culminating in the tour which he has just concluded'.[43]

This elevation is depicted towards the end of Episode 203

– with a 'mini-coronation' ceremony, complete with Philip wielding a sceptre. The invented ritual devised for the screen was built around the Duke of Windsor's 1911 investiture as Prince of Wales and was intended to give visual shape to the importance the Queen attached to honouring her husband as Prince of the Realm.

With regard to the ongoing development of the Suez Crisis in the background of all these family events, the screen timeline moves to and fro. Unlike the ballerina Ulanova in Episode 201, the Australian journalist Helen King is a fictional character, intended to embody the temptations in Philip's life and to show him making decisions based on vanity – which, he quickly learns, gets him into trouble. King also provides a vehicle to explore Philip's childhood themes, helping to explain why he was feeling homesick by the end of his tour of the southern seas.

The year 1957 brought Britain its first experience of a full-blown 'rock 'n' roll' music tour in the shape of Bill Haley and the Comets, whose pulsating 'Rock Around The Clock' never failed to get the audience out of their seats – teenagers danced in the aisles. But a minority of troublemakers took advantage of the good-natured mayhem to turn violent – slashing and even ripping out the theatre seats,[44] calling themselves 'Teddy Boys', after the supposedly Edwardian origin of their heavy-drape jackets and narrow 'drain-pipe' trousers. The 'Teds' were Britain's first youth cult of the mass-media age and they made rock 'n' roll the anthem of their rebellion. Disaffected by the inequities of post-war Britain, and sensing the revolution in young hearts everywhere, the Teddy Boys were the working-class equivalent of the 'Angry Young Men' – the theatrical rebellion started in the year of Suez by John Osborne's *Look Back in Anger*.[45]

The new Prince Philip took a keen interest in the Teddy Boys, declining to dismiss them as mere 'juvenile delinquents'. In 1955 he had launched an appeal seeking 10,000 Londoners to contribute £1 each to sponsor a Teddy Boy becoming a member of one of London's boys' clubs. The clubs were to be divided into six groups each headed by one of Britain's sporting heroes of the moment – the athletes Chris Chataway, Gordon Pirie and Roger Bannister, the first four-minute-miler; veteran footballer Stanley Matthews; the flyweight Welsh boxing champion Dai Dower; and Northants cricketer Frank 'Typhoon' Tyson, then the world's fastest bowler, who could fling down deliveries at more than 100 mph.[46]

1956 – Suez on a platter: Anthony Eden
and General Nasser

29

Philip was a pioneer in recruiting celebrities to worthy royal causes, but his scheme never flew. The 'Teds' did not prove 'boys-clubbable' – they *were* rebels, after all – and not everyone viewed them as a pressing social problem. 'Why all this fuss about Teddy Boys?' asked one letter in a London newspaper. 'The boys at Harrow wear tails, wing collars, striped trousers and straw hats. The boys at Eton dress equally as ridiculous in clothes of another century. Why nag at the Teddy Boys? Is it all right for the wealthy to dress foolishly, but wrong for those with less money and social position?'[47]

The Duke went back to the drawing board, and in February 1956 he announced his new youth scheme, the Duke of Edinburgh's Award, designed specifically to attract boys who did *not* want to join a club or dress up in the uniform of a movement like the Scouts or the Boys' Brigade.[48] The Award Scheme's ideas of individual expeditions, social volunteering and the development of personal and physical skills drew heavily on Philip's own experiences as a pupil at Gordonstoun School, which we shall be visiting in Episode 209, Chapter Nine, *Paterfamilias*. Kurt Hahn, the founder of Gordonstoun, had already created the Outward Bound scheme, which cultivated similar qualities of self-improvement to the new award – and Philip had served as Patron of Outward Bound since 1953.[49]

Much of the scheme's organisation was administered and designed by Brigadier Sir John Hunt, who had led the British attempt to climb Mount Everest in 1953 (the news of whose success had reached London on Coronation Day). Hunt expressed the hope that 'the DofE', as the scheme soon became known, would attract Teddy Boys and other individualists of a 'lone wolf' disposition – as a mountaineer, he had fellow climbers in mind – and in November 1957 he announced that girls would also be invited to participate.[50] The first DofE girls received their Gold Awards from Prince Philip personally in November 1959 at Buckingham Palace,[51] and the scheme went from strength to strength in the decades that followed. At the time of writing in 2019, Philip's Award Scheme has expanded to operate in 144 nations around the world, with hundreds of thousands of young people participating annually – quite the most successful youth and welfare organisation ever created by any member of the royal family.[52]

CHAPTER THREE

'LISBON'

DECEMBER 1956–FEBRUARY 1957

———

THE HUMILIATION OF THE SUEZ DEBACLE MADE 1956 A
year of particularly bitter disillusion in Britain, and if one
single voice expressed that discontent it was John Osborne,
the first of the 'Angry Young Men' who – with a number of
angry young women – created the sardonic plays, poems and
novels which expressed the rebellion of the rising generation
in the late 1950s. Osborne's play *Look Back in Anger* caused a
sensation when it was staged at Chelsea's Royal Court Theatre
in May 1956, creating a new, gritty and unsentimental school
of drama which summed up the turmoil of the Suez era.[53]

Always proud of possessing 'an un-tuggable forelock',
Osborne was expelled from his minor public school when he
dared to strike back at his headmaster, who had clipped him
round the ear for listening to Frank Sinatra records.[54] Osborne
found himself on the dole in his early twenties, living on a
leaky barge on the Thames, when he saw an advertisement

soliciting scripts on behalf of the newly formed English Stage Company at the Royal Court in the corner of Sloane Square, beside the tube station.

He had already tried his hand at a few plays, while working on a number of trade magazines, including *Gas World*.[55] Now, in a matter of weeks, he dashed off *Look Back in Anger*, the story of Jimmy and Alison Porter living not in Belgravia or the South of France – still the setting for so many of the Noël Coward-style drawing-room dramas of those days – but in a rented attic in the Midlands, with an ironing board centre stage, over which Alison is leaning as the curtain goes up.

'The room is still, smoke-filled,' wrote Osborne in his detailed stage directions. 'The only sound is the occasional thud of Alison's iron on the board. It is one of those chilly spring evenings, all cloud and shadows. Presently, Jimmy throws his paper down: "Why do I do this every Sunday? Even the book reviews seem to be the same as last week's, different books – same reviews ... Do the Sunday papers make *you* feel ignorant?"'[56]

Next morning's reviews of *Look Back* were far from ecstatic, and it seemed as if the struggling Royal Court, badly in debt after a succession of poorly reviewed productions, might have to close. But then came the reviews from the Sunday papers about whom Jimmy Porter had been so rude – Harold Hobson of the *Sunday Times*[57] and, in particular, Kenneth Tynan of the *Observer*, who, as a critic, was not unknown for his own flights of anger.

'All the qualities are there,' wrote Tynan in his rave review, 'qualities one had ever despaired of seeing on the stage – the drift towards anarchy, the instinctive Leftishness, the automatic rejection of "official" attitudes, the surrealist sense of humour … the casual promiscuity, the sense of lacking a crusade worth fighting for.'[58]

Tynan's glorification of Jimmy Porter's disillusion transformed the fortunes of the play – and also of the Royal Court Theatre, which spits out bravely experimental drama to this day. Osborne himself became the anti-hero of the moment and the spokesman of his generation – particularly after British paratroopers dropped into Suez that November. Dissent became big business, with 'kitchen sink drama' taking over half the theatres in Britain, and across the Atlantic onto Broadway. One impresario even enquired as to whether there might be a part in Osborne's next play for Britain's most famous thespian, Sir Laurence Olivier.

'Laurence who?' asked Osborne.

In fact, the prolific young playwright was already drafting a drama, *The Entertainer*, that contained the ideal role for the great theatrical knight – Archie Rice, a down-at-heel seaside song-and-dance man.[59] When the play later became a movie, it was filmed on the crumbling pier on Morecambe beach, Lancashire.

Drunk, promiscuous and deeply self-pitying, Archie is a thoroughly unlikeable character, whose patter relies heavily on insulting remarks about his wife. 'Why should I care?' runs his theme song – 'If they see that you're blue, they'll look down on you. So why should I bother to care?'[60] Then, in a contemporary reference, we learn that Archie's son Mick is among the British troops caught up in the ill-fated Suez adventure. We later hear that Mick has been bravely killed in action and has been awarded the Victoria Cross – but Archie is unimpressed. 'Look at these eyes,' he says in words that were much requoted as summing up the spirit of Suez Britain. 'I'm dead behind these eyes. I'm dead.'[61]

For Anthony Eden, the architect of Suez, the consequences of the adventure were disastrous. In Episode 203 we see angry demonstrators waylaying the Prime Minister as he arrives at Sandringham early in 1957 to see the Queen.

'Booooo! Shame on you! ... Eden must go!'[62]

In fact, far worse was uttered in bitter and violent anti-Suez demonstrations all over Britain. Opinion polls showed some jingoistic support for Eden's attempt to reassert British authority, but the venture was widely seen as a failure. The country's essential impotence had been underlined by the Soviet Union's forcible and brutal occupation of Budapest in November 1956 to suppress the Hungarian uprising at the very moment when British troops were occupying Suez. As Eisenhower's Vice-President Richard Nixon later put it: 'We couldn't on one hand, complain about the Soviets intervening in Hungary and, on the other hand, approve of the British and the French picking that particular time to intervene against Nasser.'[63]

American disapproval had severe consequences. In three days at the beginning of November 1956 the Bank of England lost $45 million from Wall Street speculation against the pound, and with Suez blocked, Britain's oil supply was dwindling dangerously. US–UK relations had seldom been so low. When London sought help from the International Monetary Fund, Washington actually intervened to stop the move, and the irate President Eisenhower told the US Treasury to get ready to sell its Sterling Bond holdings.

Eden's deteriorating health added to his problems. At the end of November 1956, while British and French troops were still getting established on the ground in Egypt, the Prime Minister's doctors insisted that he must take a break, and Eden transformed a political hiccup into a catastrophe when he decided that he would not recuperate in Britain. He opted to fly off instead with his wife Clarissa to Jamaica, to Goldeneye, the exotic villa of his friend the novelist Ian Fleming, the creator of the recently popular spy character James Bond, 007.

Peter Morgan imagines the suntanned Eden trying to bluff it out as he greets his cabinet on his return to London in December 1956. 'In all these months,' he pronounces complacently, 'we have been a united government.'

'But we are *not* a united government are we, Anthony?' responds his Chancellor of the Exchequer Harold Macmillan acidly. 'The war you insisted on has left us as divided as Caesar and Pompey, and the country is in chaos. There is no petrol in the pumps. There are no tins on the shelves …'

In vain, Eden protests that Macmillan and all the cabinet supported the Suez invasion – 'You would have torn off Nasser's scalp with your own fingernails, given the chance!'

Macmillan shrugs.

'Come now, Anthony, you know as well as I, there is no justice in politics.'[64]

And so Eden went to Sandringham to hand his resignation to the Queen on 9 January 1957, after just 644 days in office … [65]

The dilemma now facing Elizabeth II was the Conservative Party's total absence of any formal mechanism for choosing a successor. At Eden's suggestion, the grandest of the current

Tory grandees, Robert Cecil, the fifth Marquess of Salisbury – popularly known as 'Bobbety' – who had served with distinction in Winston Churchill's war cabinets, agreed to take 'soundings' of the cabinet. These would be backed up by an assessment of backbench MP opinion from the young Chief Whip, Edward Heath, with Winston Churchill stepping in as well from retirement to lend unspecified gravitas to the process.

It was agreed there were just two candidates, with the favourite being Richard Austen Butler, a piercingly intelligent and liberal reformer popularly known at 'Rab' (after his initials), whose great achievement was the post-war Education Act of 1944 which had extended free education to all. Rab had been serving as Eden's effective deputy while Eden had been in Jamaica – so on the face of it, the job was now his for the taking. But Rab's habitually lugubrious features lacked charisma. As Labour's Harold Wilson, who was Butler's weekly fencing partner as Shadow Chancellor of the Exchequer, cruelly put it, Rab sported 'the look of a born loser'.[66]

Butler's older rival Harold Macmillan, who had succeeded him as Chancellor in 1955, was himself often derided for his fuddy-duddy moustaches and his Edwardian courtliness, but he was blessed with an inherent nimbleness. His spring budget of 1956 had introduced the monthly prize draw concept of Premium Bonds, which were denounced by everyone from the Archbishop of Canterbury to the Labour Party as a 'squalid raffle' but had proved an instant hit with the public. Disparaged for his lack of scruple as 'Mac the Knife', the Chancellor was quite happy to be compared to a caller in one of the recently popular 'bingo halls'. While Butler's post-Suez speeches had defended Anthony Eden in a loyal but wooden fashion, Macmillan had contrived an altogether trickier mix of regret, patriotism and party loyalty – along with the suggestion, that somehow, *he* would never have got the country (or the party) into such a mess.

When the cabinet offered their soundings to 'Bobbety' Salisbury on 9 January 1957, their verdict left no doubt. Salisbury had a famous speech impediment, which became immortalised in the question that he put to the 25 or so cabinet ministers in succession – 'Wab or Hawold?'[67] The 'Hawolds' had it by an overwhelming majority. Just three or four ministers came out for 'Wab'. Edward Heath confirmed the preference from the backbench MPs in the tearooms, and Churchill supplied his own breezy endorsement. 'Sorry, old cock,' he told Butler then aged 54, 'we went for the older man.'[68] In January 1957 Harold Macmillan was just coming up to his sixty-third birthday.

Elizabeth II has frequently been criticised for her acquiescence in what have been described as the Tory Party's 'machinations' that produced Prime Minister Harold Macmillan in January 1957 – and she might, perhaps, have made a more obvious attempt to check the 'soundings' with which she was presented. But it was hardly her fault that the Conservative Party lacked a more defined leadership selection process at that date, and they did command a solid parliamentary majority of 58 in the Commons. Love them or loathe them, the Tories were clearly the democratically elected majority party, so it was their business if they chose to pick their leader – and hence the Prime Minister – in the mildly conspiratorial fashion that they did. Salisbury,

Heath and Churchill covered a broadish sample of those who counted in the party and their verdict stood the test of time. When invited to assemble a cabinet on 10 January, Macmillan told the Queen apologetically that he could not guarantee his government would last 'six weeks'.[69] In the event, Macmillan was to serve as Elizabeth II's third prime minister for more than six years.

Harold Macmillan's political style was summed up by the title of the book he had published in 1938, *The Middle Way*. Later it became a political commonplace – to seek a unifying path between left and right – but with Nazism threatening Europe in the late 1930s, it was not the message of the moment. Even the Macmillan family nanny sniffed that 'Mr. Harold is a dangerous pink'[70] – inadvertently hitting on the secret of Macmillan's long-term success. As his biographer, D. R. Thorpe, has perceptively put it, 'Macmillan was not really a Tory at all'.[71]

His First World War experience as an officer in the trenches (in which he was wounded) and the time he spent in his working-class constituency of Stockton-on-Tees – which he lost, but then recaptured by long stints of personal door-to-door canvassing in the Depression years – gave Macmillan a genuine and rather moving understanding of what 'ordinary' people wanted. In the years 1914–18, he later confessed, he learned much from reading his ordinary soldiers' private letters home, as censorship required him to do. He devised a plan to reconfigure Conservatism in a camouflaged, socialistic form, and he carried this liberalism into his foreign policy. As we shall see in Chapter Eight, Macmillan's 'Wind of Change' speech in Cape Town in 1960 boldly swept away decades of colonial tradition and waved farewell to the British Empire.

His modernism and surreptitious egalitarianism infuriated traditional Tories – to the blithe indifference of the new Prime Minister, who relished the social jumbling over which he presided. 'Mr Attlee [Labour Prime Minister 1945–51] had three Old Etonians in his Cabinet,' declared Macmillan in 1959. 'I have six. Things are twice as good under the Conservatives!'[72]

Macmillan's sweeping 101-seat victory in the October 1959 election would have been a Tory pipe dream in the months after Suez, and the credit largely went to 'Supermac', as the cartoonist Vicky grudgingly came to dub him.[73] Suez was not quite the end of the world, it turned out, when voters came to weigh up the price stability and almost full employment that Macmillan was able to achieve by 1959 with his 'Keynesian deficit financing' – the latest academic term for heavy borrowing. 'You've never had it so good,' pronounced the Conservative leader,[74] and the country agreed with him – consigning the Labour Party to an unprecedented third successive poll defeat.

In foreign policy, Macmillan deployed all his charm to patch up relations with America, building on his military dealings with General Eisenhower during the war in North Africa, then creating an avuncular relationship after 1960 with the new young President J. F. 'Jack' Kennedy, to whom his wife's family, the Devonshires, were related.[75] By agreeing to the stationing of US Polaris submarines in Holy Loch, Scotland, Macmillan could claim that Britain remained a member of the nuclear club. Largely for this reason, both Macmillan and his chief negotiator, Edward Heath, fared less well with France's anti-American President Charles de Gaulle in their attempts to negotiate Britain into the new European Economic Community. But the PM laughed off France's rejection with one of his trademark *bon mots*. General de Gaulle, he remarked, possessed 'all the rigidity of a poker without its occasional warmth'.[76]

'Quiet, calm deliberation disentangles every knot' ran a notice that the new Prime Minister had placed upon the cabinet office door.[77] Macmillan was famous for relaxing by reading Anthony Trollope's Barsetshire novels: these entertaining fables of squabbling Victorian clergymen put matters into perspective, he explained, when it came to the patronage of giving out government jobs. Tolerant of the 1960s satire boom, the Prime Minister adored Peter Cook's biting impersonations of his own bumbling style, and he warned his Postmaster General *against* any ban on the BBC's weekly satire programme *That Was the Week That Was*. It was far better, he declared, 'to be mocked than to be ignored'.[78]

The highlights of Macmillan's week were his Tuesday evening audiences at the Palace with Elizabeth II. 'The Queen is not only very charming, but incredibly well-informed,' he wrote. 'Less agreeable, are the visits and letters from the Archbishop of Canterbury [Geoffrey Fisher]. I try to talk to him about religion. He seems to be quite uninterested and reverts all the time to politics.'[79]

To judge from his prolific diaries, the Trollope-reading Prime Minister rather enjoyed his skirmishes with the Primate. Fisher had been a fierce critic of Suez, then fell out again with Downing Street over who should succeed him at Canterbury, with Macmillan favouring Michael Ramsay, the then Archbishop of York. 'Dr Ramsay,' Fisher protested, 'is a theologian, a scholar, and a man of prayer – therefore he is entirely unsuitable as Archbishop of Canterbury ... I have known him all my life. I was his Headmaster at Repton.' 'Thank you, Your Grace, for your kind advice,' replied Macmillan. 'You may have been Dr Ramsay's Headmaster, but you are not mine.'[80]

We shall discover in Episode 210 (Chapter Ten) how the racy Macmillan boom years eventually came to a scandalous bust in 1963 and 1964, but until then the slippery old showman presided over an era of remarkable national buzz and prosperity. Austerity Britain became affluent Britain – cheeky, modern, creative Britain, in fact. It took a tattered and moustachioed Edwardian Prime Minister, ironically, to leach the bitterness out of the Teddy Boys, directing the angry

1963 – Love Me Do: Beatles Paul, Ringo, George and John

energies of the new generation into the fun and youth-driven whoopee of mini skirts, Carnaby Street, pirate radio stations, The Beatles and 'Swinging Britain'.

No longer was it trendy to be 'dead behind these eyes' like Archie Rice. Quite the contrary. When Harold Macmillan retired in 1963, the mingled priorities of his 'Never Had It So Good' era were supplied by John, Paul, George and Ringo in their two massively best-selling albums of the year *Please Please Me* and *With the Beatles*. You could have it crass and materialistic – 'Gimme money, that's what I want'. Or you could have it sentimental – 'P.S. I love you'.

CHAPTER FOUR

'BERYL'

AUGUST–NOVEMBER 1957

I N JUNE 1949 THE DIARIST SIR HENRY 'CHIPS' CHANNON
attended the annual ball at Windsor Castle to celebrate
Royal Ascot race week, where he was struck by the glamour
of 'the Edinburghs', as they were then known – the young
Princess Elizabeth and her handsome husband Philip. 'They
looked divine …' he wrote, 'characters out of a fairy-tale, and
quite eclipsed Princess Margaret', who was cavorting around
the Castle with several dozen of her high-spirited young
friends – to Channon's disapproval. 'Already she is a public
character,' mused the diarist, 'and I wonder what will happen
to her? There is already a Marie Antoinette aroma about her'.[81]

Marie Antoinette was the guillotined queen of pre-
revolutionary France, notorious for her response when told
that the peasants had no bread to eat – 'Let them eat cake!'[82]
True or not, the remark and the French queen's name came
to epitomise over the years the idiot wilfulness of a detached

45

royal lifestyle, and now here was 'Chips' Channon seeing the same detached wilfulness in the behaviour of the 18-year-old Princess Margaret …

By 1949, in fact, the teenage Margaret had already embarked on the first of the ill-judged love affairs that were to characterise her highly scandalous life. Two years earlier, by her own subsequent account, she had fallen in love with her father's equerry, the handsome Group Captain Peter Townsend, on the royal tour of South Africa in 1947. She was a wayward 16, while the war hero, at 32, was precisely twice her age. As depicted in Season 1 of *The Crown*, the couple's romance became public following the coronation of June 1953, when the Princess was spotted outside Westminster Abbey brushing fluff from the group captain's lapel with over-possessive familiarity.[83]

The subsequent scandal was a royal disaster to match the Abdication Crisis. 'It has all been a silly, mismanaged lash-up,' complained the playwright Noël Coward, 'and I cannot imagine how the Queen and the Queen Mother and Prince Philip allowed it to get into such a tangle … I hope she will not take to religion in a big way and become a frustrated maiden princess. I also hope that they had the sense to hop into bed a couple of times at least, but this I doubt.'[84]

The jury is out on Coward's last, intriguing speculation. But some years later the Princess's indiscreet footman David Payne revealed that throughout Margaret's later courtship with the photographer Antony Armstrong-Jones, and even up until the couple's marriage in 1960, there were three precious items that 'never left the Princess's bedside table' – a trio of miniature portraits of Group Captain Peter Townsend.[85]

'Interesting to watch her face,' noted the waspish young Tudor historian A. L. Rowse when he spotted the Princess in July 1956 at a Buckingham Palace Garden Party, eight months after her separation from Townsend: 'Bored, *mécontente*, ready to burst out against it all – a Duke of Windsor among the Royal Family.'[86]

By this date the Queen's younger sister was becoming notorious for the boisterous antics of the friends with whom she was consoling herself – a group of high-born young folk whom the papers were starting to label the 'Princess Margaret Set'.[87] One evening in the summer of 1956 they joined her at a showing of *The Girl Can't Help It*, a recent rock 'n' roll film starring Jayne Mansfield, the American sex symbol of the moment.[88] In a state of high excitement, the Princess was reported to have put her bare feet up on the rail at the front of the circle, so she could take off her shoes and wave them extravagantly in time with the music.[89]

'When is Princess Margaret going to be her age (which is 26),' enquired Anthony Heap, a local government officer who was writing his diary for the Mass Observation Project, 'and behave like a member of the Royal Family, instead of a half-baked, jazz-mad Teddy Girl?'[90]

Back at Clarence House, halfway down the Mall attached to St James's Palace, where Margaret had been living since 1952 with Queen Elizabeth the Queen Mother, the staff were no more impressed. At the end of every evening, footman David Payne would be on duty, standing to attention and waiting for the Princess to come home with her friends, 'tumbling out of their cars, laughing and calling out to each other' – and very ready for a fresh round of drinks.

'They might even decide to have a little late dinner,' wrote Payne, who complained that 'these decisions were always a thorn in my side, for they never thought about it until 11 o'clock or so, which meant I had to wait up all evening, and then stay up to serve dinner at midnight'.[91]

Dinner would be followed by smoking, and the party would then head back to the sitting room. 'Within minutes,' wrote Payne, 'the record-player went on. Brandy and cigars were ordered in quantity, and the "Margaret Set" let their hair down, kicking off their shoes to dance on the carpets, helping themselves to drinks and sorting through the Princess's vast collection of records, from pop singers to Dixieland to real cool jazz.'[92]

It is small wonder that when, in 1961, Payne composed his revealing memoir, *My Life with Princess Margaret*, he could only get his book published in America. Citing the confidentiality conditions of his employment contract, the Queen Mother successfully secured an injunction to prevent publication in Great Britain.[93]

'My Princess's taste was definitely low-brow,' noted the footman disdainfully. Margaret had a 'very fine' collection of classical music, but when her friends came to call, 'the symphonies, concertos and arias remained solidly in their covers'.[94]

The leading characters of the 'Margaret Set' in the years 1956–9 were young aristocrats – Colin Tennant, the future Baron Glenconner; Johnny Dalkeith, the future Duke of Buccleuch; and John George Vanderbilt Henry Spencer-Churchill, the future Duke of Marlborough, who was known as 'Sunny' Blandford after one of his lesser titles as Earl of

Sunderland. Lacking a title, but not short of money, was the tall but stooping figure of William Euan 'Billy' Wallace, the son of Euan Wallace, who had been Neville Chamberlain's Minister of Transport. Shambling and languid with a receding jawline which rendered him almost chinless, Wallace was witty and well-read, with an entertaining line in repartee. He was three and a half years older than the Princess and was constantly proposing marriage to her. Early in January 1956, to their mutual surprise, she accepted him.

The brief – and secret – engagement of Billy Wallace to Princess Margaret opens Episode 304 of *The Crown*, entitled 'Beryl' after the nickname the Princess scratches out for herself, at one point, using a diamond to make her marks on a mirror. Margaret later explained to her biographer Christopher Warwick that she accepted Wallace early in 1956 (the fateful year of Suez) because she felt it was better 'to marry somebody at least one liked' than to end up on the shelf.[95] The previous August she had passed 25, the age by which society women were expected to be safely 'hitched' in the 1950s, with a couple of children. That was certainly what the Queen had managed to accomplish, and Margaret had always fancied herself rather niftier than her sister.

Billy Wallace was amusing and original. He used to turn up at Clarence House in his little Italian 'bubble car', whisking Margaret off to his South Street townhouse in Mayfair, where they were served by liveried flunkies, or down to Beechwood near Petworth in Sussex, well positioned for the polo at Cowdray Park and the races at Goodwood. Wallace's four brothers had all died in the course of the Second World War, leaving him sole heir to his father's seven-figure fortune.

With his faux-diffident style, which some compared to P. G. Wodehouse's bumbling Bertie Wooster – 'I know perfectly well that I've got, roughly speaking, half the amount of brain a normal bloke ought to possess' – Billy was fondly known among Margaret's friends as her 'Old Faithful'.[96]

Faithful, heh? After her experience with Peter Townsend, Margaret had told Wallace that she would only marry him if she had her sister's express blessing and provided that no obstacles were found to the marriage. Elizabeth and Philip were then away on a state visit to Nigeria, not scheduled to return for the best part of a month, so Billy took himself off to the Bahamas – to recover from the recurring kidney infections that plagued him, according to some sources or, according to the columnist Nigel Dempster, to enjoy a final 'bachelor' holiday before marriage.[97] The young man did this in style, staying with friends at Lyford Cay, an exclusive new development comprising a golf club and villas near Nassau that had been started by the Canadian brewer E. P. Taylor – with a beautiful daughter Louise, whom Billy promptly seduced.

'Flushed with his conquest,' Colin Tennant later related, Billy 'didn't even bother to call Princess Margaret on his return. She naturally soon heard that he was back, and telephoned to ask him if he was doing anything that evening. He said, "Nothing much," so she asked him to Clarence House to have an egg or something for supper, and when he arrived he told her all about his fling. She was furious and threw him out … He told me he was rather surprised by her attitude.'[98]

Margaret did not speak to the wayward Wallace for more than a year. According to another friend and member of the 'Margaret Set', the publisher Jocelyn Stevens, the Princess 'became very bitter about Billy'[99] – although she did eventually come to realise what a lucky escape she had had, and even forgave him. Besides, by the early months of 1958, Margaret had developed other interests. Her new lady-in-waiting Elizabeth Cavendish had made efforts to introduce Margaret to a less chinless and rather more socially representative group of friends, some of whom are imagined in this episode: film director Ken Russell; jazz singer George Melly; painter Lucian Freud; pianist and comedian Dudley Moore – and an unconventional young photographer, Antony Armstrong-Jones, of whom we shall hear a great deal more in subsequent episodes ...

On Saturday 23 August 1958, a group of nine white youths armed with iron bars, blocks of wood, an air pistol and a knife, set out on what one of them described as a 'nigger hunting expedition' in the streets of Notting Hill, little more than a mile north of Kensington Palace. By the time the 'hunters' were finished that Saturday night, five black men lay in hospital, three of them in a serious condition.[100]

Matters worsened the following Friday when a mob of two hundred or more whites armed themselves with sticks and butchers' knives to parade aggressively through the streets with shouts like 'Go home you black bastards!'[101] The riots that followed were the worst racial violence that Britain had ever seen – the beginning of a series of conflicts both in Notting Hill and more widely across the country that would provide a sorry sub-plot to much of the reign of Queen Elizabeth II.[102]

Preserved today in the National Archives, the papers that document the first Notting Hill riots make clear that the aggression that summer originated with neo-Nazi, 'Keep

Britain White' activists.[103] There were three more days of rioting, in which local Jamaicans retaliated by hurling homemade Molotov cocktails and by wielding machetes of their own. By the time the violence was over, 108 people had been arrested, with dozens hospitalised[104] – and in the agonised debate that followed, comparisons were inevitably made to the Suez Crisis of two years earlier.[105] In 1956 Britain had forfeited her foreign reputation in the sands of Egypt. Now she had lost what remained of her moral prestige as well. What price the 'Mother' country?

Britain's 'Immigration Issue', as politicians described it, could be traced back ten years to 22 June 1948, when the troopship *Empire Windrush* arrived at Tilbury Docks in Essex carrying 492 Jamaicans who had embarked at Kingston.[106] The image of the new, non-white arrivals filing down the gangplank of the *Empire Windrush* with their suitcases has come to symbolise the beginning of modern British multicultural society. But 20 years later opinion polls showed discouraging support for the views expressed by Enoch Powell, MP, former Health Minister and Shadow Defence Secretary, in his inflammatory 'Rivers of Blood' speech of April 1968, when he criticised current rates of immigration and opposed the anti-discrimination laws that were being proposed at the time.[107]

The Windsor response to the issue has always been to remain resolutely colour-blind, with Elizabeth, Philip and the entire royal family exuding genuine warmth towards a succession of black African activists and, quite strikingly, as we shall see in Chapter Eight, towards Ghana's firebrand leader Kwame Nkrumah. In her 1961 Christmas broadcast, the Queen paid tribute to 'the quiet people who fight prejudice by example'.[108]

But when it comes to racial relations inside Britain, Elizabeth II's own example, certainly as an employer, has been quiet to the point of silence. Through the racially turbulent second half of the twentieth century when the nation's buses, trains and hospitals relied heavily on African-Caribbean workers, there was a striking absence of black faces at Buckingham Palace, with just 6 per cent of domestic staff coming from ethnic backgrounds, by one estimate – and plain zero per cent of the senior courtiers and private secretaries.[109] Only with the marriage of Prince Harry to Meghan Markle in 2018, and the birth in the following year of their son Archie, the first mixed-race member of the modern royal family, has the contentious question been laid, to some extent, to rest.[110]

In the late 1950s Princess Margaret was unique among the modern young Windsors for her obvious non-white interests and friendships. She attended concerts by the American jazz trumpeter and singer Louis 'Satchmo' Armstrong, who hailed

1948 – New arrivals: *HMT Empire Windrush* docking at Tilbury

her loudly from the stage as 'one hip chick',[111] and she was a similar fan of Count Basie and his orchestra who, in 1957, recorded the song 'H.R.H.' in her honour.

Closest of all was the Princess's friendship with Grenada-born Leslie Hutchinson, 'Hutch', the tall and handsome black crooner who had been popular with King Edward VIII and also with Dickie Mountbatten's wife, Edwina – with whom 'Hutch' was rumoured to have had a lengthy affair.[112] Although Buckingham Palace refused, as a consequence, to allow 'Hutch' on the bill of any Royal Command Performance, Margaret always insisted on sitting as close as she could to the singer's trademark white grand piano whenever he was performing at Quaglino's, the St James's restaurant favoured by the 'Margaret Set'. She would chat animatedly with 'Hutch' between songs, and sometimes dance with him, inviting him to go with her and the rest of the party to round off the evening at the Colony Club, George Raft's nightclub in Berkeley Square.[113] But whenever 'Hutch' came and went from these establishments without Princess Margaret, it was usually via the tradesmen's entrance.[114]

Tony Armstrong-Jones may or may not have encountered Princess Margaret at the April 1956 wedding of the Tennants in a significant fashion. Both were certainly present as friends of the couple, and Tony had been commissioned to take the wedding pictures. Tony *did* meet Margaret at a dinner party at the home of her lady-in-waiting, Lady Elizabeth Cavendish, as depicted, though this was in early 1958, several months after the other events in this episode. The image of Vanessa Kirby as Princess Margaret, which closes the episode, is based on one that Tony took of Margaret published in 1959 – his first official birthday portrait of his future wife.

CHAPTER FIVE

'MARIONETTES'

AUGUST–DECEMBER 1957

'THERE ARE PROBABLY QUITE A LOT OF PEOPLE,' WROTE THE journalist and commentator Malcolm Muggeridge in October 1955, '... who, like myself, feel that another newspaper photograph of a member of the royal family will be more than they can bear. Even Princess Anne, a doubtless estimable child, becomes abhorrent by constant repetition. Already she has that curious characteristic gesture of limply holding up her hand to acknowledge applause. The Queen Mother, the Duke of Edinburgh, Nanny Lightbody, Group Captain Townsend – the whole show is utterly out of hand ...'[115]

Thirty months after her coronation of June 1953, the new Queen Elizabeth II and her family were still basking in the ongoing warmth of national veneration, and Muggeridge was a rare voice in arguing that Britain's slavish cult of royalty was both unnatural and foolish – and could even be dangerous. As editor of the satirical magazine *Punch*, charged with what he later described as the doomed occupation of 'trying to make the English laugh', Muggeridge felt that exposure of the royal family to humour and caricature was, in fact, a *healthy* thing, since it emphasised that the royals were 'mortal men and women like the rest of us'.

'To put them above laughter,' he wrote, 'above criticism, above the workaday world, is, ultimately, to dehumanise them.' Such idolatry, he contended, was actually a threat to the monarchy's very survival.[116]

Entitled 'Royal Soap Opera', Muggeridge's article attracted little notice when it appeared in the *New Statesman* in 1955, ignored by all the newspapers[117] and shunned by the BBC as just the sort of diatribe that a one-time Communist sympathiser might well compose in a journal for lefties.[118] Muggeridge gave shape to the discomfort that a minority had come to feel at the 'royalty worship' of the coronation era, but it took the 1956 humiliation of Suez to open more people's eyes and minds – along with the publication in August 1957 of a special issue of a small circulation journal, the *National and English Review* (formerly the *National Review*), that was devoted to 'The Monarchy Today'.[119]

Founded in 1883, the *National Review* sought to promote ideas of social reform within the Conservative Party, notably under the editorship of Edward Grigg (1879–1955), a progressive Tory MP for the Manchester suburb of Altrincham, who had been raised to the peerage as Baron Altrincham in 1945 in recognition of his services to Churchill's wartime government.[120] His son John, the second Lord Altrincham, pursued the same liberal agenda when he took over the *Review* in 1954, attacking Suez when it happened, then deciding to investigate the work and purpose of the crown the following summer because, as he later put it, 'I was rather worried by the general tone of comment, or the absence of comment really in regards to the monarchy – the way we were sort of drifting into a kind of Japanese Shintoism' (Shinto being the traditional religion of Japan that glorifies the emperor with rigidly ritual practices).[121]

Most of Altrincham's contributors to the August 1957 issue were rising Conservatives of a reforming frame of mind, notably Humphry Berkeley, a future MP who provided an article about the royal finances in which he argued that the royal family gave good value for money.[122] The journalist B. A. Young was not so approving in his analysis of recent royal public engagements, suggesting that 34 public appearances in 90 days was 'hardly a back-breaking programme for a company whose principal *raison d'être* is the making of public appearances'.[123] Looking more closely at those 34 royal engagements listed for the May–July 1957 Season, Young noted that only three could be considered 'cultural' activities – adding that if those particular three performances reflected Buckingham Palace's idea of 'culture', then one could only conclude that the royal family had 'deplorably bad taste'.[124]

But it was editor Altrincham who really landed the issue's knockout blow in an unashamedly personal analysis of Queen Elizabeth II that has never been equalled in its directness and vigour – starting with all the hoo-ha of the 'New Elizabethan Age' which had set the theme for the coronation four summers earlier: '"Crawfie" [the young Elizabeth's nanny], Sir Henry Marten [her constitutional history teacher], the London season, the race-course, the grouse-moor, Canasta, and the occasional royal tour,' wrote Altrincham scathingly, '– all this would not have been good enough for Queen Elizabeth the First! It says much for the Queen that she has not been incapacitated for her job by this woefully inadequate training. She has dignity, a sense of duty, and (so far as one can judge) goodness of heart – all precious assets. But will she have the wisdom to give her children an education very different from her own? Will she, above all, see to it that Prince Charles is equipped with all the knowledge he can absorb without injury to his health, and that he mixes during his formative years with children who will one day be bus drivers, doctors, engineers, etc. – not merely with future land-owners or stockbrokers? These are crucial questions.'[125]

Altrincham made clear his sympathy with the royal dilemma – 'the seemingly impossible task of being at once ordinary and extraordinary'[126] – and he acknowledged that the Queen was not helped in this respect by the exclusive and upper-crust character of her advisers. They 'are, almost without exception,' he wrote regretfully, 'the "tweedy" sort'.[127] But he did not shrink from blaming Elizabeth herself for the monarchy's central passivity and lack of initiative. When she has 'lost the bloom of youth,' he wrote, the Queen would have 'to say things which people can remember and do things on her own initiative which will make people sit up and take notice'.[128] So far, she had signally failed to do this, in Altrincham's opinion, and he was particularly critical of her public speaking style and content – or, rather, the lack of either.

'She will not ...' he wrote, 'achieve good results with her present style of speaking, which is, frankly, "a pain in the neck".

Like her mother, she appears to be unable to string even a few sentences together without a written text ... But even if the Queen feels compelled to read all her speeches, great and small, she must at least improve her method of reading them ... The personality conveyed by the utterances that are put into her mouth is that of a priggish schoolgirl, captain of the hockey team, a prefect, and a recent candidate for Confirmation.'[129]

The newspapers that had ignored Malcolm Muggeridge's criticisms two years earlier now leapt on Altrincham's remarks about the royal speech-making with delight and fury – his 'priggish schoolgirl' remark drew particularly gleeful repetition[130] – and Episode 205 of *The Crown* opens with the widespread outrage that the peer's remarks provoked. We see Philip Kinghorn Burbidge, a member of the League of Empire Loyalists (an anti-immigrant group with Fascist origins, which would later merge with other right-wing organisations to form the National Front), striding up to Altrincham as he left the studios of ITV where he had just been interviewed by the news presenter Robin Day. Burbidge struck the peer forcefully across the face, then spat on him derisively, shouting, 'You traitor!'[131]

Imposing a nominal fine of 20 shillings on Burbidge for his assault, the Chief Metropolitan Magistrate expressed his sympathy for the defendant's patriotic feelings. 'Ninety-five per cent of the population of this country,' he declared, 'were disgusted and offended by what was written.'[132] Up in Cheshire, the town council representing 'the ratepayers of this ancient town of Altrincham' joined in the protests, summoning a meeting 'completely to disassociate from' the young scoundrel who, thanks to his father, their former MP, just happened to carry their name. 'No town has a greater sense of loyalty to the Crown,' they proclaimed, 'than the Borough of Altrincham'.[133]

But as the storm calmed, it turned out that quite a number of people actually *agreed* with Altrincham's sentiments. Bill Connor ('Cassandra' of the *Daily Mirror*) reported that readers' letters were running thirteen to two in the peer's favour[134] – and Altrincham's comments appeared to strike a special chord with the young. Forty-seven per cent of 16–34-year-olds agreed with him, according to the *Daily Mail*, as compared to 39 per cent disagreeing – while there was widespread support across all age groups, by a ratio of 55:21, for his arguments that the court's social circle should be widened beyond 'a tight little enclave of English ladies and gentlemen'.[135]

Altrincham had been particularly scornful of the annual summer 'debutante' parties, where hundreds of wealthy and aristocratic young women came to the Palace to be 'presented' to the Queen in a ceremony at which, in all but words, she initiated them as new members of the nation's 'upper' classes, blessing them in a lace-gloved laying-on of hands. In the swing round of press opinion that followed, *Reynolds News* congratulated the rebel peer for 'saying out loud what many people are thinking'.[136]

As it happened, some people were already thinking these things inside Buckingham Palace – starting with the Queen herself, who had from the start of her reign disliked the facile and empty 'debutante' parties where she was required to sit motionless, nodding like a totem, while hundreds of simpering young women, noble, rich and nouveau riche, filed and curtseyed in front of her. Aware of the need to widen her court circle, she had already set up a slightly more relaxed system of welcoming people to the Palace – over informal luncheons where professionally qualified guests like the managing director of Wembley Stadium and the chairman of the National Coal Board could offer her a different perspective from the traditional stuffed shirts.

Elizabeth had already agreed to the televising of her Christmas speech that year, and plans were also under way to rebuild the bombed chapel at Buckingham Palace as a picture gallery in which the royal art treasures, hitherto reserved for the eyes of visiting heads of states and special guests, would now be accessible to ordinary visitors, with the novel and mildly populist possibility that there might be a shop where members of the general public could buy 'royal' souvenirs. Finally, in November 1957, the Lord Chancellor announced that, after 1958, the 'deb' presentation rituals would come to an end, to be replaced by additional garden

1957 – Elizabeth II's first televised Christmas broadcast

parties to which 'guests from more varied backgrounds and walks of life' could be invited.[137]

Some courtiers whispered snidely that the 'deb' parties might actually have been ended a year earlier if the Palace had not wished to avoid being seen dancing to Lord Altrincham's tune, but others were more generous. Many years later in 1988 Martin Charteris, the most beloved and trusted of all the Queen's private secretaries, happened to be on the platform of a well-attended meeting at Eton College with Altrincham, where he told him for the record – 'You did a great service to the monarchy, and I'm happy to say so publicly.'[138]

We know that Altrincham was certainly invited to Buckingham Palace in 1957 to meet Martin Charteris in the middle of the furore over his article, and there is some suggestion that he may also have met the Duke of Edinburgh at that time, off the record. It seems unlikely that he would have met the Queen, but later evidence does suggest that Elizabeth retained over the years a particular interest in her strangely loyal critic, and came to admire Altrincham for the causes and reforms that he championed – not least his proposals for the reform and modernising of her monarchy.

By 1988 Altrincham had long ceased to be a lord. On 31 July 1963 he had taken advantage of the new Peerage Act, which passed into law that day, to renounce his title – becoming the second English peer to seek to step 'down' into normal, non-titled life.[139] Narrowly preceding him in the renunciation stakes was Anthony Wedgwood Benn, the former Viscount Stansgate, whose efforts over several years had brought about this important change in the hereditary system.[140]

Like Altrincham, Wedgwood Benn was the son of a middle-ranking politician – in his case, William Wedgwood Benn (1877–1960), who had served as Secretary of State for India in Ramsay MacDonald's short-lived Labour government of 1929–31. Both fathers had been awarded their peerages in the 1940s (Benn/Stansgate in 1942 and Grigg/Altrincham in 1945) for the same basic reason – to boost their respective political party's numbers in the House of Lords, where hereditary peers continued to exercise the ancient voting majority that they would maintain for most of the century.

Both sons wished to shed this 'honour' acquired by their fathers – the Conservative Altrincham for simple reasons of principle and preference, the Labour Stansgate for additional political motives. In November 1960 Anthony Wedgwood Benn's rising career as the Labour MP for Bristol South East had been abruptly halted by the death of his father and his automatic succession to the Stansgate title, which he found impossible to escape. The Speaker of the Commons denied Stansgate any further access to his Commons seat, or even the right to make a plea from the bar of the house. But the young activist did manage to get his name onto the ballot paper for the Bristol South East by-election that followed his 'elevation', and there he garnered 23,275 supporters – nearly 70 per cent of the vote.[141]

It was clearly ridiculous that the electoral court should nonetheless award the seat in Westminster to his Conservative opponent, who had polled only 10,231, and Benn's right to commoner status and a seat in the Commons became a national issue.[142] In 1963 Harold Macmillan's government agreed to make parliamentary time for the new Peerage Act which would make renunciation possible (and also admit hereditary peeresses to the Lords), and they decided *not* to run a Tory candidate when the no longer noble Mr Wedgwood Benn went down to Bristol again, to be triumphantly re-elected that August at the age of 38. In later years, 'Wedgie' Benn would drop his double-barrelled name as well as his title, to become plain Tony Benn, serving as Labour's Minister for Industry as well as for Energy in the 1970s, then challenging Neil Kinnock unsuccessfully for the leadership of the Labour Party as he moved politically ever leftwards.

John Grigg, the ex-Lord Altrincham, aged 39 in 1963, chose to walk away from partisan politics. Mild-mannered and bookish, with a fondness for Scottish hill-walking, Grigg devoted his life to liberal and humane causes – starting with the challenge of capital punishment, which had been a principal focus of his attention since the early 1950s. 'The gallows is a piece of medieval furniture completely out of place in a civilised modern society,' he wrote in one of the many campaigning articles he published on the subject. 'When it has gone the way of the rack and the block, those who now firmly believe in it will soon be wondering why it was retained for so long.'[143]

Grigg's passion had been captured by the fate of Timothy Evans, a troubled and handicapped character – 'weak in mind and body', as Grigg later wrote[144] – who was hanged in 1950 for the death of his infant daughter Geraldine, in a case linked to evidence that he had also killed his wife. Three years later, Evans's neighbour, ex-Special Constable John Christie, who had given crucial testimony against Evans, was convicted of murdering his own wife in a trial in which he confessed to having murdered a number of other women – including Mrs

Evans, with subsequent enquiries establishing that Christie must also have murdered the Evans's baby, Geraldine. Evans had gone to the gallows protesting his innocence, but the judge had directed the jury to believe the false evidence provided by Christie.

Working with Ian Gilmour, owner and editor of The Spectator, Grigg co-wrote The Case of Timothy Evans: An Appeal to Reason, an eloquent pamphlet that convinced many of Evans's innocence.[145] Then in October 1955 Grigg joined Gilmour and the editors of The Observer and The Yorkshire Post in a delegation to the Home Secretary, Major Gwilym Lloyd George, to request a review of the case. Their request was rejected, but both men continued to argue on the basis of other miscarriages of justice – notably the hangings of Derek Bentley in 1953[146] and Ruth Ellis in 1955[147] – with Altrincham serving as treasurer of the National Campaign for the Abolition of Capital Punishment (NCACP).

Their persistence was rewarded with the new Homicide Act of 1957,[148] which significantly reduced the number of offences punishable by execution, followed eight years later by the Murder (Abolition of Death Penalty) Act 1965,[149] guided through the Commons by the veteran Labour campaigner Sydney Silverman. This Act suspended capital punishment for five years (abolition became permanent in 1969), and in October 1966, Labour Home Secretary Roy Jenkins formally recommended a posthumous royal pardon for Timothy Evans that was granted in October 1966.[150]

'Man is born to err,' wrote Grigg in The Guardian a few days later, 'yet it is the hardest thing in the world to persuade officialdom (which includes the legal establishment) to admit that it has made a mistake. Ordinary people were convinced long ago that Timothy Evans was probably innocent, and they welcome the Home Secretary's decision – so prompt by him, so belated by the State.'[151]

In his moment of triumph after a dozen years' hard fighting, it was typical that John Grigg should take no credit at all for himself and his fellow campaigners, choosing instead to bestow praise on Roy Jenkins. 'In his short time at the Home Office,' he wrote, 'he has already given clear evidence of being the best man in the job this century, and quite possibly the best since [Robert] Peel.'[152]

In 1960 Grigg had had to close down his *National and English Review* for lack of funds, but he continued his social campaigning through the pages of *The Times,* The *Spectator,* and particularly *The Guardian*, where, for more than a decade, his eloquent weekly columns helped nudge late twentieth-century Britain into being a fairer, calmer and more equal place: justice for Timothy Evans, the end of the gallows, racial equality, homosexual law reform, divorce law reform, women priests in the Church of England – many were the causes for which John Grigg (who died in 2001, aged 77) fought bravely and successfully over the years.

But people always tended to remember the former Lord Altrincham as the naughty young peer who had once dared to criticise the Queen, often asking him to explain why he had so hated the monarchy. To which the erudite Grigg liked to reply briefly with a question: 'Does a literary critic hate books?'[153]

CHAPTER SIX

'VERGANGENHEIT'

AUGUST 1957

———

Documents on German Foreign Policy 1918–1945: Series D, Volume X *(1937–1945), The War Years, June 23–August 31, 1940,* Editor-in-Chief (Great Britain) – The Hon. Margaret Lambert, published by Her Majesty's Stationery Office, August 1957 …[154]

It was hardly the shortest or snappiest of titles for a book, and it was certainly not the most fashionable of publishers, but HMSO's tenth collection of Nazi wartime documents caused something of a stir when it landed in London at the end of the summer after Suez. For there on page 2 (and appearing on 17 other pages), nestling cosily in the company of Hitler, Goering, Hess, Himmler, Ribbentrop and the very worst villains of the Third Reich was the name of His Royal Highness Edward Albert Christian George Andrew Patrick David – Prince of Wales, King Edward VIII and Duke of Windsor – along with that of his wife Wallis, the Duchess.[155]

Little more than a decade following the desperate and bloody events of the Second World War, people could read in black and white how the exiled Windsors had welcomed and negotiated quite seriously with Nazi agents in 1940, not treating them as Britain's mortal enemies – but, quite the contrary, as their friends.

The papers documented a series of secret negotiations between the Duke and Duchess and German diplomats in Madrid and Lisbon in the first summer of the war, at one of the darkest moments in the hostilities, when, far from offering the slightest disagreement with the Axis mission to subjugate Britain, the couple had conferred in cordial terms with Hitler's Iberian emissaries – and had even offered them advice on their war strategy.[156] It seemed to be smiles all round, in fact, whenever these two Windsors and Fascists met.

Episode 206 of *The Crown* opens with the literal unearthing of these sinister revelations – in US-occupied Thuringia, central Germany, on 14 May 1945, a few days following Hitler's suicide and the Axis surrender of German forces to Britain's General Bernard Montgomery.[157] We find ourselves in a bright, sunlit pine forest, following a convoy of US Jeeps and other military vehicles through the woods as captured Nazi translator, Carl von Loesch, speaking impeccable English, guides the victorious US and British intelligence officers to a small clearing, where he points to a spot beneath the trees. Digging reveals a metal can wrapped in an old waterproof cape, and when the can is taken back to the nearby castle of Marburg it is opened to reveal Nazi documents and numerous metal canisters containing microfilm.[158]

We watch analysts thread the microfilm into a reader,

scanning the copied documents – letters and despatches dated June, July and August 1940 – until they come across the names 'Hitler', 'Windsor' and 'Ribbentrop' appearing alongside each other in typewritten German script, not just in one document but in a whole sequence relating to a series of Windsor–Nazi flirtations that had taken place five years earlier while the Duke and Duchess were staying in Lisbon.[159] We see the documents being gathered together into one dossier – known henceforward as the 'Marburg File' – and we follow the file as it makes its way up through the ranks of US and UK intelligence to end up in front of the Duke's horrified brother, King George VI.

The pictures of this opening sequence closely trace what happened in real life – right down to the can of documents and microfilms wrapped in the old waterproof cape. Carl von Loesch was an assistant to Hitler's chief interpreter, Paul Schmidt, and, to sidestep war crimes charges, he had parlayed his knowledge of where he and Schmidt had buried Ribbentrop's most sensitive archives, including such treasures as the secret protocols of the Nazi–Soviet Pact negotiated with Soviet Foreign Minister Molotov in August 1939.[160] Also in the cache were the damning details of Ribbentrop's dealings with the Duke and Duchess when they took refuge in Spain and Portugal the following summer.

The Duke and Duchess had headed for Fascist Spain at the end of June 1940 as German armies swept across France, fleeing from their villa near Cannes to stop in Barcelona and Madrid, then moving south to Portugal, where they took up residence in a villa in Cascais, just outside Lisbon. They were scared for their own safety, they were worried about the fate and contents of their two houses in German-conquered territory and the Duke was also seeking a new wartime role (he had previously been attached to the headquarters staff of the defeated Allied troops in France).

But when Winston Churchill telegraphed urgently to offer the couple immediate sanctuary in England, with a plane to bring them home, the ex-King refused – on the grounds that his brother George VI and his family, and particularly his mother Queen Mary, were still declining to accord Wallis the full royal dignity of 'Her Royal Highness' status, and would not receive her at all, in fact. The Duke preferred to stay out of the country and risk enemy capture rather than accept that 'dishonour' to his wife[161] – though he had not done much for his own honour by forsaking his military post as the Germans approached France. Any regular staff officer would have faced court martial for such unauthorised desertion.

With the Battle of Britain raging in the skies overhead, and the British Army struggling to get home from Dunkirk, it might be imagined that Winston Churchill had better things to worry about in the summer of 1940 than squabbles in the royal family. But early that July the Prime Minister sat down with the war cabinet to puzzle out an ingenious solution to assuage royal pride – and also limit the Duke and Duchess's ability to connect with the enemy. The former King would be offered the plumed pomp of colonial governorship in the Bahamas, an archipelago a few hundred miles off the coast of Florida (and within flying distance of the shops of New York). The Duke would become Governor, while the Duchess could play Her Grace (*not* Her Royal Highness) with the local community more than 4,000 miles away from London. George VI – and his mother Queen Mary – gave the plan the nod.

Yet the Duke continued to say 'No'. He yearned for more recognition from his family, and he had come to feel affronted by the absence of his personal bagpiper and batman, Alistair Fletcher, who had been called up for military duty. The ex-King grudgingly accepted the idea of service in the Bahamas – but he declined to travel there until Piper Fletcher had been discharged from his regiment and was back polishing his shoes again. The highlight of any evening with the Duke and Duchess was the moment when Fletcher – or, on occasions, the Duke himself – piped the guests in for dinner.

To seek to blackmail the British government at such a perilous moment over the services of an able-bodied young serviceman surely verged on sabotage, if not downright treason on the Duke's part – 'It's incredible to haggle in such a way at this time,' wrote George VI's private secretary, Alec Hardinge.[162] And it was at this point in Lisbon that local German agents who were aware of the stand-off with London – though not of the scarcely believable detail of the bagpipe-playing batman – stepped forward on German Foreign Minister Ribbentrop's behalf.

Ribbentrop had socialised with the Duke and Duchess when they visited Germany in October 1937 to be lionised by Hitler and other leading Nazis, and he had first-hand knowledge of their pro-Fascist and dismissively anti-Semitic views.[163] He got on well with the couple. There were even rumours that he had enjoyed an affair with the Duchess during visits to London in the early 1930s – with the picturesque legend that he sent her a bouquet of 17 carnations to commemorate the number of times that they had slept together.[164]

This seems more than fanciful. There is little evidence to

show that the Duchess and Ribbentrop were in the same place at the same time frequently enough to consummate an affair once, let alone 17 times. But less than a year after the Abdication, the exiled couple had been delighted to find a friendly head of state willing to receive them with full honours – and when he met Hitler, the Duke had even ventured a tentative, raised-arm Nazi salute.[165] Two and a half years later, in July 1940, Ribbentrop continued the conversations that were to be republished so damningly in the *Documents on German Foreign Policy, Series D* Volume X.

The Duke had already expressed himself in Madrid '... in strong terms against Churchill and against this war'.[166] Now Spanish agents in Lisbon reported that 'the Duke intends to postpone his departure for the Bahama Islands as long as possible ... in hope of a turn of events favourable to him'.[167] What could that 'turn of events' possibly be, after the retreat from Dunkirk and with Britain on the verge of collapse? 'He characterises himself as a firm supporter of a peaceful arrangement with Germany,' reported Oswald von Hoyningen-Huene, the German ambassador to Lisbon, who concluded his report with an encouragingly disloyal titbit: 'The Duke definitely believes that continued severe bombings would make England ready for peace.'[168]

Ribbentrop's agents warmed up the Duke and Duchess by allowing the Duchess to send her maid Jeanne-Marguerite Moulichon to Paris to retrieve some treasured possessions, and by promising to maintain 'an unobtrusive observation of the residence of the Duke' throughout the German occupation of the city.[169] Then they got serious, inviting the Duke and Duchessto leave Lisbon and come back to Spain, 'since the

Duke was likely yet to be called upon to play an important role in English policy and possibly to ascend the English throne'.[170] This intriguing idea, noted the German ambassador Eberhard von Stohrer – the notion that the Germans were planning to depose George VI in the event of conquering Britain and to restore the crown to his elder brother – caused both Windsors to fall silent. 'The Duchess especially became very pensive.'[171]

When these damning revelations were published in 1957, the Duke of Windsor issued what he called a *démenti*, describing the German allegations as 'in part complete fabrications and in part gross distortions of the truth',[172] and the Foreign Office of the time backed him up, shrugging the charges off as enemy fantasy and malice. But after the Duke's death, the FO would disclose the compelling testimony of a *British* source, Marcus Cheke, a junior diplomat at the Lisbon embassy, who painstakingly noted the ex-King saying in July 1940 very much the same thing that the Germans had claimed. According to Cheke's informant, 'the Duke predicted the fall of the Churchill government, and its replacement by a Labour government which would negotiate peace with the Germans. The King [George VI] would abdicate, there would be a virtual revolution, and he (the Duke) would be recalled. Britain would then lead a coalition of France, Spain and Portugal, and Germany would be left free to march on Russia.'[173]

The Duke of Windsor was planning, in other words, to become London's equivalent of Vidkun Quisling, the Norwegian politician who ruled wartime Norway for Hitler and who made the name 'Quisling' a byword for 'collaborator' or 'traitor'.[174] The Duke's defeatist attitude hardly matched the stirring spirit that Winston Churchill had famously put into words in the House of Commons on 4 June 1940 a few weeks earlier: 'Even though large tracts of Europe and many old and famous states have fallen or may fall into the grip of the Gestapo and all the odious apparatus of Nazi rule,' he declaimed, 'we shall not flag or fail. We shall go on to the end ...'[175]

The Duke and Duchess of Windsor did not appear to find the prospect of the Nazi grip so odious. When Winston Churchill ordered the couple to make their way to the Bahamas without delay in the early days of July 1940, the Duke threatened to resign all his military ranks, while also demanding full financial compensation from the Civil List or other public funds for any move that might jeopardise his non-resident taxation status. He refused to leave Lisbon, and, as July advanced, he kept playing for time, talking to Ribbentrop's messengers while awaiting the return of his wife's maid from Paris, and also keeping a sharp eye on events in Britain.

Towards the end of the month, however, Windsor confided to von Stohrer that he *would*, in fact, now embark for the Bahamas since 'no prospect of peace existed at the moment'.[176] In the Duke's latest judgement, 'the situation in England at the moment was still by no means hopeless. Therefore, he should not now, by negotiations carried on contrary to the orders of his Government, let loose against himself the propaganda of his English opponents ... He could, if the occasion arose, take action even from the Bahamas.'[177]

On the very last day of July 1940, the day before he was due to set sail for Nassau, the Duke had a final meeting with his Lisbon contact, assuring him that he paid 'full tribute to the Führer's desire for peace, which was in complete agreement with his own point of view. He was firmly convinced that if he had been King it would never have come to war', and he promised that he stood ready to return to England as soon as the moment was right.[178] The Duke had exchanged secret contact details with his confidant, 'and had agreed with him upon a code word, upon receiving which he would come back over'. These statements, concluded the dispatch, were 'supported by firmness of will and the deepest sincerity, and had included an expression of admiration and sympathy for the Führer'.[179]

It seems astonishing today that not a word of these startling Windsor promises to enemy agents found their way into the newspapers when they were revealed a decade and a half later. Whether totally true, totally imagined by the Germans, or something in between, the ex-King's words were set out for all to read and judge in the official 615-page Stationery Office volume published in August 1957, and they remain to this day as authentic historical documents in the public domain. But Fleet Street chose to avoid controversy in the touchy months following Suez, taking its cue from the Foreign Office and noting the ex-King's fondness for libel actions – he had enjoyed some success before the war suing the publishers William Heinemann for mildly adverse suggestions about his drinking habits.[180] The press parroted the official line that the Duke had 'never wavered in his loyalty to the British cause ... The German records are necessarily a much-tainted source' – while the BBC steadfastly looked the other way.[181]

The Duke's old chum Noël Coward was not fooled for a minute. The playwright treated the non-scandalous scandal as a huge joke, noting in his diary how 'Secret papers have disclosed his pro-Nazi perfidy which, of course, I was perfectly aware of at the time. Poor dear, what a monumental ass he has always been!'[182]

Not such an ass, however, that the Duke did not, in the end, get exactly what he had really wanted. For, even as Churchill's secretary Jock Colville was noting that 'the Duke of Windsor is being cantankerous and maddening',[183] and Churchill himself turned down the Duke's request that Piper Fletcher should be released from his regiment, the Prime Minister took soundings with the ex-King's best friend, the politician Walter Monckton, as well as with the Duke's sworn enemy, his former private secretary 'Tommy' Lascelles. From their very different points of view, both men explained to Churchill that 'HRH had to be treated as a petulant baby ...', warning that 'there was a by no means remote possibility that he was prepared to force a break on this subject'.[184]

Churchill drew a breath and relented. The Prime Minister had a war to fight, and he decided that he had already wasted enough time on the matter. 'I have now succeeded,' he telegraphed to the Duke in Lisbon on 24 July 1940, 'in overcoming War Office objection to departure of Fletcher.' So, throughout the remaining course of the Second World War, the new royal Governor of the Bahamas would be able to welcome guests to his table with his bagpipe-playing batman.[185]

After the war, it was George VI, rather than Elizabeth, who actually had to deal with his elder brother's efforts to secure some sort of job or public role in Britain, and it was the King who had to make clear to the Duke that the disclosures of the Marburg File ruled out any chance of his acceptance or special status at home: the job prospects described in the episode are based on the sort of positions the Duke had previously been offered and which still existed in 1957.

But Elizabeth was always close to her parents on issues involving her troublesome uncle, and her mother and father would certainly have briefed their daughter fully on the Duke's compromising contacts with the Nazis. Her senior staff – notably private secretary Tommy Lascelles – would also have considered it their duty to make their boss aware of all the most discreditable details known about the Windsors at the time of her accession in 1952, when assessing whether to invite the Duke and his wife to the coronation the following year. The couple were *not* invited.

The theme of forgiveness is introduced into this episode by the American evangelist Dr Billy Graham, whom Elizabeth II invited to visit her at Windsor and Sandringham more than once in the course of her reign. She was – and is – a believer, personally subscribing to his fundamentalist gospel. The first of her encounters with Dr Graham was during his London Crusade in 1954, and the timing of this meeting has been shifted to 1957 to fit with the August publication of the Marburg File.

During one visit the Queen invited the evangelist to help her with the preparations for her Christmas broadcast. 'To illustrate a point,' recalled Dr Graham, 'she wanted to toss a stone into a pond to show how the ripples went out farther and farther. She asked me to come and listen to her practice the speech by the pond and give my impressions, which I did.'[186]

On another occasion, Dr Graham was sitting beside the

Queen at lunch at Windsor, having preached the Sunday sermon in the Chapel Royal. He told her he had been undecided until the last minute about his choice of sermon, and had almost preached about Jesus's healing of the crippled man beside the pool at Bethesda, as related in the Gospel of Saint John: '*Arise, take up thy bed and walk!*'[187]

The Queen's eyes sparkled, he later related, and she bubbled over with enthusiasm.

'I wish you had!' she exclaimed. 'That is my favourite story.'[188]

1954 – Dr Billy Graham preaches on his first
London crusade

CHAPTER SEVEN

'MATRIMONIUM'

AUGUST 1959–MAY 1960

———

ANTONY ARMSTRONG-JONES, THE PHOTOGRAPHER AND MAN about town who married Princess Margaret in May 1960, was the first commoner to marry a senior member of the royal family since Anne Boleyn married Henry VIII in 1533.[189] Then, when the couple broke up in 1978, they achieved another landmark – the closest-to-the-top royal divorce since Henry parted from Anne of Cleves in 1540.[190] Inasmuch as we can tell from the murkily available evidence, the photographer and the younger sister of the respectable Elizabeth II leapt into more sexual shenanigans with more varied partners in their one single marriage than the Tudor 'Merry Monarch' managed in six.

Well, that is the historical context. In future episodes, *The Crown* will be exploring some of Princess Margaret's midlife sexual adventures. But let us start here with Episode 207 and the story of how she decided to marry her highly attractive – and highly dangerous – husband. Talk about 'Free Love'! For Antony Armstrong-Jones and Princess Margaret, the shenanigans were there from the very start, inherent in their complex characters and personal histories. We have already studied the Princess's troubles with Group Captain Townsend,[191] followed by her failed engagement to Billy Wallace and her life in Episode 204 as a 'half-baked, jazz-mad Teddy Girl'.[192] Now let us turn to the equally challenging and curious case of her incredibly talented and – as it proved – incredibly troublesome husband.

The parents of Antony Armstrong-Jones separated almost as soon as he was born on 7 March 1930, and had divorced by the time he was five, so Tony, as he was known, and his elder sister Susan (b. 1927) experienced a life of conflict and unhappy compartments, moving from one temporary home to another. Theirs was a loveless and emotionally deprived childhood, shuttling between bitter, feuding parents who specialised in the clever verbal put-down and the 'blanking' of each other with flinty superiority – weapons that would become Tony's own waspish trademarks in later life.

His father Ronnie was a successful barrister, the gregarious, chatty son of a Welsh doctor who had hyphenated Armstrong into the family name in 1913 to distinguish himself from legions of other Welsh Dr Joneses. By one count, Ronald Armstrong-Jones QC changed addresses as many as 27 times in his life,[193] and he enjoyed the changing company of almost as many girlfriends – a parental example that Tony would certainly absorb and seek to emulate in his own spectacular love career.

His mother Anne Messel was a polished figure, presented

at court in 1922 and a famous society beauty – a 'Deb of the Year',[194] in fact. She was the elder sister of Oliver Messel, the celebrated stage and costume designer who helped shape her widely admired wardrobe. Anne soon tired of the amusing but relatively impecunious Ronnie Armstrong-Jones, moving on to Michael Parsons, the sixth Earl of Rosse, an Irish peer based in the handsome seventeenth-century castle of Birr, Co. Offaly, with a West Yorkshire stately home, Womersley Park, to match. She wasted no time bearing her earl an heir and spare – two handsome young men who, being titled, instantly became her favourite offspring. Anne Rosse was a snob from her ovaries to her fingertips.

'These are my sons,' she would say, introducing her two Rosse children. 'Oh, and this is my other son' – indicating Tony.[195] Throughout his life, recalled his friends, the usually ebullient Armstrong-Jones was terrified of his mother. 'Anne Rosse just had to walk into the room,' recalled his friend the journalist Francis Wyndham, 'and Tony would freeze. The impact she had upon him was uncanny.'[196]

As Tony's authorised biographer Anne de Courcy has perceptively remarked, young Armstrong-Jones was simultaneously entranced by his mother's glittering figure, while nursing the pain of her rejection of him as a child: 'A child who has not had proper mothering often not only cannot form a proper relationship with a woman in later life,' wrote de Courcy, 'but also cannot trust women – sometimes to the extent of wanting to be first to strike a blow.'[197]

When he was 16 and had just been given his first motorbike, Antony Armstrong-Jones contracted polio. In later years doctors would link the two events – the strain of repeatedly kick-starting the awkward 250 BSA having created the muscle trauma onto which the polio virus could get attached in those pre-vaccination days. The teenager nearly died. Polio – also known as infantile paralysis – was a plague in the 1940s: one day you had a headache, and an hour later you were paralysed. How far the virus crept up your spine determined whether you lived or died, and how much you could breathe or walk afterwards.[198] Tony was rushed by ambulance to the Liverpool Royal Infirmary, where he would spend the next six months, emerging with a withered left leg that was an inch shorter than his right. Throughout his life he had a permanent limp.

He also emerged with a command of deaf and dumb sign language that he learned from one of his fellow patients, and a deep empathy for the disabled which would come to inspire his charity work as a royal. 'Disabled people are not rejects,' he would later write. 'They are not manufacturers' seconds, to be treated cheaply. Their rights and opportunities must be the same as the rest'[199] – and he would campaign to the end of his life for the improvement of disabled access everywhere,[200] from trains (where, even at the end of the twentieth century, wheelchair users had to travel in the unheated and loo-less metal guard's cage) to cinemas, theatres, the Chelsea Flower Show and London taxi cabs (all of which now accommodate wheelchairs).

The most affecting aspect of Tony's six long months of convalescence, however, was the fact that his mother never once visited him in hospital – and nor did his father. His jolly uncle Oliver Messel arranged for some of his theatrical friends – Noël Coward, Beatrice Lillie and Marlene Dietrich – to visit the boy when their tours took them through Liverpool: Marlene sat by his bedside and sang him 'The Boys in the Back Room'.[201] But his only family visitor was his sister Susan, for whom he spent hours knitting enormous scarves, while also stitching petit point.

It was hardly surprising that the 16-year-old's long spell in solitary confinement should encourage a profound scepticism towards the conventional bonds of affection. He clearly came to resolve, consciously or otherwise, that he was emotionally on his own, and that he would play by different rules when it came to matters of what other people called 'the heart'. This sometimes chilling cynicism also contributed, he would later acknowledge, to his steely-eyed proficiency as a photographer. 'Taking photographs,' he liked to say, 'is a very nasty thing to do.'[202]

Tony had acquired his first camera soon after he started at Eton in 1943 – a cheap device he had swapped with another boy in exchange for a microscope that had been an expensive present from his grandfather. Rapidly discovering how much of the artistry lay in the developing and printing, he filled his seven-foot-long school bedroom with trays and chemicals, plus a homemade enlarger built from old biscuit tins and tomato soup cans. In the course of his school career he revived the moribund Eton Photographic Society, and when he went up to Cambridge (Jesus College) in October 1949, he started taking pictures for *Cameo,* a small magazine started by his friend Jocelyn Stevens.

There he developed his own edgy style of portraiture, letting his subjects stew, rather than putting them at their ease. 'I'm not a great one for chatting people up,' he would later say, 'because it's phony. I don't want people to feel at ease. You want a bit of edge. There are quite long, agonized silences. I love it. Something strange might happen … It's very cruel.'[203] Early on he discovered that black and white images were his forte, rather than colour.[204]

He came down from Cambridge 'without taking a degree' – he failed his exams, in other words. But he had enjoyed some success on the river, coxing the Light Blues to a three and a half-length victory over Oxford in the 1950 Boat Race – and he had no doubt about his destiny: to work as a photographer. Just before Christmas 1950, not yet 21, he got a job working as an assistant in the studio of the society photographer Stirling Henry Nahum – the Duke of Edinburgh's friend, 'Baron'. Tony's weekly wage as one of Baron's 30 or so skivvies, setting the lights and loading the film for wedding and debutante photographs, was £2 15s. 1d.,[205] but he rapidly launched into a freelance career, taking bread and butter society pictures of his own, while also contributing to *Tatler* and *Picture Post* and later to Jocelyn Stevens's stylish and successful *Queen* magazine.

After work he would go out many nights to the Café de Paris near Leicester Square, photographing cabaret artists from the balcony – where he got a break from one of his Liverpool hospital visitors, Marlene Dietrich, who agreed to give him half an hour one afternoon on the empty stage.

'I wanted smoke in the picture,' he later recalled, 'but as there wasn't enough from her cigarette, I had three people under the piano puffing out cigar smoke.'[206]

Nearly 12 hours later, after the last show was over, Tony was back at the Café de Paris in the small hours of the morning, showing Miss Dietrich his sheets of contact prints, which she examined with a forensic eye.

'All right, my dear boy,' she said in a low, seductive voice that Tony liked to imitate whenever he repeated the oft-told story. 'I like my *face* in this-a-one, but I like the *smoke* in that-a-one.'

'But Miss Dietrich,' Tony replied, 'these pictures have to go to press at nine o'clock. It's frightfully difficult, and I really don't know how to do it.'

'My dear,' she told him, 'all you do is put the negative of my face in the enlarger and shade *this* part back with your hands. All right? Then you take the negative of the smoke and print *that* one, shading the other bit. You have four hours, so go along and do it.'

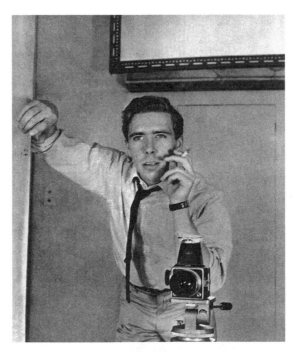

1960 – New recruit: Antony Armstrong-Jones
at work

'I followed her instructions,' Tony would conclude, 'and she was absolutely right.'[207]

The moody Dietrich photograph – the singer later used it for one of her album covers[208] – got Armstrong-Jones firmly noted in Fleet Street as the celebrity snapper of the moment, and in June 1956 came *Photocall*, the first public exhibition of his work, at the prestigious Kodak Gallery in Kingsway.[209] The show featured striking portraits of ballerina Anya Linden, dress designer Christian Dior, the painter Pietro Annigoni, actresses Edith Evans and Ingrid Bergman and, most memorable of all, Laurence Olivier playing an angry Archie Rice in the film of John Osborne's *The Entertainer*. For this, Tony had indulged in a rare piece of retouching to enlarge the natural gap between Olivier's front teeth, emphasising the decaying doom of his character's ferocity.[210]

With fame and money, Tony was able to step up the tempo of his already busy love life. Work and sex were his guiding lights – a day without either, he used to say, was a day wasted. To start with, his companions were mainly men: the interior designer Tom Parr with whom he frequently holidayed, the stage designer Carl Toms with whom he later shared a flat in New York, the choreographer John Cranko, whom he would welcome to his studio with a full-blooded kiss on the lips – to the delighted horror of his female assistants – and his gloriously camp uncle Oliver Messel, who would invite his nephew to Venice, wandering the canals and alleyways with him through the night. 'We would end up in some gay bar,' Tony fondly recalled, 'at five in the morning.'[211]

So, was Antony Armstrong-Jones gay? Many years later his biographer Anne de Courcy dared to put the question directly to the great man in one of their weekly conversations, prompting a very, very long pause as he stared out of the window.

'I didn't fall in love with boys,' he eventually replied. Then he added reflectively, after another long pause – 'But a few men have been in love with me.'[212]

That is certainly not a 'Yes'. But if you study the words carefully, it is definitely not a 'No' either. In his memoir *Redeeming Features*, interior designer Nicky Haslam writes of enjoying 'a very brief romance' with Armstrong-Jones about a year before the photographer's marriage to Princess Margaret[213] – and when Margaret herself first met her future husband, over dinner in 1958 at the Chelsea home of her lady-in-waiting Elizabeth Cavendish, 'she was far from convinced,' in the words of *her* approved biographer, Christopher Warwick, 'that he was interested in women'.[214]

The issue became public – though the newspapers at the time politely declined to air it in any detail – when Tony's close friend, the chocolate heir Jeremy Fry, had to step down as best man for the royal wedding in May 1960. A criminal conviction had been discovered in his past – a £2 fine at Marlborough Street Magistrates Court for 'importuning for immoral purposes' (soliciting a man for sex).[215]

This is the Jeremy Fry whom we meet in Episode 207 of *The Crown*, cavorting in bed with his wife Camilla and making up an energetic sexual 'threesome' with Tony to the music of Henryk Górecki's Third Symphony (*Lento Cantabile Semplice*). Over the music, the two Frys take a break from their exertions to congratulate Tony on how much more expert his lovemaking has become since he started dating the flower-like

Jacqui Chan (Trinidad and Tobago-born of Chinese descent), then starring in the West End in *The World of Suzie Wong*.

'I really can't keep up anymore,' says Jeremy.

'And you're more imaginative ...' adds Camilla. 'So, don't give her up. Whatever you do.'[216]

The scene is 'invented', but it is also the truth, for Tony Armstrong-Jones's sexual appetites were, by all accounts, omni-voracious. 'If it moves, he'll have it,' explained one of Tony's friends and sexual partners to Anne de Courcy in the early 2000s – and that was when the photographer was over 70.[217] His lifelong amatory energies made distinctions between homo- and hetero-sexual activity irrelevant.

'He couldn't buy a packet of cigarettes,' recalled the young actress Gina Ward, 'without flirting with the man or woman behind the counter.'[218] In her case, the flirting was while watching Alfred Lunt and Lynn Fontanne act Dürrenmatt at a Boxing Day matinee in 1957. She had only met Tony that morning in his studio.

The man himself was most generously endowed physically, according to those who knew him intimately. 'It was like having a baby backwards,' recalled one lady, smiling broadly, decades later, at the memory of her three weeks of romps with the future Lord Snowdon.[219] Princess Margaret soon discovered that the apparently gay photographer she had met at dinner was most definitely interested in women, and she wasted no time. Their affair took off passionately through the spring and summer of 1959 – though Her Royal Highness occupied just one compartment of Tony's life in those summer months, along with Gina, Jacqui, the two Frys and goodness knows who else, parcelled out to separate compartments of their own. Each and all of them, for the most part, along with the now-rampant Princess Margaret, were jumping into bed with Tony in total ignorance of the others.

'He's a monster,' said his friend Andy Garnett, the furniture designer – a platonic friend – when once discussing Tony's promiscuity and deep-rooted emotional deceptiveness. 'But I love him.'[220]

Another platonic friend who knew Tony very well took a less indulgent view. When Jocelyn Stevens, who might have been expected to welcome the huge boost to the fame of his star *Queen* photographer, heard the news of Tony's engagement to the Princess at the end of February 1960, he declined to join in the general rejoicing. 'NEVER,' he cabled gravely from his estate in the Bahamas, 'WAS THERE A MORE ILL-FATED ASSIGNMENT.'[221]

Suddenly Tony seemed to feel the same. Had he trapped himself? When he rang up to share the news with Francis Wyndham, then an editor on *Queen*, his voice was shaking, and he wondered if he was having a nervous breakdown. Wyndham suggested that he should get away for a break. 'But I'd only have to come back,' Tony replied.[222]

Getting practical, he went around to Tom Parr's flat to ask, apparently on a whim, if he could look through Parr's photograph albums of all their holidays together as an 'item'. He then delved fixedly through the three large volumes, page after page, studying every little photograph with surprisingly detailed interest. Later Parr realised that his old partner must have been searching for snapshots from the early years of their relationship that might have been deemed compromising in some way.

Gina Ward was dealt with over the telephone – 'broken into a hundred pieces,' as she later recalled, by the total surprise and harshness of the news. 'You're in love with me!' she cried out. 'You'll have an awful life!'[223]

Jacqui Chan did not even receive the courtesy of a phone call. She was told by the photographer Robert Belton on the evening before, just hours ahead of the announcement, dispatched by Tony down to Pinewood where she was filming. 'Well,' she responded, sitting in Belton's car in the pouring rain, 'I hope she can cope better than I could.'[224]

There was another girlfriend, unnamed, who later told the writer John Moynihan how Tony had broken the news to her while they were in bed together – weeping his tears, she recalled with some precision, onto her 'bare breasts' as he bemoaned the prospect of his forthcoming royal servitude.[225]

So that makes at least three women – Gina Ward, Jacqui Chan and Ms 'Bare Breasts' – who all believed that they were enjoying close and committed sexual relationships with Tony in the very months when he was sleeping with the Queen's sister and was getting ready to propose to her – as Margaret would later put it to Christopher Warwick, 'in a roundabout way. It was very cleverly worded.' The unusual marriage proposal sequence depicted in the episode, with the couple lying side by side in bed together, seeks to reflect that: 'Will you forgive me if I don't go down on one knee?'

And then there was Camilla Fry. We do not know how or when she and Tony said goodbye to each other. But at the end of May 1960 – three weeks into the royal couple's honeymoon – Camilla gave birth to a daughter, Polly, who, DNA tests would later establish beyond doubt, was the child of Antony Armstrong-Jones.[226]

Episode 207's depiction of the official engagement party draws its inspiration from a formal reception held at Buckingham Palace two days prior to the wedding on 6 May 1960, along with an earlier private celebration for the couple held at Clarence House on 31 October 1959 by the Queen Mother, who was an enthusiastic champion of both Tony and the marriage.

Senior courtiers at the Palace, on the other hand, troubled by rumours of the new recruit's promiscuity. At the time of the engagement, Sir Alan 'Tommy' Lascelles, the Queen's private secretary from 1952–3, who had retired in 1953, confided to the diarist Harold Nicolson that 'the boy Jones has led a very diversified and sometimes a wild life and the danger of scandal and slander is never far off'.

Nicolson himself went on to note: 'At least Mr. Jones is not a homo, which is rare these days.' As already discussed, however, Nicolson's assumption has been largely disproved by the evidence of the 'homos' who were close to Tony in the 1950s. So their testimony would seem to add an intriguing strand of bisexuality to the complex mixture that was Antony Armstrong-Jones.

CHAPTER EIGHT

'Dear Mrs Kennedy'

June 1961–November 1963

———————

'THE "WIND OF CHANGE" IS BLOWING THROUGH THIS continent,' Harold Macmillan historically announced to the assembled members of the South African Parliament on 3rd February 1960. '... Whether we like it or not, this growth of [African] national consciousness is a political fact, and we must all accept it as a fact.'[227] Listening in Cape Town, the British Prime Minister's immediate audience – the Anglo-Dutch enforcers of apartheid, 95 per cent male and 100 per cent white – did not like what they heard, and they acknowledged his message with lukewarm applause.[228]

But further north the cheers rang out – starting with the new, would-be independent nations of 'black' Africa, for here was the current chief executive of the British Empire effectively throwing in the towel. Macmillan was saying that Britain's African colonies could now have their freedom whenever they wanted – with no haggling or bloodshed – a momentous and

93

historical declaration. And in 1960 few people welcomed that declaration more warmly than Macmillan's own boss and Sovereign, Queen Elizabeth II, the custodian of Britain's imperial crown.

Episode 208 of *The Crown*, 'Dear Mrs Kennedy', examines Elizabeth II's pioneering endorsement of African liberation in the 1950s and 1960s, suggesting that it may have been influenced by the Queen's personal contacts with America's glamorous First Lady, the wife of President Jack Kennedy, who features in part of this episode. But this is dramatic invention.

Peter Morgan has explained how he wished to highlight the post-1960 advent of Jackie Kennedy on the world scene – super-model and, apparently, super-brain – suddenly a rival to Elizabeth II's hitherto unchallenged pre-eminence. Jackie had recently enjoyed a huge triumph in Paris, charming and winning over the previously anti-American General de Gaulle, by speaking fluent French to the grumpy French president so dazzlingly that JFK joked that he was just a sideshow. It would be quite natural, Morgan suggests, for Elizabeth II to have felt a little up-staged by the First Lady's talents, and this episode shows how her own diplomatic work in Africa solidly outshone anything that Jackie Kennedy ever accomplished.

Queen Elizabeth II was firmly committed to the cause of liberating Africa's colonial states long before she met Jack and Jackie Kennedy in London in June 1961. In fact, her own liberal attitude towards the break-up of the British Empire would certainly have played a role in what her Prime Minister knew he could say in Cape Town – since, as head of Her Majesty's Government, Macmillan was speaking in the name of the Crown. And the domestic corollary of this – the Queen's consistent stance throughout her reign in support of racial equality – has also been part of her personal lifelong vision, for which she alone deserves the credit.

At the end of the 1950s, Kwame Nkrumah was the proud President of Ghana, the former West African colony of the Gold Coast that had become Britain's first African colony to win its independence in 1957. This was largely thanks to Nkrumah's own fighting attitude – Ghana means 'Warrior King' in the language of the Soninke people who ruled the ancient empire of Ghana from the eighth to the thirteenth centuries. Nkrumah twice spent some time in a British jail, and, outside Africa, he was seen by many as an anti-Western troublemaker in the mould of Egypt's President Nasser. Nkrumah encouraged this comparison – he had been drawn to his Egyptian wife Fathia on the basis of her pro-Nasser and anti-colonialist views.

Nkrumah spoke out loudly for pan-African unity, just as Nasser championed pan-Arabism to counteract the infiltrating power of the West. And like Nasser, Nkrumah built much of his foreign policy around playing off the US and the Soviet Union, the two major Cold War powers, against each other in order to finance his new nation's self-sufficiency with the favoured 'open sesame' of the day – a hydroelectric power project. It was America's refusal to finance Egypt's Aswan Dam that had provoked Nasser's occupation of Suez in 1956. Now, early in 1960, Harold Macmillan was worried that American failure to finance Ghana's Volta Dam project might provoke a similar backlash by Nkrumah, turning him permanently towards the Soviet Union and prompting him to stalk out of the British Commonwealth – taking other black African leaders with him.

Nkrumah's surprising and sentimental disappointment as an African mover and shaker was that he had never had the chance to meet Queen Elizabeth II herself. He felt let down when Downing Street and the Palace had cautiously sent her aunt, the Duchess of Kent, to attend Ghana's independence celebrations in 1957,[229] consoling himself with the promise that Her Majesty would visit Ghana's capital, in 1960 as part of the tour she was already planning of Britain's West African connections and dependencies to start the new decade.

But in the summer of 1959, Elizabeth fell pregnant with the child who would turn out to be Prince Andrew (b. February 1960). She would not be able to travel for more than a year, and she had studied the dispatches from Accra sufficiently to know what a disappointment that would be to Ghana's President. 'I'm going to have a baby,' she told Martin Charteris, her assistant private secretary, 'which I have been trying to do for some time, and that means I won't be able to go out to Ghana as arranged. I want you to go and explain the situation to Nkrumah and tell him to keep his mouth shut.'[230]

The courtier duly flew out to Accra to pass on the message to the Prime Minister, who, as Charteris later related to the Queen's biographer Ben Pimlott, received the news in silence. After several minutes, Charteris felt he should try repeating the message — to be greeted by still more profound silence. After waiting several further minutes, Charteris tried for a third time, asking the great man, then just approaching his fiftieth birthday, if he understood the situation.

'I put all my happiness into this tour,' Nkrumah finally replied. 'Had you told me my mother had just died, you could not have given me a greater shock.'[231]

By the time Elizabeth was finally ready to visit West Africa in November 1961, the Ghanaian situation had changed. In January that year Nkrumah had joined up with Nasser and other 'Third World' nationalist leaders to sign the African Charter of Casablanca, which courted Soviet Premier Khrushchev and took an aggressively anti-Western line. Nkrumah's foreign policy was pro-Soviet in many respects. Before the Queen's arrival, he had been on a lengthy tour through Communist Eastern Europe, proclaiming Ghana's solidarity with the Soviet Union and the People's Republic of China.

More seriously, Nkrumah had abolished Ghana's network of regional assemblies and altered the constitution to create what was in effect a one-party state. As President of the new republic of Ghana, he still paid nominal homage to the Queen, but only just – raising the question in London as to whether a state whose leader made anti-British speeches while denying traditional British civil liberties to its citizens was entitled to stay inside the Commonwealth.

Days before Elizabeth was due to depart on 9 November 1961, Nkrumah arrested 50 of his most prominent domestic opponents and also expelled all his British military advisers. Then a terrorist bomb went off in Accra, blowing both legs off his grand presidential statue – which raised serious questions about the safety of the Queen if she were to go out with him in public. Macmillan dispatched his Commonwealth Secretary Duncan Sandys to inspect and check the Queen's intended route, but it was Elizabeth herself who took the crucial decision.[232]

'How silly I should look,' she said to her Prime Minister, 'if I was scared to visit Ghana, and then Khrushchev went and had a good reception!'[233]

'What a splendid girl she is!' said Macmillan to his press secretary Harold Evans, describing how, at his final Palace audience before the journey, the Queen had been positively 'indignant' at the idea of cancelling the trip. She took her Commonwealth responsibilities 'very seriously …' recalled the Prime Minister.[234] As Macmillan later wrote in his diary, Elizabeth had no patience with the attitude 'to treat her as a *woman*' – and he went on to set down some surprisingly spikey thoughts that could only have come from the Queen herself in the personal audience that he had described to Evans.[235]

'If she were pressed too hard,' he noted, 'and if Government and people here are determined to restrict her activities (including taking reasonably acceptable risks) I think she might be tempted to throw in her hand. She does not enjoy "society". She likes her horses. But she loves her duty and means to be a Queen and not a puppet.'[236]

Travelling through the streets of Accra a few days later, Elizabeth showed no hesitation in sitting in an open car beside Nkrumah, smiling broadly – bombs or no bombs. She had read all the telegrams about her host's Russian flirtations and she had also been briefed on the local security concerns: Nkrumah's regime was far from universally popular or stable. But she betrayed no sign of anxiety. Her courage was the more remarkable for being so unassuming – 'I have to be seen to be believed,' as she said on another occasion.[237]

Elizabeth's Ghana visit of November 1961 proved to be a turning point in the building of the British Commonwealth that had meant so much to her since her accession in 1952. It was the moment when Black Africa came onside – an historic illustration of the strength in what had often been accounted her weakness, her essential passivity of character. Elizabeth II triumphed just by 'being' there.

Then at the state ball that final evening in Accra came a still stronger illustration of what could be achieved by the unspoken and the symbolic – the white Queen surrendered herself into the arms of the black President. When the band struck up 'The High Life', a popular West African reggae-style shuffle,[238] the Queen rose to her feet in white gloves, tiara and sash to dance happily with President Nkrumah, laughing and joking for the best part of ten minutes,[239] while Prince Philip boogied energetically beside them with First Lady Fathia.[240] There is no evidence that Elizabeth discussed with Nkrumah the wider implications of the pair of them dancing together, but both Queen and President must have been fully aware of the message they would send out at that stage in history by dancing in each other's arms as two people of different races.

1961 – Elizabeth II dances with President
Nkrumah of Ghana

The photograph went around the world – to be greeted with predictable outrage in apartheid South Africa (which had voluntarily left the Commonwealth the previous year before it could be thrown out for its racial policies). 'This spectacle of the honored head of the once-mighty British Empire dancing with black natives of pagan Africa is extremely scandalous ...' complained the nationalist newspaper *Die Oosterlig* in an editorial headed 'Her Black Dancing Partners'.[241]

'Trumpeting forth that the Queen apparently enjoyed it is just as bad,' continued the complaint. 'While realizing that Britons do not recognize colour differences, it remains in our opinion a pitiful outrage of the dignity one associates with a white royalty. Britain has given cause for shame in exchange for the good will of black tyrannies ... It is just as well that we in South Africa are no longer linked to a Commonwealth where such things are becoming the fashion to an increasing extent.'[242]

America's segregationist press did not rise to the bait, but at that date interracial marriages were still forbidden by law in 31 American states.[243] In 1959 the black singer Sammy Davis Jr had delayed his marriage to a white woman, the Swedish actress May Britt, so as not to jeopardise the electoral prospects of his friend Jack Kennedy. Davis had campaigned tirelessly for Kennedy in black districts through much of 1960, but after his 13 November marriage to Britt (the presidential election had been on 8 November), he was removed from the list of entertainers – and even from the guest list – of the inaugural celebrations in Washington on 20 January 1961.

Elizabeth II's gesture of dancing with Kwame Nkrumah was an expression of personal principles that she went on to uphold all her life. 'On racial matters she is absolutely colour-blind,' said David Owen, her Foreign Secretary from 1977 to 1979.[244] It went back to her first experiences of South Africa in her early twenties with her father George VI in 1947, when the King – on a post-war victory tour to thank the imperial dominions for their help – became infuriated at the racial restrictions that stopped him presenting medals to non-white troops.

'Gestapo!' he harrumphed when Afrikaner police kept him away from the 'native' sections of the crowd – and he sniffed derisively when he spotted South Africa's motto *Ex Unitate Vires*, 'Strength from Unity', on a tablecloth.

'Huh!' he exclaimed. 'Not much bloody *Unitate* about this place!'[245]

Over the years Elizabeth II would get as close to some of her black African premiers – Kenneth Kaunda, Julius Nyerere and, later, especially, to Nelson Mandela – as to any of her middle-class Anglo-Saxon prime ministers. 'It's the one-man, one-vote principle,' explained David Owen.[246]

Well, perhaps. But there is also the practical matter of one tribal totem recognising another – along with the role played by the Queen's personal Christian faith.[247] As we saw in Episode 206, Elizabeth II was much influenced by the American evangelist Dr Billy Graham. She invited the preacher to Windsor three times when he brought his crusades to Britain in the late 1950s[248] – the same years in which Graham became a vehement anti-segregationist, preaching in Harlem and working alongside Dr Martin Luther King.[249] 'The ground at the foot of the cross is level,' Graham liked to say, and his royal admirer worked to that very same principle.[250]

Decades later the Queen finally put definitive words to

what she believed about race, touchingly revealing an unusual perspective of where she stood – and, we can presume, had always stood – on issues of discrimination and multiculturalism.

'Everyone is our neighbour,' she declared in her Christmas broadcast of 2004, 'no matter what their race, creed or colour … And it was for this reason that I particularly enjoyed a story I heard the other day about an overseas visitor to Britain who said the best part of his visit had been travelling from Heathrow into Central London on the "Tube".

'His British friends were, as you can imagine, somewhat surprised, particularly as the visitor had been to some of the great attractions of the country. "What do you mean," they asked?

'"Because," he replied, "I boarded the train just as the schools were coming out. At each stop children were getting on and off – they were of every ethnic and religious background, some with scarves or turbans, some talking quietly, others playing and occasionally misbehaving together – completely at ease and trusting one another.

'"How lucky you are," said the visitor, "to live in a country where your children can grow up this way …"'251

This snapshot of the give-and-take racial jumble on the Tube every day around teatime at Hounslow, Middlesex, exemplified the principles that Queen Elizabeth II tried to put into practice all those decades ago in Ghana with Kwame Nkrumah – and had also come to cherish as an ideal for her own country and its children.

'I hope they will be allowed,' she concluded in 2004, 'to enjoy this happy companionship for the rest of their lives. A Happy Christmas to you all.'252

CHAPTER NINE

'PATERFAMILIAS'

1937 AND 1962

B ORN ON 10 JUNE 1921 ON THE ISLAND OF CORFU, THE blond-haired and blue-eyed Prince Philip of Greece looked rather Danish or even German – and he was, in fact, both. His father Prince Andrew was a member of the Danish royal family, the house of Glücksborg, and his mother Alice, one of 'Dickie' Mountbatten's two sisters, originally hailed from the Battenberg clan from Hesse in central Germany. Educated principally in English-speaking schools, from Paris, France, via Cheam in Surrey to Gordonstoun in north-eastern Scotland, the young Greek prince spoke perfect English, while claiming in later life that he could understand 'a certain amount' of Greek.[253] But, as we noted in volume 1, 'Phil the Greek' had not a drop of Greek blood in his veins. ('Phil the Greek' was the nickname devised for the Prince by the satirical magazine *Private Eye* in the early 1960s. They also tried calling him 'Keith' for a period – but that did not stick.)

For a variety of reasons the ill-fated Kingdom of Greece, which lasted, on and off, until 1973, preferred non-local sovereigns, opting for a succession of royal families who came from anywhere but Greece. Following their hard-won war of independence that had ended four centuries of Turkish domination in 1830, they first tried a German, Prince Otto of Bavaria, who became King Otto the First – and also Otto the Last, following his deposition in 1862. After a referendum in November that year, the throne was then offered to Prince Alfred, the second son of Britain's Queen Victoria, but she prudently declined on her son's behalf, leaving the way clear for the 18-year-old Prince William of Denmark, who ascended the throne in 1863. As a gesture towards Greece's patron saint, William took the title of King George I. Prince Philip was his grandson.

The young Prince Philip was not high in the order of succession, but that was no bar to him becoming King of Greece at some later stage, since kings tended to come and go quite rapidly in his family. His grandfather, George I,[254] had been assassinated in 1913, and his uncle Constantine I[255] was deposed four years later. His cousin Alexander I died in 1920 of blood poisoning following a monkey bite,[256] and his uncle Constantine abdicated for a second time in 1922, having been briefly restored to the throne. Then his cousin King George II abdicated in 1923, to be successively recalled (1935), expelled (1941) and then restored again in 1946.[257] As the commander of the British light cruiser HMS *Calypso*, remarked when he carried the 18-month-old Philip away from Greece in an improvised cot constructed from orange boxes in December 1922, this royal family seemed philosophical about being exiled – 'for they so frequently are …'[258]

Calypso's commander was Captain H. A. Buchanan-Wollaston, who was picking up Prince Philip, his mother and four sisters in a daredevil rescue operation inspired from London by no less a figure than King George V. Philip's father, Prince Andrew, was in prison in Athens, under threat of execution for his role in the recent defeat of Greece's armies by Kemal Atatürk and his ferocious Turkish troops. Six other Greek scapegoats for the debacle – five cabinet ministers and the army's commander-in-chief – had been shot in November, and Philip's father would almost certainly have met the same fate had it not been for the arrival in Athens of an undercover British agent, Commander Gerald Talbot.

Talbot had been sent out to Greece, complete with disguise and false papers, at the personal instructioin of George V, intervening as Andrew's first cousin as well as uncle to Alice. Exercising the royal prerogative in a way that was, strictly, unconstitutional, the King had bypassed government channels to telephone the Admiralty directly and instruct that a British warship be sent to Greece to assist Talbot's rescue mission. Talbot knew General Pangalos, the leader of the Greek revolutionaries, personally, but Pangalos was actually refusing all clemency at the moment when the cruiser – Captain Buchanan-Wollaston's *Calypso* – steamed unexpectedly into the Bay of Athens. As Talbot later described it to the royal family, there was a dramatic scene when Pangalos, vehemently insisting that Prince Andrew had to die, was interrupted by an aide rushing into the room with news of the British warship in the bay.[259]

The Greek general's attitude changed immediately and now it was Talbot's turn to give the orders. He instructed Pangalos to release the prince from prison and to drive him down to

105

the quay. So, in what was one of Britain's last effective acts of gunboat diplomacy, Prince Philip's father, and hence young Philip himself, were saved by the Royal Navy, thus making possible the baby prince's destiny as future husband to Queen Elizabeth II.

But this providentially preserved baby was still a waif in many senses – and if it has sometimes seemed that Prince Philip, Duke of Edinburgh and royal consort, has punched his way through adult life with an over-toughened emotional detachment, then that toughening and detachment were born in these difficult years. He left Greece in an orange crate and never really found a better or more permanent home until his marriage in 1947.

In England his uncles George Milford Haven and Lord Louis 'Dickie' Mountbatten did provide generous and supportive foster care for the growing boy. But his own parents were less sheltering. Having been married for 18 years and raised four daughters, Andrew and Alice had exhausted their affection for each other by the time of Philip's arrival, and had effectively separated. The baby's four elder sisters – aged 16, 15, 9 and 6 at the time of his birth – were the closest thing to parents that Philip ever had.

The newborn's father, Prince Andrew, was poleaxed by the humiliating and nearly fatal end to his military career. It was not so much the danger of execution, but the public shame of his court martial after a lifetime of seeking to shape himself into the ideal soldier and commander. Andrew devoted his early years of exile to writing an angry and self-justifying memoir, *Towards Disaster*, whose unfortunate title proved all too apt. His cantankerous outpouring only served to convince the world of his resentment and self-pity – and those who have detected these qualities in his son's tendency to bearishness might dip into the book with profit.[260]

Prince Andrew's public humiliation was made worse by his reliance on the charity of others. From the moment he left Greece he was virtually penniless, dependent for his living expenses – along with costs such as Philip's school fees – on handouts from rich relations like the anglicised Battenbergs, the Mountbattens. Over time the ignominy of exile beat down his outrage to shoulder-shrugging indifference, and his emotional detachment became physical so far as his family was concerned in the late 1930s when he gravitated to Monte Carlo.

Young Philip's cousin and childhood playmate, Alexandra of Yugoslavia (later considered, pre-Princess Elizabeth, as a candidate for Philip's hand in marriage),[261] recalled how Andrew became no more than 'a debonair and distant presence' to his children. On the rare occasions they saw their father in Monaco, they tended to find him presiding over a white restaurant tablecloth with his latest lady friend and something on ice in a silver bucket close to his elbow – somehow the prince had reconciled himself to the charity of others – exhibiting a compulsion to keep everyone around him laughing continuously, a custom maintained by his son.

Prince Andrew also passed on his short-sightedness to Philip. Andrew's trademark monocle or pince-nez made an elegant virtue for his necessity for spectacles, but his son would choose to be more discreet. Prince Philip became an early customer for contact lenses, often lost when playing polo.[262]

Alexandra remembered her playful cousin as a mischievous character, running into the Baltic on one occasion fully clothed, or falling into a muddy pigsty simply to annoy his English nanny, Nurse Roose, who liked to serve her charges cauliflower for lunch. Philip was the ringleader of the retaliation – 'Whoosh, we simultaneously upturned our plates on the snowy tablecloth.'[263] As the boy reached double figures, the family consensus was that more discipline was called for, and in 1933, aged 12, he was sent to the academy at Schloss Salem near Lake Constance on the border of Bavaria, founded by the legendary educator Kurt Hahn.[264] All Philip's sisters had married Germans who owned castles, and the largest of all was Schloss Salem – bigger than Buckingham Palace and the home of the Margrave of Baden, who had married Philip's sister Theodora in 1931.

Born in Berlin in 1886 to a prosperous family of German-Jewish industrialists, Kurt Hahn sought to bring together what he saw as the best in British and German traditions of character-building, and by 1933 he had developed Salem into a 500-pupil college that was attracting interest from educators around the world. But Hahn's Jewish descent and scathing critique of the rising National Socialist (Nazi) Party meant that he had already spent a spell in prison before Philip's arrival, accused of 'the decadent corruption of German youth'.[265] Hahn had to leave Germany. So Philip did just one year at Salem, where he spent a happy and stable 12 months in the home of his sister Theodora and her young family, before moving to join Hahn's new venture at Gordonstoun House (as it was originally known) in north-east Scotland. He was one of a select group of 24 young pioneers.

This is where we join Philip in Episode 209, and we listen to Kurt Hahn as he sets out his educational ambitions. 'On its current path,' he tells Philip, 'the world will fill with anger and soon will be destroyed. So here, away from the madness, we must build a new way. A new school. A new philosophy. A new ethos. The world needs saviours. A generation of remarkable young men ...'[266]

Of Hahn's first 24 young saviours a dozen or so were German, brought over, like Philip, from Salem, two were Spanish and the remaining eight or so were English and Scottish. German had been the school's language at Salem. In Bavaria Philip had spoken nothing but German for a year – 'Phil the Kraut'.[267] But now in Scotland, German was banned to help the foreign students perfect their English, with just four teachers to cover conventional subjects like mathematics, geography and geology. Alongside these were a range of especially Hahn-inspired topics – forestry, seamanship, firefighting, mountain climbing and, most important, 'expeditions'.[268]

Hahn brought to Gordonstoun his 'Seven Laws of Salem',[269]

1938 – Prince Philip as Donalbain in
Macbeth at Gordonstoun

based on educational ideas ranging from Plato to St Benedict and Rudyard Kipling – 'If you can dream – and not make dreams your master'[270] – along with some dippings into the British public school system, which he admired with reservations. 'Every girl and boy has a "grande passion",' he wrote, 'often hidden and unrealised … It can and will be revealed by the child coming into close touch with a number of different activities.'[271] Hence the forestry, firefighting and expeditions.

Young people, Hahn felt strongly, should experience defeat as well as victory. 'Salem believes you ought to discover the child's weakness as well as his strength,' he wrote. 'It is our business to plunge the children into enterprises in which they are likely to fail, and we do not hush the failure up.'[272] The sensitive child must learn 'to defeat his own defeatism' the hard way, or risk being 'crippled for the battle of life'.[273]

This 'tough love' principle, Hahn's second law of Salem, is what we see causing such problems for Prince Charles in this episode – a reflection of how the Prince, the first heir to the British throne ever to be sent away to school, experienced the cold showers and short, hairy tweed trousers of Gordonstoun when he became a pupil 30 years after his father. 'Literal hell',[274] and 'Colditz with kilts'[275] were two of the Prince's choicer verdicts. 'He was bullied,' recalled Ross Benson, the *Daily Mail* journalist who was his contemporary at the school. 'He was crushingly lonely for most of his time there. The wonder is that he survived with his sanity intact.'[276]

Charles was not given his father's old bed when he went to Gordonstoun in 1962, as depicted in this episode, nor was Kurt Hahn still the headmaster – he had retired in 1953. But Hahn has been retained as a character through the school careers of both father and son to provide a constant against which to compare their very different experiences.

The annual 'Challenge' in which Charles is shown participating is original to the drama, as is the presence of Prince Philip. But the 'Challenge' faithfully reflects the testing ethos of Gordonstoun's cross-country races – as well as the school's famously rugged expeditions – while also allowing the viewer to imagine Charles's experience of not living up to his father's glittering legacy.

Hahn's third law of the Salem-Gordonstoun code was that pupils should learn to put pursuit of the common good before personal ambition – with the help of the fourth law: that they should make time in their lives for silence and contemplation. 'Unless the present-day generation acquires early habits of quiet and reflection,' Hahn wrote, 'it will be speedily and prematurely used up by the nerve-exhausting and distracting civilisation of today.'[277]

Law five emphasised every child's need to develop their imagination – 'You must call it into action, otherwise it becomes atrophied like a muscle not in use.' Law six was that sports and games should be 'important' but never 'predominant'. 'Athletics do not suffer,' wrote Hahn, 'by being put in their place.'[278] The purpose of sport at the school was to promote teamwork rather than competitive achievement – the third and fourth cricket teams should be cheered on just as much as the first. Heads of house were called 'Helpers', and the head boy was the 'Guardian'. The captain of rugby was, in theory, no grander than the captains of lost property, the linen room or bicycles.

Finally, the children of the rich and powerful must be 'liberated' from their privilege. 'Rich girls and boys wholly thrown into each other's company are not given a chance of growing into men and women who can overcome,' wrote Hahn, whose ambition was that a third of pupils should ideally come from 'normal' or poor backgrounds.[279] In reality, however, Gordonstoun never became a comprehensive school. Its fees were among the highest in Britain – higher than Eton's – and it remained an eccentric 'posh' college in the eyes of its critics, with its hair-shirt philosophy and even hairier shorts.

The school's incontestable failing was its shunning – certainly in Hahn's day – of emotional intimacy of any sort. Never married nor seen relaxing in female company, Hahn made no attempt to help his boys investigate what women thought or felt – in fact, he fiercely banned any mention of sex, let alone sex education, from the school. Noting how their boss was visibly uncomfortable with women unless they were middle-aged mothers, most of his staff assumed that Hahn was of confused or uncertain sexual identity. The Founder could also be a stern disciplinarian, wielding the cane as a punishment for smoking offences.[280] Sexual indiscretions merited expulsion.

The child psychologist Oliver James has suggested that Philip's striking lack of emotional education 'might have rather diminished his capacity to have faith in intimacy or love or closeness … If you throw in the disappearance of his father … there's a fairly high probability that he would have developed what psychologists call a "highly defended personality". That's to say that he doesn't want to know about his emotions or other people's emotions.'[281]

As Philip's confidential aide and naval best friend, Mike Parker, put it: 'He doesn't wear his heart on his sleeve. I always wanted to see him put his arms around the Queen and show her how much he adored her – what you'd do for any wife. But he always sort of stood to attention. I mentioned it to him a couple of times. But he just gave me a hell of a look.'[282]

Philip would direct the same 'hell of a look' at anyone who dared criticise Gordonstoun or its founder, to whom he felt he owed so much. 'I was wet, cold, miserable, probably sick, and often scared stiff,' he later wrote of the school's notorious 'challenges', 'but I would not have missed the experience for anything. In any case, the discomfort was far outweighed by the moments of intense happiness and excitement.'[283]

As a father, Philip wanted his eldest son to be enriched by all these experiences, with the miserable outcomes that we see on screen. Prince Charles's 'death of the soul' at Gordonstoun was not just a metaphor; it was the painful, real-life consequence of his father's own emotional aloofness. How could Prince Philip with his effectively unparented childhood, give or teach his son the things that he had never been given or taught himself?

Kurt Hahn, however, had no such reservations about his star pupil. He always gloried that Philip had proved a living example of his highest hopes during his Scottish academy's pioneering years. 'Often naughty, never nasty' was his verdict on the future Duke of Edinburgh[284] – though he was not blind to his protégé's shortcomings, noting how Philip's positive leadership qualities could be 'marred at times by impatience and intolerance'.[285] In his final report, Hahn sounded another warning note, suggesting that Philip, like his father, leaned just a little too heavily on the game going his way: 'Prince Philip is a born leader,' he wrote, 'but [he] will need the exacting demands of a great service to do justice to himself. His best is outstanding – his second best is not good enough.'[286]

Philip was never punished at Gordonstoun by being detained over half-term. Thus, his sister Cécile did not die as a result of Philip's misbehaviour at school, as depicted on the screen. She and her family were killed in November 1937 when their plane hit a factory chimney in fog near Ostend, Belgium, travelling to a wedding in London. When *The Crown* departs from historical accuracy, this reflects a deliberate creative choice by Peter Morgan and his team, so this dramatic invention has been devised to emphasise the despair that Philip felt at the tragic loss of his favourite sister – along with the irrational self-blame that children often develop psychologically when a parent or close family member dies.

Philip had already effectively 'lost' his mother for a long period to mental illness, making Cécile and her husband his surrogate parents in many ways. Now they too were gone, and one practical consequence of their deaths was to cut him off from his European life and to point the 16-year-old even more directly towards 'Dickie' Mountbatten as his parental figure.

In Chapter Fourteen we shall be examining Prince Philip's other parent, his eccentric mother, the deaf and distrait Princess Alice – much of Episode 304 is devoted to her complex character and her relationship with her complex son. But when it came to fathering there can be no doubt that Philip considered Kurt Hahn to be the father he never had – his 'paterfamilias', in fact.[287]

Prince Charles, of course, did not view that particular fathering connection with any special warmth at all …

CHAPTER TEN

'MYSTERY MAN'

APRIL 1962–MAY 1964

W HEN PLATO WAS ASKED BY A FRIEND TO RECOMMEND the best book to explain the ins and outs of ancient Greece, the philosopher suggested the comic satires of Aristophanes.[288] It is through satire, he liked to teach, that we can edge closest to the truth.[289] So if Plato had been asked the same question about Britain at the beginning of the 1960s, he would certainly have pointed the way to London's Covent Garden and the Fortune Theatre on Russell Street, where the groundbreaking satirical review *Beyond the Fringe* opened in 1961, starring the impertinent young Alan Bennett, Peter Cook, Jonathan Miller and Dudley Moore.[290]

'We are greatly enthused,' declares Queen Elizabeth II (played by Dudley Moore), 'by the prospect of our forthcoming trip to India and Pakistan. Prince Philip tells me that he is very much looking forward to taking me up the Khyber Pass.'[291]

Laughter all round! Sitting in the Fortune Theatre as Episode

210 opens, we see the Prime Minister of the moment, Harold Macmillan and his wife Lady Dorothy, in an imagined scene, enjoying a lesson in what distinguishes satire from standard humour. With standard humour, you laugh. With satire, you may laugh but you wince as well – and somewhere in your brain, consciously or unconsciously, you also resolve that some sort of action is required beyond laughter. Successful satire is a challenge to change things. It is a call to reform and improve the society that produces it – and one of the questions that this episode asks is how satire should have become such a distinguishing feature of the second Elizabethan age.

Britain's modern satire boom exploded into life in the early 1960s. *Private Eye* – a more scabrous and investigative version of *Punch* – published its first issue in 1961, and in the following year even the BBC got in on the act with David Frost and Ned Sherrin's *That Was The Week That Was*. Not afraid to ridicule the Corporation's own deferential coverage of royal events, the late-night TV review produced a sketch that depicted the royal barge sinking – with the entire royal family on board. As the national anthem played, Frost intoned with solemnity: 'And now the Queen, smiling radiantly, is swimming for her life! Her Majesty is wearing a silk ensemble in canary yellow ... Perhaps the lip-readers among you can make out what Prince Philip, the Duke of Edinburgh, is saying to the captain of the barge as she sinks.'[292]

Episode 210, '**Mystery Man**', concludes Season 2 of *The Crown* with the political events of 1963 that many people at the time considered beyond satire: the bungling collapse of Prime Minister Harold Macmillan, the backstairs intrigues leading to the 'emergence' in October of his aristocratic successor Sir Alec Douglas-Home, the former fourteenth Earl of Home, and the scandal that provoked both these events – the Profumo affair of March in that year. The outdated and incompetent manoeuvrings of the Conservative Party seemed purpose-built for laughing at.

The roots of the Profumo Scandal had been laid down two years earlier in the 1961 liaison between John Profumo, 45, the hitherto high-flying Secretary of State for War in Harold Macmillan's Conservative government, and Christine Keeler, a teenage model and show girl – at the same time that Keeler was involved with Captain Yevgeny Ivanov, a Soviet naval attaché at the Russian Embassy in London.[293] This created an obvious security risk, and when suspicions emerged in March 1963, Profumo at first denied any involvement with Keeler, only to admit a few weeks later that he had lied to the House

1963 – Sitting pretty: Christine Keeler, aged 21

117

of Commons. He had no choice but to resign humiliatingly from both the government and from Parliament.[294]

When Macmillan had first cross-questioned Profumo on the issue, however, he had accepted his War Minister's assurances without serious questioning, and Profumo's bare-faced duping dealt a body blow to the Prime Minister's reputation. Macmillan had little choice but to resign himself in October 1963. He tried to use an operation that month on a benign prostate complication as an alibi for his departure,[295] but in truth his own reputation and that of the Tory Party had been shattered by the affair.[296]

The scandal had high-society and even royal ramifications that were gleefully exploited by the press. Keeler, Profumo and Ivanov had been brought together at louche parties and country house gatherings organised by Stephen Ward, a fashionable society osteopath, who built on his skill at manipulating bones and tendons to create a social circle of aristocrats, diplomats and good-time girls like Keeler and her friend Mandy Rice-Davies. Ward's party venues ranged from his mews house in Marylebone to the Thames-side cottage that he rented on Lord Astor's country estate at Cliveden in Buckinghamshire, where he assembled his glamorous and high-powered guests essentially for the purposes of sex.[297]

The censorious considered the osteopath to be no better than a high-society pimp, and, after the scandal became public, Ward faced charges at the Old Bailey for profiting from the immoral earnings of Keeler, Rice-Davies and others. Condemned for plumbing 'the very depths of lechery and depravity' and found guilty on the charges relating to Keeler and Rice-Davies, Ward took an overdose of sleeping pills and died on 3 August 1963, aged 50, before he could be sentenced to what would certainly have been a lengthy term of imprisonment.[298]

As the scandal spread wider – the screen timeline has been compressed into a few weeks rather than a few months – the cast of characters came to include Lord Astor himself (a patient of Ward's and a political ally of Profumo); Peter Rachman, the infamous slum property landlord and a former lover of Keeler's; Aloysius 'Lucky' Gordon, a flamboyant Jamaican jazz singer with a history of petty crime; Johnny Edgecombe, an ex-merchant seaman from Antigua who contrived to knife Gordon in a row over Gordon's behaviour towards Keeler; several call girls – and Prince Philip, the Duke of Edinburgh.[299]

The Prince had certainly rubbed shoulders with Ward in the mid-1940s when both were young men about town, but Philip never received any medical treatment from Ward as an osteopath as shown in this episode's opening scenes. Both had attended lunches at their friend Baron Nahum's colourful Thursday Club,[300] and then, on 9 June 1961, Ward paid Philip a visit at Buckingham Palace. The osteopath had developed a sideline in graceful sketches that could capture a flattering likeness, and he had secured a commission from the *Illustrated London News*, then the glossy staple of every dentist's waiting room, to execute portraits of several members of the current royal family, ranging from Princess Margaret and Princess Marina of Kent to the Duke of Edinburgh himself.[301] That 9 June Ward spent some 20 minutes with Philip sketching out several studies for an elegant portrait that featured on the opening page of the *ILN* two weeks later.[302]

119

Episode 210 opens a year before these events in April 1962, with Prince Philip waking up in bed with a crick in his neck, which gets worse as he puts himself through his regular morning routine of commando exercises – the star jumps quite finish him off. But a visit to Stephen Ward's clinic in Marylebone resolves the pain with the skilful neck manipulation and bone 'clicking' for which Ward was renowned. All this is dramatic invention – but mischievous observers of some photographs taken at Ward's indiscreet parties later identified the shadowy dark silhouette of a faceless figure who, gossip asserted, was actually Prince Philip. Hence the title of this episode – *Mystery Man*.[303]

In June 1963 a Conservative Party gathering in the Midlands made reference to 'a rumour floating around the country that a member of the Royal Family is involved' with Christine Keeler, and the *Daily Mirror* jumped forward ostensibly to defend the Prince's reputation with a lurid front page – 'Prince Philip and the Profumo Scandal'. This rumour, it stated, was 'utterly unfounded', and the *Mirror* went on to set out the story of the royal sketches for the *ILN*. 'Apart from these private sittings,' the paper stated, 'there were no further contacts between Dr. Ward and the members of the Royal Family concerned', and that put paid to Prince Philip's involvement with regard to the media.[304] There were no more newspaper stories.

Unfortunately, the Queen's involvement in the political ramifications of the scandal were not so easily disposed of. By 1963 Elizabeth II had been working with Harold Macmillan for half a dozen years, her longest relationship with any of her prime ministers to that date, and they had come to appreciate each other's company. When he fell ill on one occasion, the

Claire Foy is made up for her role as the 30-year-old Queen Elizabeth II
in Episode 201 of *The Crown* – 'Misadventure'. © Des Willie / Netflix, Inc.

In 1957 Elizabeth II proclaimed her husband 'Prince of the United Kingdom' – without ceremony.
The Crown imagined how a princely crowning might have been. © Robert Viglasky / Netflix, Inc.

While Elizabeth II shivered at Sandringham (left) through the winter of 1956-57,
her husband Philip, played by Matt Smith (above and lower right), enjoyed the pleasures of
the South Pacific with his naval chum Mike Parker (lower left), played by Daniel Ings.

Left © Stuart Hendry / Netflix, Inc. Right both © Coco Van Oppens / Netflix, Inc.

Antony Armstrong-Jones, played by Matthew Goode (above) in Season 2, first met
Princess Margaret (right) played by Vanessa Kirby, at a dinner party in London in 1958.
Their romance took off after he photographed the princess later that year.

'Unintelligent and unremarkable' was the verdict of Jackie Kennedy, played by Jodi Balfour (above), when she met Elizabeth II at Buckingham Palace in June 1961. © Alex Bailey / Netflix, Inc.

Security fears meant that the long-delayed visit of the Queen and Prince Philip to Ghana in West Africa had its difficult moments in November 1961 … © Coco Van Oppens / Netflix, Inc.

... until Elizabeth II stepped into the arms of President Nkrumah and the couple danced 'The Highlife' together. In an age when racial segregation was often the practice – and actually the law in South Africa and numerous US states – it was a gesture that made headlines around the world, and firmly established Queen Elizabeth II's leadership of Britain's multi-racial Commonwealth of nations. © Alex Bailey / Netflix, Inc.

The early 1960s saw the arrival of Philip and Elizabeth's 'new' family – the Queen pregnant (above) with Prince Andrew (born 1960), then celebrating the christening of Prince Edward (below) at Windsor in May 1964. Both © Alex Bailey / Netflix, Inc.

Queen sent him what she called a 'small "reviver"' – a bottle of champagne, with a handwritten note.[305] Their weekly audiences expanded happily as Macmillan, 67 in 1963, enjoyed his fatherly tutelage of the still young Queen, 37, while Elizabeth herself grew in confidence – though not becoming so confident, at the end of the day, that she could challenge the arrangements which he would make for his own succession.

Until the Profumo Scandal, Macmillan had enjoyed a more successful premiership than many would have anticipated after the debacle of Suez. Growing affluence in the late 1950s floated the Tories to victory in the 1959 general election under Macmillan's catchy slogan, 'You've never had it so good!'. When *The Adventures of Superman* reached British television in the mid-1950s, that suggested an obvious nickname for the premier, and 'Supermac' he became – until the summer of 1963 when the Profumo Scandal brought him down.[306] The arrogance of Ward and his hedonistic upper-class circle reflected the less attractive aspects of Tory affluence, and it seemed to hit the normally resilient Macmillan harder than many expected. Some wondered if he had taken the betrayal by his War Minister as a personal blow, although he had never been especially close to Profumo.

On 20 September 1963, in their weekly audience, Macmillan told the Queen he had come to feel – and was informing his colleagues – that he should leave Downing Street within a few months, and Elizabeth duly voiced her sadness and thanks.[307] But Supermac was canny enough to realise that whatever polite regrets the Queen might express about the news, her deeper worry was the personal role that she would now have to play in choosing his successor, since the Conservatives still had no set mechanism for selecting a new leader. As the confusion following Eden's departure six years earlier had made clear, the ill-defined Tory process of 'emergence' could verge on chaos, and Elizabeth was desperate to avoid the same mess again. For her part, she preferred not to get involved at all, if she could help it.

'She feels the great importance of maintaining the prerogative intact,' noted Macmillan. 'After all, if she invited someone to form a government and he failed, what harm was done?'[308]

As we saw in Chapter Three, it had been the Tory grandee Lord Salisbury, with his semi-comical speech impediment, who had quizzed the cabinet and other grandees in 1957 as to whether they preferred 'Wab' (R. A. Butler) or 'Hawold' for the leadership of the party, and hence the premiership.[309] Six years later Macmillan wanted to play the grandee himself – with the principal aim of keeping his deputy and long-time rival 'Rab' Butler out of Downing Street. 'From the first day of his premiership to the last,' wrote Iain Macleod, a rising star on the liberal wing of the party, 'Macmillan was determined that Butler, although incomparably the best qualified of the contenders, should not succeed him'.[310]

Macleod was correct – and also correct in his inference that Macmillan was personally jealous of his deputy. Butler's visionary 1944 Education Act that had extended free secondary education to all gave Butler a far better claim than Macmillan to being seen as the post-war father of modernising Conservatism. But in 1963 the so-called 'Butler Act' was nearly 20 years in the past, and despite recent good work as a reforming Home Secretary, Rab lacked the panache to lead the Tories into the election they would have to fight by the

October of the following year – he was 'a slab of cold fish' in the acerbic opinion of the former Defence Minister, Walter Monckton.[311] Labour's recently elected leader Harold Wilson was licking his lips in anticipation.

Macmillan changed his mind about resigning – the whiff of the hustings quite revived the old bruiser's battle spirits. He decided that he would fight the next year's election, after all. But on 7 October, the night before he was due to inform the cabinet of his new resolve, he was laid low with a prostate attack – 'I found it impossible to pass water and an excruciating pain when I attempted to do so,' he noted in his diary. 'I was seized by terrible spasms.'[312] The PM was in agony throughout the cabinet meeting, having to leave the room twice, and that evening his doctors ordered him straight into hospital for surgery. Macmillan now finally accepted that the moment had presented itself for his resignation, but he was still determined that he should oversee the choice of his successor – a process complicated by the fact that the entire Tory Party was just moving up to Blackpool for its annual conference.

There, in the Winter Gardens' Empress Ballroom, the ebullient Lord Hailsham, campaign manager of the Tories' sweeping election victory of 1959, was already campaigning on his own behalf, planning to take advantage of the recent legislation that allowed peers to renounce their titles.[313] Other candidates included Iain Macleod, then Secretary of State for the Colonies; the Chancellor of the Exchequer, Reginald Maudling; and another up-and-comer, Edward Heath, who would have been a stronger candidate if his negotiations to join the Common Market had not been recently rebuffed by General de Gaulle.

None of these candidacies, however, were really thriving. Hailsham's blustering style – at one point he brandished his nappy-clad daughter in front of the Blackpool delegates and fed her with a baby bottle – was falling flat, while the consensus was developing that Heath, Macleod and Maudling were just a bit too young. There was no one to match the sober – and rather depressing – gravitas of Butler.

A few weeks earlier, Macmillan would happily have gone with Hailsham, to whom he had recently entrusted a number of special assignments for unemployment and higher education. But with Lord Hailsham sabotaged by his over-flamboyant campaigning, and Macmillan sharing the view that Heath, Maudling and Macleod should wait their moment, the Prime Minister turned to another aristocrat, the fourteenth Earl of Home who had, like Hailsham, just acquired the legal option of resigning his title through the Peerage Act of July 1963.

It was Macmillan himself who had plucked Home from comparative obscurity to take over the Foreign Office only three years earlier, and the peer had proved a loyal and solid colleague. 'Alec' Home was no genius, but he was steady and straightforward, coming across as a friendly doctor as he peered over the top of his trademark half-moon spectacles. As Foreign Secretary, Home had played a constructive part in the negotiations for the Partial Nuclear Test Ban Treaty of August 1963 – whose success had earned the government some respite from the ramifications of the Profumo Scandal. But insiders wondered whether the Prime Minister had not really picked out Home as the best available opponent to thwart the ambitions of his own long-term rival and adversary R. A. Butler – and so it now proved.

On 9 October 1963 the ailing Macmillan was admitted to King Edward VII Hospital for Officers in Marylebone, near Harley Street, ready for surgery next day. There he wrote to the Queen to tell her that his resignation now seemed inevitable, and he summoned Alec Home to his bedside, giving him a letter to be read out to the party conference publicly announcing the news. He had wanted and had intended to stay in office to fight next year's election, Macmillan explained, but his imminent surgery now made that impossible. He also urged Home strongly to throw his own hat into the leadership ring. Having this letter to read out to the 4,000 delegates in Blackpool would be a very good start to his campaign.[314]

The missive had the intended effect. Although Butler, as deputy premier, was technically in charge of the conference, Home's shock announcement and his reading out of the Prime Minister's personal letter of wishes to the awe-struck delegates quite took the wind out of Butler's sails – and, indeed, of his other rivals. Home's fatherly manner played well in the crisis, and by the end of the conference he was being rated as strongly as anyone – with the added impetus of the horse that makes its bid on the final bend.

Back in London on 14 and 15 October, all the leadership contenders and other Tories – the Chief Whips and senior party officials – commenced their pilgrimages to Macmillan's bedside at King Edward VII's. The Prime Minister was 'still woozy from the anaesthetic ...' according to his biographer, Alistair Horne. But 'it was now clear that, sick as he was, Macmillan was still going to hold all the strings in his hand until the very last minute, controlling events from his bed'.[315]

While putting on a tantalising show over the days that followed for the reporters and photographers gathered outside the hospital, Macmillan's ostensible purpose was to take 'soundings' from all these comings and goings in order to prepare the advice that he could give to the Queen – and at 11.15 on the morning of Friday the 18th, Elizabeth duly arrived.

'She came in alone,' wrote Macmillan later, 'with a firm step, and those brightly shining eyes which are her chief beauty. She seemed deeply moved; so was I.' According to Sir John Richardson, Macmillan's doctor, the young Queen had tears in her eyes. (According also to Richardson's later account, Macmillan's prostate complication was 'benign' and he could easily have resumed his official duties two weeks later if he had not decided to step down for political reasons.)[316]

Once Prime Minister and Sovereign were alone, Macmillan asked if he could read out the memorandum he had put together over the past few days, apologising that he did not feel strong enough to speak without a text. 'She expressed her gratitude, and said that she did not need and did not intend to seek any other advice but mine. I then read the memorandum. She agreed that Lord Home was the most likely choice to get general support, as well as really the best and strongest character ... I said that I thought speed was important and hoped she would send for Lord Home immediately – as soon as she got back to the Palace. He could then begin to work. She agreed.'[317]

Macmillan added, both verbally and in the second part of his memorandum, that the Queen should *not* appoint Home as Prime Minister at this first audience, but should use the old-fashioned formula of 'inviting him to form an administration', so he could consult his colleagues before giving a final answer.

Could Home, in other words, get Butler and his other competitors on board, since without their support he could not command a majority in his party or in the Commons?

To round off the proceedings, Macmillan handed over his memorandum to be kept in the royal archives as justification for whatever action Elizabeth might now take on his advice. Unfolded, the document filled a large white envelope which the Queen took from her ex-Prime Minister and passed on to her private secretary, Sir Michael Adeane, who was standing by the now-open door. As Adeane received the envelope, its huge size 'made him look,' thought Macmillan, 'like the Frog Footman'.[318]

Alice in Wonderland? Alice Through the Looking Glass? Many were the unflattering analogies made in the days that followed about Macmillan's hospital bed theatrics – and they have intensified as historians have analysed these events over the years. The crucial detail is that the Prime Minister had formally resigned at 9.30 that morning.[319] So, the 'advice' handed over two hours later by Harold Macmillan, ex-Prime Minister, had no constitutional status whatsoever. Elizabeth was *not* compelled to accept it, as she was normally bound to accept and follow the advice of an elected Prime Minister. Indeed, her responsibility was actually to step back and take a hard look at what this ex-official with no government status was proposing.

The truth was, however, that Macmillan's personal preference was the Queen's as well. Elizabeth had established no closeness at all with the damp and complex deputy premier. 'Rab wasn't her cup of tea,' explained one royal aide to the historian Ben Pimlott. 'When she got the advice to call Alec she thought

"Thank God". She loved Alec – he was an old friend. They talked about dogs and shooting together. They were both Scottish landowners, the same sort of people, like old school friends.' While the Queen knew very well that she would have been 'constitutionally justified in sending for Rab', she felt no temptation whatsoever to do so.[320]

In the opinion of Ben Pimlott, Elizabeth II's unquestioning acceptance of Harold Macmillan's advice to pick Douglas-Home was 'the biggest political misjudgement of her reign'.[321] But as events turned out, the retiring Prime Minister's advice proved quite shrewd – in hard political terms, at least. As 1963 moved into 1964, the Conservatives made a remarkable recovery under Douglas-Home's leadership, losing the 15 October election by the merest whisker – 0.7 per cent of the vote. As we shall see in the next chapter (covering Episode 301, the start of Season 3), Harold Wilson's Labour Party enjoyed an overall majority of just four seats. If only 900 voters in eight constituencies had switched their votes, Supermac's aristocratic and apparently eccentric hospital choice would have remained Prime Minister.[322]

Episode 210 concludes with the unresolved dramatic strand left over from Episode 201 – Elizabeth's 1956 discovery in her husband's briefcase of the photograph of the Russian ballerina Ulanova. The couple's reconciliation over this imagined incident must, by definition, be fictitious, but it does provide a dramatic device to reflect the refreshed closeness that the Queen and her husband enjoyed in the early 1960s with the birth of their 'new family' – the princes Andrew (b. 19 February 1960) and Edward (b. 10 March 1964).

CHAPTER ELEVEN

'OLDING'

OCTOBER 1964–FEBRUARY 1975

Season 3, Episode 301, opens with the Queen inspecting a new issue of postage stamps, giving her the chance to comment on how the passing years have changed her appearance 'from young woman,' as she puts it, '... to old bat'. 'Age is rarely kind,' she reflects '... to anyone.'[323]

1967 – Profile of Elizabeth II, 41, on UK stamps to this day

Meanwhile, we, the viewers, can reflect on this new season's change in casting, from Claire Foy to Olivia Colman, as she inspects her new postal profile. The timing of this new issue, based on the famous Arnold Machin silhouette of Elizabeth that features on British stamps to this day, has been brought forward to coincide with the 1964 opening of Season 3, and the Postmaster General's name has been changed accordingly. There would not normally have been so many officials present for the inspection, and they almost certainly would not have included the Surveyor of the Queen's Pictures, Sir Anthony Blunt. But Anthony Blunt, as we shall see, will play a crucial role in the drama of this episode...

Much of *The Crown* is set in Buckingham Palace – you could hardly fail to have noticed that – but a fair proportion of the drama also unrolls in the Palace of Westminster (the Houses of Parliament) and inside No. 10 Downing Street, the residence of the Prime Minister, since much of the ongoing narrative revolves around *Politics* with a capital 'P'. Season 1 was built around Winston Churchill, Elizabeth II's first Prime Minister, with all the grumblings and grandeur of the great man's final spell in office. Season 2 has recounted the adventures and misadventures of Churchill's less imposing Conservative successors – Sir Anthony Eden, Harold Macmillan and the fourteenth Earl of Home, who renounced his peerage to serve as Sir Alec Douglas-Home. Now Season 3 introduces us to Britain's version of socialism and the '14th Mr Wilson', as Alec Douglas-Home derisively called his opponent in the 1964 general election, when Britain voted out the Tories and entrusted its destiny for the next five years to Harold Wilson and the Labour Party.[324]

The contest was a cliffhanger, as we have already seen at the end of Chapter Ten – but Mr Wilson was ready for his encounter with history. At 2.47 on the afternoon of Friday 16 October 1964, Labour gained the 316th seat it needed to secure a majority in the 630-seat House of Commons,[325] and the Downing Street civil servants promptly instructed Wilson to don the striped trousers and long morning tailcoat that tradition required a prime minister to wear for his audience at the Palace. Wilson's Tory predecessors Churchill, Eden, Macmillan and Home had all dressed themselves in that gear whenever they went to see the Queen – sometimes with a top hat as well.[326]

But Mr Wilson politely declined. Striped trousers, perhaps – long coat, certainly not. Not for the leader of the triumphant People's Party. The new Prime Minister had a short black jacket brought down from his wardrobe in Hampstead Garden Suburb, and that was how Wilson dressed when he went to kiss hands with the Queen.[327] The brilliant first-class, alpha-plus Bachelor of Arts (Philosophy, Politics & Economics) – Oxford's youngest don since Cardinal Wolsey, and a lecturer in Economic History at the age of 21 – jealously guarded his image as a plain and everyday man: tinned salmon, please, not smoked; holidays in a bungalow on the Isles of Scilly; khaki shorts in August to recall his Boy Scout days; then an hour or so with the Meccano set, enlivened by some Gilbert & Sullivan on the gramophone. Most famously of all, Harold Wilson insisted on being photographed puffing on his battered old pipe – though, as we see in this Episode 301, the premier smoked Havana cigars in private and greatly preferred cognac to beer.[328]

When Wilson arrived at the Palace that Friday afternoon, he discovered that, in fact, Elizabeth II could be quite as relaxed about etiquette as he was. In view of the clear Westminster majority that the Labour Party now commanded, she simply asked its leader to form a government, without ceremony. The hand-kissing, he later recalled, was taken 'as read'.[329] Nor was the Queen disconcerted by her new Prime Minister's request that he might bring along his wife for the occasion – another innovation – with his father and his sister turning up in another car.[330]

But the Queen did have some surprises in store for him. With his anti-elitist disdain for the rituals of monarchy, the new Prime Minister had not bothered to research precisely what was involved in his audience at the Palace every Tuesday. He arrived for his first encounter anticipating some cosy round-up of the political situation in general terms – with a cup of tea as well, perhaps.

Elizabeth II had other ideas, for she had been reading the contents of her red leather 'boxes' more carefully than ever. The arrival of a socialist government had prompted fierce speculation against sterling, and Wilson had generated additional gloom by harping on about the £800 million balance of payments deficit which was the legacy of 'thirteen years of Tory mis-rule'.[331] This might not be Wilson's fault, but Her Majesty wished to know precisely what her First Lord of the Treasury now intended to do about the problem. She was the Queen, not some television interviewer to be fobbed off with platitudes. She expected her Prime Minister to take her into his confidence – and to know his facts, as Wilson discovered in another audience a week or so later.

'Very interesting,' said the Queen, 'this idea of a new town in the Bletchley area.' The Prime Minister looked blank. It was the first he had heard of the proposal to build the new town in Buckinghamshire that became known as Milton Keynes. The plan was set out in a Cabinet Committee paper which the Queen had studied, but which Wilson had set aside to read at the weekend.[332]

'I shall certainly advise my successor to do his homework before his audience,' he said a dozen years later in his retirement speech, 'and to read all his telegrams and Cabinet Committee papers in time, and not leave them to the weekend, or he will feel like an unprepared schoolboy.'[333]

From this uncomfortable start, Elizabeth II's relationship with her first Labour Prime Minister could only improve. Alec Douglas-Home compared the Queen's handling of her audiences to a friendly headmaster receiving the head prefect in his study, listening hard and asking shrewd direct questions, but always being supportive – while being especially understanding of the difficulties that politicians can get themselves into for politics' sake.[334] Now Harold Wilson found the same. It was a sustaining element of his working week that he had not anticipated. The Queen, he discovered, was on his side in a fundamental fashion. She was the one working colleague, he confided once to the Prime Minister of Eire, to whom he could take his problems without feeling that he might be sharpening a knife for his own back. The most trustworthy of fellow ministers had their own axes to grind, personal or political, but the Queen's preoccupation quite simply started and ended with the welfare of her nation.[335]

Wilson and monarch soon became a surprising – and surprisingly effective – team. Elizabeth 'tamed' the awkward Labour man to use the word coined by the Queen Mother.[336] Following the death of Winston Churchill in January 1965, the Queen gave a reception for the world leaders attending the funeral – among them Ian Smith, the defiant white settler leader of Southern Rhodesia that was still part of the Commonwealth, but only just. Wilson was hoping to repair the situation through informal contact with Smith, and he asked the Queen if she could invite him to the reception, though Smith was technically ineligible, not being the head of a Sovereign government. Elizabeth agreed – then noticed after an hour or so of drinks and small talk that she could see no sign of their quarry. Having conferred with Wilson, she summoned an equerry to seek out Mr Smith immediately.[337]

The Rhodesian leader was duly discovered enjoying a steak in the restaurant of the Hyde Park Hotel and was hauled sheepishly to the Palace swearing that he had never received the invitation – though his High Commissioner had seen him put it into his jacket pocket. The Queen chose to be gracious as he stammered his apologies, and Wilson then had the chance of the private conversation that he had been seeking.[338]

Peter Morgan opens Season 3 by looking at the 'pre-taming' differences and mistrust that were hovering between Harold Wilson and Elizabeth II in 1964, as played out through the most notorious spy scandal of the era – the betrayals of the 'Cambridge Four', who would later become 'Five'. At the start of Elizabeth's reign there had only been 'Two', when early in the summer of 1951, just three months after the young Queen's accession, Britain and America – and the West as a whole – had been rocked by the defections to the Soviet Union of Guy Burgess, a high-ranking member of MI5,** and Donald Maclean, Head of the American Department in the Foreign Office. Burgess and Maclean, it seemed, had been systematically betraying British secrets to the Soviets throughout the Second World War and the Cold War for the best part of 20 years, taking flight to Moscow that May on the point of being unmasked.[339]

It was known that the two men had been friends at Cambridge University in the early 1930s, part of a circle of gifted young left-wingers who feared the rise of the Fascist dictators on the Continent and despised the old British Establishment's torpor in response to the misery of the Depression. Idealistically, they looked for salvation to the new factories and collective farms of the Soviet Union, where, at that date, the crimes and mass murders of Stalin were not widely known.[340]

Kim Philby, a senior officer in MI6, had been one of Burgess and Maclean's closest associates, both at Cambridge and thereafter. So when the pair defected in order to forestall discovery, suspicions started to drift towards Philby as people tried to work out who was in the know and might have tipped the men off.[341]

** 'MI5' is the name of Britain's domestic counter-intelligence and security service which still operates today, while 'MI6' designates the British intelligence service operating abroad. MI6 are 'our' spies, it has been said, while MI5 exists to catch 'their' spies. Until the end of the Second World War there were also Military Intelligence Sections 1 (Code-Breaking), 2 (Russia and Scandinavia), 3 (Eastern Europe), and 4 (Aerial Reconnaissance) with sections 7–19 covering projects like Propaganda, Signals and Aid to European Resistance Movements. MI5 and MI6 remain today as the only survivors of this numerical system.

Questions were asked in Parliament a few years later about the possible existence of a 'Third Man' – i.e. Kim Philby – working as a double agent inside the Foreign Office,[342] following a gloating Moscow press conference in which Burgess and Maclean had criticised the 'senselessness and danger' of Western policy. We know from their Moscow friends that the pair were bitterly disillusioned by the harsh realities of Soviet life – 'Can you imagine Glasgow on a Saturday night in the nineteenth century?' Guy Burgess once asked his fellow exile Jim Riordan who would serve as a pallbearer at his funeral in 1963.[343] But that was not their message to the world's press as they contrived to make British intelligence appear especially hapless.[344]

The problem for London was the mistrust – and the possible withdrawal of collaboration – that Britain's incompetence risked provoking in her main Cold War ally, the United States. But in 1963 help arrived in the confession of Michael Straight, a long-time Soviet agent operating in America, who is depicted in this episode making mysterious telephone calls in Washington.

Born into a family of immense wealth – his father Willard was a partner at J. P. Morgan – Straight had arrived at Trinity College, Cambridge, in 1934, and soon became a friend of Burgess, Maclean and Philby through the 'Apostles', the elite intellectual society whose past members had included Bertrand Russell, and which contained only 12 members at any one time.[345] By 1934 the ruling ethos of the Apostles was unashamedly Marxist, with members like Anthony Blunt, a brilliant young mathematician-turned-art historian, who soon became a lover of Straight and recruited the American for

Russian intelligence. In 1937 Straight returned to America, and the Cambridge spies could congratulate themselves on their first major infiltration when Straight almost immediately became a speechwriter for President Franklin D. Roosevelt, at the very heart of Washington policymaking.[346]

But the Nazi–Soviet Non-Aggression Pact of 1939 that enabled Hitler to swallow Poland undermined the Marxist sympathies of Michael Straight. He joined the US Army Air Corps as a bomber pilot in the Second World War, and when, after the war, he became publisher of his family's magazine, *The New Republic*, he steered its editorial policy towards an anti-Stalinist stance.[347] One of the triggers of Guy Burgess's defection to Russia in 1951 had been a chance encounter with Straight in Washington, and Burgess's realisation that his fellow Apostle was no longer a Communist, and that Straight might well take steps to reveal the dark secret of the past they shared.[348]

Straight himself later claimed in *After Long Silence*, his self-justifying autobiography, that he actually drove to the British Embassy on three occasions in the years 1949–51 to do precisely that, before losing his nerve.[349] In the event, it was a 1963 offer from the Kennedy administration of a position on the prestigious National Endowment for the Arts that prompted the now-remorseful spy into action. Realising that one passport to this plum job would have to be FBI security clearance, Straight decided to volunteer the truth.[350]

In January 1963 Kim Philby had defected to Moscow, confirming to the world that he was indeed the 'Third Man'. Now Michael Straight could reveal who was the 'Fourth' – his former lover, Anthony Blunt, who had not only become

Professor of Art History at the University of London and a director of the prestigious Courtauld Institute of Art, but had also, since 1945, occupied an office at Buckingham Palace. The fellow Apostle and Cambridge co-conspirator with Straight, Philby, Burgess and Maclean, had risen to become Sir Anthony Blunt KCVO (Knight Commander of the Royal Victorian Order), Surveyor of the Queen's Pictures, and hence curator of one of Britain's most prestigious art collections – knighted by Her Majesty in 1956 as a particular sign of her personal favour and gratitude.[351]

By the time the security services brought this shocking news to Elizabeth's private secretary, Michael Adeane, they had already worked out a deal with Blunt. The spy would confess all in interrogation over the following years, and in return for his confession and silence he would be spared prosecution. Blunt would be allowed to retain his prestigious position at Buckingham Palace,[352] since this would help British 'intelligence' to conceal their incompetence – just as they had deliberately allowed the compromised Kim Philby to evade their clutches and board a Soviet freighter in Beirut at the beginning of 1963. In both cases, they preferred to let the traitors escape judgement in order to avoid the embarrassment of public revelation and the inevitable trial and retribution that would follow.

In the case of Blunt, it seems likely that MI5 decided to conceal his double identity from the Queen, instructing Adeane *not* to pass on the truth about the spy to his boss. When Mrs Thatcher finally unveiled Blunt's treason in 1979, angrily stripping him of his knighthood, the Queen told her Prime Minister 'It doesn't surprise me one bit' – which was hardly the response of someone who had been privy to the full and unpleasant truth about her Surveyor of Pictures for the past 16 years.[353]

Nor was the Queen alone in her probable ignorance. Official documents have since made very clear – astonishingly – that neither Alec Douglas-Home *nor* Harold Wilson, Britain's two prime ministers in these years, was ever told about the high-level treachery of Blunt. MI5 limited the truth to the narrowest possible circle, and one focus of Margaret Thatcher's particular anger in 1979 was the arrogance of civil servants in concealing such dangerous betrayals – and their own mistakes – from their elected superiors.[354]

In this context, however, there is another more challenging interpretation of the Queen's ambiguous 'It doesn't surprise me ...' remark – namely that Michael Adeane *did* brief her about Blunt's treachery in the spring of 1964, but warned her that she should not share it with her current Prime Minister Alec Douglas-Home, nor, more importantly, with his likely successor, Harold Wilson, who was under some suspicion at that time of being himself a Soviet spy. As early as 1946, British intelligence had opened a file on Harold Wilson's activities, tracking the contacts of the new young president of the Board of Trade (then aged 30) in the post-war Labour government as he started travelling to and from the Soviet Union. In 1956 the KGB (the Russian Committee for State Security, recently formed in 1954) opened an agent recruitment file of their own on Wilson, under the code name 'Olding', the title of this episode.[355] And then, in 1964, US intelligence decided to focus their own high-powered attention on this potentially subversive new British Prime Minister, filing him as 'Oat Sheaf'.[356]

The basis of all this suspicion were the frequent journeys – 20 or so in less than a dozen years – that Wilson made to Russia in the late 1940s and early 1950s, in the course of which he met such prominent Soviet statesmen as Anastas Mikoyan, Vyacheslav Molotov and Nikita Khrushchev, and delighted in introducing his Russian friends to the joys of cricket beside the Moskva River.[357] The purpose of the journeys was to arrange timber sales to satisfy the demands of Britain's post-war housing reconstruction – first on behalf of the government, then, after Labour's 1951 loss of office, as the representative of various private firms and agencies.[358]

Though much-probed by all manner of intelligence agencies and journalists, no dishonestly pro-Soviet or anti-British purpose was ever linked to Harold Wilson's commercial ventures in Russia – while as a Labour politician he gave little indication of pro-Soviet leanings. Through the 1950s Wilson distanced himself steadily from Aneurin Bevan's radical left wing of the Labour Party, moving rightwards to join forces with the centrist and 'safe', Winchester-educated Hugh Gaitskell, Labour leader from 1955 and leader of the opposition. Wilson made his name while serving as Gaitskell's clever and eloquent Shadow Chancellor of the Exchequer – joining his colleague George Brown in deriding Swiss bankers who speculated against the pound and seemed to be holding British fortunes to ransom as the 'Gnomes of Zurich'[359] – while shrugging off whatever attempts that Russian agents may have made to recruit him. The Soviet recruitment file on 'Olding' was eventually closed with the regretful comment: 'The development did not come to fruition.'[360]

Then, out of the blue on 18 January 1963, at the age of only

56, the previously healthy Hugh Gaitskell died unexpectedly of an obscure illness – systemic lupus erythematosus (SLE) – and Harold Wilson was elected his successor as leader of the Labour Party a few weeks later. Instantly the Soviet rumours revived again, though this time with a more conspiratorial – and even melodramatic – edge: that the Soviets had poisoned Gaitskell in order to get their own man in place as leader of the opposition, poised for the imminent occupation of Downing Street.[361] Anatoliy Golitsyn, the highest level KGB agent ever to defect to the West, gave credence to the accusation when he was interviewed by MI5 in the spring of 1963.[362]

But though Golitsyn provided MI5 with solid insight into the Cambridge 'Ring of Five' and other spy scandals of the time, his allegations against Wilson were no more solid than the suspicions surrounding Wilson's timber trade travels. When pushed, the Russian defector confessed he had only heard a rumour that the KGB were planning a political assassination 'somewhere in Europe'. He could produce no solid evidence about Hugh Gaitskell's death – and lupus was an unpredictable cause of fatality in 1963, as it is today.

Nor could Golitsyn, or anyone else, explain why the Russians should want to murder Hugh Gaitskell in January 1963, when the solid-gold Labour No. 2 and favourite to succeed him at that time was the outspokenly anti-Soviet right-winger George Brown. Harold Wilson's leadership victory had come as a last-minute surprise against the odds, after a succession of Brown's mercurial and drunken gaffes had sabotaged his own cause.[363] Courtesy of *Private Eye*, George Brown's alcohol-fuelled behaviour came to inspire the expression 'tired and emotional'.[364]

So, as events turned out, Britain's most eminent Russian double agent of the mid-1960s did *not* occupy No. 10 Downing Street. As we see in this episode, the real double agent stalked the hallowed corridors of Buckingham Palace.

CHAPTER TWELVE

'MARGARETOLOGY'

NOVEMBER 1965

B Y THE AUTUMN OF 1965 PRINCESS MARGARET AND TONY Armstrong-Jones were the swingingest couple in all of 'Swinging London', both 35 years old, with two healthy children as evidence of their happy and loving marriage – to that date, at least. 'Tony and Margaret were so good together,' remembers their friend interior designer and torch singer Nicky Haslam. 'They made a marvellous double-act, playing off each other with a rivalry that, in those days, was rather charming. There was always huge humour and great fun buzzing between them'.[365]

In exploring the ambiguous role which Princess Margaret played throughout her life as younger sister to Elizabeth II, Episode 302 contains a number of incidents that are not factually 'true'. But the overall purpose of the episode is to explore the larger truths inside the Princess's complicated character and royal role – starting with the episode title,

'Margaretology'. An article in The *New York Times* in these years quoted someone who described himself as 'a self-confessed "Margaretologist"', and who could thus be defined as a devotee of 'Margaretology' – though it is difficult to say how many others belonged to this rarefied cult.

In the mid-1960s, Apartment 1A, KP (Kensington Palace) was the smartest address in London, where guests might encounter Dudley Moore playing the piano of an evening, or the glamorous Cleo Laine singing to the accompaniment of her jazz musician husband John Dankworth. Peter Sellers would roll out his 'Bluebottle' to Spike Milligan's 'Moriarty', with the two comics wickedly embellishing the surreal humour of their groundbreaking *The Goon Show* that had come to command nearly two million listeners on the BBC Home Service – 'You dirty rotten swine! You have deaded me!'[366]

Margaret and Tony shared a sense of style and a mutual love the arts, along with a sexual chemistry that was clearly visible in their inability to keep their hands off each other. In 1965 Tony's usually catty rival Cecil Beaton captured the image of the perfect family in a photograph that was taken outside Apartment 1A – with firstborn David (three) on Tony's shoulders, and baby Sarah (one) sitting solidly in her mother's arms while husband and wife both exude glamorous and well-groomed lovingness.[367]

There was, however, a sardonic edge to this togetherness. The clever couple had a code – 'the bread game' – by which they communicated with each other at dinner parties. Whenever someone round the table uttered a particularly fatuous remark or cliché, a piece of bread would be subtly torn off and quietly pushed across the table in that direction. The person with the most pieces of bread accumulated by supper's end was the 'winner'. The fun, of course, was that no one else was supposed to realise that the contest was in progress – but as the years unfolded the joke turned nasty, with the couple starting to play the game against each other.[368]

Tony's success in the months following the couple's May 1960 marriage was busy and spectacular. In rapid succession he became a consultant to the Council of Industrial Design, artistic adviser to the glamorous new *Sunday Times Colour Magazine,* and was commissioned in 1963 to co-design an angular and much-praised aviary for the London Zoo – Tony affectionately called it his 'bird cage'.[369] As a mark of her

1965 – Smiling Snowdons: Margaret, Sarah,
Tony and David

145

mildly surprised pleasure with her brother-in-law, Elizabeth ennobled him as the Earl of Snowdon in 1961 and appointed him Constable of Caernarfon Castle two years later – in preparation for the investiture ceremonies of Prince Charles as Prince of Wales that were planned for the end of the decade. Welcome to the royal family, Lord Snowdon![370]

Tony's glamorous projects took him here and there – and quite often abroad when he carried out his photographic assignments for *The Sunday Times*. But they also took him increasingly away from his wife – who, in striking contrast, found it difficult to occupy her days. Margaret would seldom rise before 11am, taking tea in bed and completing *The Times* crossword before making contact with the world. Once dressed and downstairs, she might 'do her desk' for an hour or so, then go out to lunch, at which, friends noticed, she was developing the habit of drinking quite heavily. Back home she probably spent the rest of the day inventing things to do, like washing her collection of coral and seashells or shampooing her spaniel Rowley in the bath – she liked to finish Rowley off with a blow-dry.[371]

When her husband did get home, Margaret's welcome could often be needy, demanding reassurance from which Tony sought to escape. He had a studio and metal-welding workshop at KP to which he would retreat for entire evenings with his friend and fellow designer James Cousins, working on his furniture into the small hours. Taking pity on Margaret, Cousins might join her for dinner – through most of which the Princess sat watching the television. But Tony stayed resolutely working in the welding room.

The tension erupted in February 1965 when the family

gathered for their annual service at Windsor to commemorate the death of the revered King George VI. Margaret wanted to stay at Windsor that night, but Tony insisted that he had to go down to Old House, his former family home in Sussex. The couple were with the Queen Mother when the row broke out, and they stalked up and down her drawing room at Royal Lodge shouting fiercely at each other – as if she were not there.

This uncontrolled rancour in front of a family member – Margaret's own mother and the number one fan of 'dear Tony' – was the start of a downward spiral charted by Tony's biographer Anne de Courcy, who spent many hours interviewing her subject.[372] Now arguing in front of other people came to be something of a Snowdon performance – it was almost as if the pair of them took pleasure in it. That summer they got into an argument at the home of Margaret's friend Judy Montagu in Rome, where Tony climbed out of a window and took refuge on the roof, shouting, 'It's the only place I can get away from her!'[373] Later that summer, he also cut short his stay with the whole family up at Balmoral. In the early to mid-1960s the royal sisters had been enjoying their family time in Scotland with their husbands and growing broods of young children, but now Tony slipped away two weeks early.

This was the background for the Snowdons' visit to New York and Washington in November 1965, the subject of Episode 302.[374] The couple had made two overseas tours before – to Denmark and Uganda – but America was the big time. The serious political setting was provided by Britain's ongoing economic difficulties – a combination of the debts run up by Harold Macmillan to fund his 'Never Had It So Good'[375] years, and the mistrust with which the banks and other financial institutions were viewing Harold Wilson's new Labour government.[376] Where better to visit and generate monetary goodwill than in the very heartland of American capitalism?

Harold Wilson had been working hard with the Queen to charm Jack Kennedy's Texan successor in the White House, Lyndon Baines Johnson, who had taken over after JFK's 1963 assassination. The possibility that Elizabeth could help Wilson secure a US financial bailout by issuing a highly coveted invitation to President Johnson to some intimate royal event, like a weekend of shooting in Balmoral, may or may not have been discussed. But LBJ's description of Elizabeth and Wilson operating as a 'double act' does correspond to the historical evidence. After their initial difficulties, which we witnessed in the previous episode (301), the Queen and her Labour Prime Minister could fairly be described as acting, in LBJ's words, like 'tag team wrestlers'.

In November 1964 'LBJ' had been re-elected in his own right by a landslide. With over 60 per cent of the popular vote, the new President had won the largest share of the US electorate for more than a century, and his triumph encouraged his already assertive style.[377] In this episode we see him coarsely discussing the Queen, Harold Wilson and the Brits in general with his old friend Marvin Watson – all while urinating. This crude display was a lifelong habit that started when Johnson was a young senator and used to make use of his office wash basin for this purpose – during meetings. In mixed company, the President might pull down his trousers to scratch his rear end, and he once mortified his National

Security Advisor McGeorge 'Mac' Bundy by demanding that he should deliver an important set of documents to him in the toilet stall – while he was still moving his bowels.[378]

LBJ's crudity knew no bounds. Arthur Goldberg, the US ambassador to the United Nations, recalled a White House meeting in which a group of journalists asked Johnson why America was involved in Vietnam. The President unzipped his fly, according to Goldberg, drew out his substantial organ (which he liked to call 'Jumbo') and declared, 'This is why!'[379]

The Vietnam War was the tragedy that came to define the Johnson presidency – in 1968 it would bring him down[380] – and it was the underlying theme of his relations with Harold Wilson and Britain. US military involvement in Southeast Asia to hold back Communist China and North Vietnam had been a staple of US foreign policy going back long before Kennedy. It was a cornerstone of Western Cold War strategy, in Washington's view, and Johnson's response to Harold Wilson's perpetual pleas for financial bailouts was that Britain should repay the favour by sending troops to help the effort in Vietnam.

Over the months, the President moderated his requests – from an aircraft carrier and fighter squadron down to one regiment, the Black Watch, and eventually to just a few token pipers. But Wilson consistently refused. Popular feeling in Britain was running high against Vietnam, and inside his own party in particular. Wilson knew he would be finished as Labour leader if he conceded to the US – which only made LBJ more furious. 'We've got enough pollution around here already,' he complained in response to yet another London request for a meeting, 'without Harold coming over with his fly open and his pecker hanging out, peeing all over me.'[381]

This backdrop presented the two flying Snowdons with quite a challenge when they landed in New York for their three-week tour in November 1965, and Episode 302 depicts them pulling off the trick with some elan. Harold Wilson's exuberant descriptions of drinking and limerick contests, with Margaret kissing LBJ, are fictitious – but we do know that the occasion was judged a jovial success, with dancing into the small hours. Margaret's role in procuring the financial bailout is original to the drama, and while there were, in fact, three economic rescue efforts – one in November 1964, one in September 1965 and one in July 1966 – none was as a result of this dinner.

In reality, the Snowdons' mishmash of private parties and official events failed to excite many Americans – and generated active hostility back in Britain. Elizabeth had welcomed the idea that her brother-in-law should celebrate the New York publication of his new book of photographs, *Private View*, but the British press saw this as an abuse of the £30,000 or so that taxpayers had stumped up to facilitate the 'jolly'.[382] Margaret and Tony were becoming increasingly unpopular with the press – or, rather, increasingly popular as an easy target. Criticism had started with complaints about the expense of renovating Apartment 1A in 1961[383] – now this US tour marked a further shift in media hostility. The Queen was still off limits, but the Snowdons, it seemed, were not.

Towards the end of the episode we sit in with Philip and Elizabeth as they discuss the Snowdon problem. 'Margaret does suffer more than anyone else by not having a more meaningful role ...' says Elizabeth sympathetically. 'She IS overlooked. And in terms of ability and character and intelligence and flair, she doesn't *deserve* to be overlooked. So why shouldn't we consider expanding the role? Sharing the job a bit more?'

'There are two answers to that question,' replies her husband. 'Neither makes for pretty listening. Yes – the system IS unequal. And unjust. And cruel. Primogeniture divides and destroys families. The system stinks. But in its cruelty and injustice, it reflects something brutal and unfair which no one is suggesting we rearrange – LIFE. We all desire equality, but here's the thing, we weren't born equal.'

Then Philip moves on to his second answer, which turns out to be a story about 'that God-awful monster, Tommy Lascelles', the courtier with whom viewers of *The Crown* will be familiar from Season 1.[384] Sir Alan Frederick Lascelles (1887– 1981), 'Tommy' to his friends since his days at Marlborough College and Oxford, was the long-serving private secretary to the Sovereign from 1943 to 1953. And he certainly ran Buckingham Palace – and just about the whole monarchy – for both King George VI and then for the new young Queen Elizabeth II, steering the crown through the Second World War, the challenges of the post-war Labour government and the coronation of 1953.

If anyone knew the different faces of the house of Windsor it was 'Tommy', and Philip relates how he got drunk one night with the old courtier, who divulged his personal theory about the family that he had studied at such close quarters – 'which I've not repeated to anyone since'.

'Go on,' says the Queen, intrigued.[385]

These speeches are all fictitious, remember, as invented by

writer Peter Morgan, but the Lascelles theory, as now repeated by Prince Philip, is solidly based on historical fact. Start by imagining, says Philip, that exotic creature of royal heraldry, the imperial double-headed eagle, or *Reichsadler*, as it is known in Germany. 'For the purposes of this conversation, I should like you to think of this eagle as representing us – this family. YOUR family. One body, two heads. One name. But two minds. Two characters. Two personalities. Two strains. There have always been the dazzling Windsors and the dull ones.'[386]

Philip then goes on to show how the 'dull' Windsors and the 'dazzling' Windsors have often tended to operate side by side, like the double-headed eagle, in a set of contrasting pairs: 'For every Victoria, you get an Edward VII. For every George V, you get a Prince Eddy. For every George VI, you get an Edward VIII.'[387]

To explain these comparisons – let us start with the dazzling delinquents as listed by Lascelles and Philip: King Edward VII (1841–1910) was Queen Victoria's playboy son and successor as monarch, compelled in 1891 to appear in court following his involvement in the illegal card-playing 'Baccarat' scandal;[388] Prince Eddy (1864–92) was Edward's eldest son, Prince Albert Victor, implicated in the Cleveland Street homosexual brothel scandal and unfairly rumoured – but *popularly* rumoured just the same – to be the (unidentified) Victorian serial killer Jack the Ripper;[389] while Edward VIII (1894–1972) was the dashing but wilful Edward the Abdicator, the Duke of Windsor who, as we have seen in previous chapters, was very happy to suck up to Hitler.[390] Tommy Lascelles had worked for Edward VIII on two occasions, actually resigning from his service in 1929 in protest at his poor behaviour as Prince of Wales, then returning to steer the monarchy through the abdication.[391]

To match these erratic shooting stars, Philip lists the dull but dependable Queen Victoria (1819–1901), who gave the name 'Victorian' to an entire style of smug, boring and priggish behaviour;[392] her plodding grandson King George V (1865–1936) stolidly sticking stamps into his stamp album;[393] followed by *his* equally unexciting son King George VI (1895–1952) stuttering his way to anonymity[394] – all three of them combining, says Philip, to create a thoroughly reliable but 'uninterrupted line of stolid, turgid, dreariness…'

'Culminating in me!' says Elizabeth ruefully, as she understands where her husband is leading.

'For every Lilibet,' smiles Philip, 'you get a Margaret.'

'Let's not delude ourselves,' he continues. Margaret and her glamorous husband might attract some headlines in America, but 'this is no time to rewrite the constitutional rule book … You are the Queen – and she is your dangerous baby sister.'[395]

As future episodes will show, the theory of the double-headed eagle will provide a shrewd insight into many of the dramas confronting the house of Windsor as it continues its progress into the final quarter of the twentieth century.

CHAPTER THIRTEEN

'ABERFAN'

OCTOBER 1966

FIRST PUBLISHED IN 1939, RICHARD LLEWELLYN'S *How Green Was My Valley* romanticised the mining villages of South Wales to the world – via a bestselling novel, a Hollywood movie, two BBC TV drama series and even a musical that opened on Broadway on 21 May 1966. Llewellyn painted an idealised picture of the coal-mining communities whose back-breaking labour underpinned Britain's industrial greatness – all thanks, of course, to the 'black gold' that was hacked out so painfully, shovel by shovel, from beneath the green grass of the picturesque surrounding hills.[396]

But those valleys seemed a good deal less green after 21 October 1966 – five months to the day, by chance, following the New York opening of the musical – when the pupils of Pantglas Junior School wended their way through the pouring rain to school in the little village of Aberfan. 'All Things Bright and Beautiful' was the hymn that they sang every morning – composed in another Welsh valley, as it happened, just 20 miles away beside the River Usk, in Monmouthshire.[397] But the hymn was postponed that Friday. With school due to end at midday to mark the start of half-term, the headmistress decided to delay the singing until the farewell assembly, when she could wish all her charges a safe and enjoyable holiday. The children never sang the hymn.

Sometime around 9.15 a 'rumbling, rumbling, rumbling' was heard, as if a jet plane was passing low overhead.[398] 'It's only thunder, it will go soon,' said young Jeff Edwards' maths teacher reassuringly, as he started chalking on the blackboard. But the next thing Jeff remembered was waking up on the floor, only alive and able to breathe because he was trapped in the air pocket beneath his desk. His classmates were dead around him, as was his maths teacher, swallowed in a glistening black avalanche of colliery rubbish and mud that had overwhelmed the school and was already starting to harden like cement.

'My desk was pinned against my stomach, and a girl's head was on my left shoulder,' remembered Edwards. 'She was dead. Because all the debris was around me, I couldn't get away from her. The image of her face comes back to me continuously.'[399]

A huge refuse tip of colliery rubbish – discarded, unmarketable pit dust – had come roaring down the hillside through the mist like a river of slime, engulfing rocks, trees and cottages, then rupturing a water main which engorged the flood still further and speeded the velocity of its murderous descent. The powdery waste combined with the water to form a lethal flood of sludge that killed 20 people in the flattened hillside homes and village houses beside the school – all creatures great and small.

Inside the school, the death toll would total five teachers and 109 pupils – almost half the children in the village. Nansi Williams, the school's beloved dinner lady, threw herself on top of five children as they walked down the corridor to save them from the debris of a collapsing wall, and they lay stunned and flattened beneath her body as she took the full impact. After a while, the children began to recover and call Nansi's name, then started tugging at her hair to get some response – 'She wasn't saying anything to us.' After more calling and tugging, the children came to realise that their protector must be dead.[400]

'It was black all around me,' recalls Jeff Edwards of the small space below his desk. 'But there was an aperture of light about ten foot above … I remember seeing particles of dust spinning and glistening where the light caught them. I could hear crying and screaming. As time went on, they got quieter and quieter as children died. They were buried and running out of air.'[401]

Edwards lay for 90 minutes or so beneath the hardening muck, gasping for breath, with death on his shoulder. Rescuers had dived bravely into the wreckage within minutes. The crash had been heard more than a mile away. But it was hard-going to fight a path through the chaos.

'I heard the men breaking a window and someone said, "There's someone down here …",' the boy remembered. 'They started to remove all the girders and debris from around me, but they still couldn't get me out. The firemen got their hatchets out and hacked away at my desk.'[402]

Jeff Edwards was the tenth child to be brought out of Pantglas alive – and the last. By the time the final corpses had been recovered, the rapidly congealing slag which had a bone-hardening and also a corrosive effect, had eaten away at their skin and their features. Wrapped in blankets, the little bodies were taken to a makeshift mortuary in the Bethania Chapel, where grieving parents queued for hours to identify their children.

'I saw such dreadful things, Mummy,' wrote Alix Palmer, a trainee journalist who was confronted by the heartbreaking corpses of children on her first major assignment for the *Daily Express*. 'They brought out the deputy headmaster, still clutching five children, their bones so hardened that they first had to break his arms to get the children away, then their arms to get them apart. And the mothers of two of them watched it happen.'[403]

Palmer reported on the rescue operations, with firemen, police and desperate parents tearing away at the sweating and solidifying tar. 'Every now and again, the organiser of the operation would yell through a loud-hailer for quiet. That was the most terrible moment of all. Someone had seen an arm or a leg, and everyone longed for the sound of a child crying.' But after Jeff Edwards there were no more...[404]

Episode 303's account of the Aberfan disaster closely follows the dateline of 21 October 1966 and the other events reported through the days that followed, together with the evidence heard during the subsequent tribunal of investigation. All the Aberfan characters in the episode are identified by invented names in order not to cause any further distress to survivors and families of the victims. To this day, as a mark of respect to their classmates who died, Pantglas survivors decline to specify names when discussing the incident.

Some details about the tip have been changed, including the description of how the start of the subsidence was identified – in reality, the coal tip supervisor, whose name has been changed, had travelled up to the tip that morning, so he was the first witness to see the disaster unfold.

Harold Wilson is shown hearing the news of the tip slide at the opening of a hypermarket (a term not established in the UK until 1970) in Skelmersdale New Town, Merseyside. In reality the Prime Minister was in Wigan, next door to Skelmersdale, having lunch with the local corporation, and he completed his visit while receiving updates on the disaster, before flying to Aberfan – four hours after first hearing the news.

Tony Armstrong-Jones, Princess Margaret's husband Lord Snowdon, was among those early on the scene, having rushed from London to Aberfan the moment he heard the news. The various details of his dramatic visit have been reconstructed from his original itinerary and from press accounts. He went straight to the Bethania Chapel, where 50 or so parents, mostly fathers, were still waiting to identify their children's bodies and were emerging quite shattered. Leaving the trained rescue teams to do their job, Snowdon concentrated on those who wanted to pour out their feelings.

'He had gone spontaneously,' wrote Harold Wilson in his diary, 'and instead of inspecting the site, he made it his job to visit the bereaved relatives, sitting holding the hands of a distraught father, sitting with the head of a mother on his shoulder for half an hour in silence.

'In another house he comforted an older couple who had lost thirteen grandchildren – in another where they were terribly upset, he offered to make a cup of tea, went into the kitchen and returned with a tray with cups for them all. He helped an older man persuade his son, who was clutching something in his tightly clenched fist, to open his hand. It was a prefect's badge, the only thing by which he had been able to identify his child ...'[405]

Prince Philip arrived the next day, but Elizabeth II held back, actually refusing her staff's suggestions that she should go down to South Wales.

'We kept presenting the arguments,' recalls one adviser, 'but nothing we said could persuade her.'

'People will be looking after *me*,' she objected. 'So perhaps they'll miss some poor child that might have been found under the wreckage.'[406]

Elizabeth's imagining of the lost child showed the reality of her concern – and she could not imagine why her own particular presence should matter. 'She has no vanity,' said one of the advisers involved in the daily meetings which tried to get the Queen to budge. 'She can't understand why people *should* want to see her. She is not an actress like her mother. She has a horror of what she calls "stunts", and she simply has no sense or instinct for the balm that her presence brings.'[407]

Episode 303 suggests that Marcia Williams and other Labour Party conspirators attempted to shift newspaper attention away from the government and towards the Queen, but there is no evidence for this. The big question is why Elizabeth II waited eight days before she went to Aberfan. Did she care too much – or too little? What problem did the monarch have with the knotting of her inner impulses? Or is that her strength? The depiction of her eventual visit to the home of an Aberfan resident is based on her visit to Councillor Jim Williams, where she stayed and spoke with the family for nearly 20 minutes and emerged visibly emotional. She is known to have prayed for the victims of the catastrophe so she is shown as saying her prayers inside one of the five chapels in the village.

Perhaps the most useful perspective that history can lend is to note that, unlike many who got there ahead of her in 1966, the Queen has since been back to revisit the village at least three times. She returned in March 1973 to open the new community centre; in May 1997, when she planted a tree in the Garden of Remembrance; and most recently in 2012,

October 29, 1966 – Elizabeth II and Prince Philip at Aberfan

when she met some of the remaining survivors for a fourth time in 46 years.[408]

Hoping to diffuse the dismay that Aberfan provoked around the country, Harold Wilson immediately set up a tribunal of enquiry under Lord Justice Edmund Davies QC, a Welshman born two miles from Aberfan. It was his brief to start investigating and come to some conclusions as rapidly as possible. The tribunal convened initially at nearby Merthyr Tydfil and then, after Christmas, in Cardiff, hearing evidence for 76 days and delivering its conclusions on 3 August 1967.[409] The problem, it turned out, with all the towering piles of coal waste that ringed so many British mining communities at that date, was that they were not really composed of coal – that is, not the nice large *lumps* of coal that people then liked to burn in their fireplaces, or which factories and locomotives could usefully employ. In 1966 British Rail trains were still powered by steam engines burning 'big-lump' coal.

It was mining waste and discarded 'tailings' – the fine particles left after the washing process – that had been dumped in the Aberfan valley by Merthyr Vale Colliery on sloping, low-value land: highly porous sandstone riven with streams and underwater springs, whose water had liquified the tip dust into the thick, black quicksand that came pouring down into the valley to flood over the school and had then solidified so quickly around the victims in the classrooms.

Aberfan had been expressing concerns about these 'spoil tips' for years, particularly 'Tip 7' which had been started in 1958 and had risen eight years later to a mini mountain, 111ft (34m) high, containing some 300,000 cubic yards (229,300 cubic metres) of damp, powdery waste.[410] Tip 7 had been piled up on the sloping hillside above Pantglas School on top of a running stream that was actually marked on the Ordnance Survey map. Children used to play in the water where it emerged from the tip, collecting tadpoles in the spring. In 1963 the school had organised a petition protesting at the ugliness and dangers of the slag heaps that surrounded the village, but the National Coal Board (NCB) had brushed all complaints aside.[411]

As the tribunal scandalously revealed, the NCB had no policy at all, and not even safety guidelines, for the scores of waste tips with which it had littered Great Britain's mines and excavations for the past 20 years. Merthyr Vale Colliery had operated tip safety guidelines when it was in private hands, but these had been discarded when the mine came under public ownership, along with 957 others around the country – the property of some 800 private companies all nationalised by Clement Attlee's post-war Labour government. 'This colliery is now managed by the National Coal Board on behalf of the people,' proclaimed a notice proudly posted at Merthyr and at every colliery in the country on 1 January 1947.[412] But it was difficult to detect much care 'on behalf of the people' from the NCB's conduct in Aberfan.

Lord Alfred – 'Alf' – Robens, Baron Robens of Woldingham, the former trades union official who was given a life peerage when he became chairman of the NCB in 1961, was heading towards Guildford in Surrey on that Friday morning when he received news of the Aberfan tip collapse, but he decided to keep on travelling. Robens was due to be installed as the first chancellor of the new University of Surrey. That was his priority on 21 October – and he did not arrive at Aberfan until the evening of the following day. There he immediately raised hackles by saying that his NCB staff could not possibly have foreseen the danger of the tip collapsing, claiming in a later interview that the trouble was down to 'natural unknown springs' beneath the tip. When told that the course of his 'unknown' stream that helped generate the lethal flood could clearly be traced on the Ordnance Survey map, he was not embarrassed.[413]

Lack of embarrassment was Alf Robens' style. Once considered a possibility for Labour Party leadership, he hugely enjoyed the trappings of his lofty position, which included a Daimler with the registration number 'NCB 1', an executive aeroplane – a six-seater De Havilland Dove – and a flat in Eaton Square.[414] Robens' £10,000 a year salary, along with subsequent business interests, enabled him to retire to the stately Laleham Abbey in Surrey, once the home of the Earls of Lucan. Not for nothing did Lord Alf earn the nickname from his detractors of 'Old King Coal'.

Worse was to come. When the question arose of financial compensation for the loss of life at Aberfan, the Charity Commission proposed asking the grief-stricken parents 'Exactly how close were you to your child?' – with the idea that those considered not close to their children would not need to be compensated. In the event, the NCB stepped in to offer £50 per life lost (£900 per life in 2019 monetary values) – £5,800 for all 116 children, a little over half of the chairman's annual salary. Such was the outrage that Lord Alf was shamed into a more 'generous' offer – £500 per head (£9,000 per life in 2019). A more substantial sum, it was explained, would have confused working-class recipients not used to handling large amounts of money.[415]

Justice Edmund Davies' tribunal was scathing in its condemnation of the NCB's incompetence, indifference and inhumanity – 'a terrifying tale of bungling ineptitude by many men charged with tasks for which they were totally unfitted,' as the judge put it baldly in his opening statement. The tribunal listed a damning catalogue 'of failure to heed clear warnings', and deplored 'a total lack of direction from above' – which presumably referred to Lord Robens.[416] Worse, it noted how the NCB had actually hampered the tribunal's enquiries, prolonging its work by weeks and costing even more taxpayers' money by declining to cooperate from the start. Only towards the end of the hearings did Robens grudgingly admit the inescapable – that the NCB had entire responsibility for the existence, siting, maintenance and safety of Tip 7, and thus had to assume entire responsibility for the tragedy.

Not a single NCB official, however, was dismissed or even disciplined for his role in the catastrophe, and not one resigned, with the exception of Lord Robens – after a fashion. Lord Alf did write to the Minister of Power, Richard Marsh, offering his resignation in September 1967, but papers released in 1997 under the Thirty-Year Rule revealed that he only did so after agreeing the wording of the letter that his colleague and fellow Labour grandee would write in gracious refusal of the resignation.[417] In 2006 Marsh (created a life peer himself in 1981, as Baron Marsh of Mannington in the County of Wiltshire) confirmed in a broadcast interview that he had discussed everything with Robens in advance: 'I said, "Well, you send me in your resignation, and I will send you back a letter saying, 'Quite understand it, but I don't accept it'" ... All 'on behalf of the people', of course.[418]

The final wrinkle in the saga was the question as to when and how the remains of Tip 7 and the six other piles of waste around Aberfan would be removed. The first news of the tragedy had prompted the setting up of an Aberfan Disaster Fund to which ordinary people around Britain – and abroad – rushed to subscribe. Over 90,000 donations soon reached a total of £1.75 million, an estimated £20 million-plus in 2019 values – only the Diana, Princess of Wales Memorial Fund has ever outstripped it.[419] Most donors must have imagined that their money would be going directly to help the bereaved families, but the NCB had other ideas. They insisted that the Disaster Fund should contribute £150,000 towards the removal of the remaining waste tips, and this injustice was not corrected for more than 20 years when Tony Blair made repayment – albeit without accounting for interest or inflation.

It seems reasonable to suggest that the scarcely believable heartlessness of the NCB's behaviour in 1966 and 1967 as a public agency that was charged with 'caring' for the workers and welfare of Aberfan was a contributory factor in the demise of Britain's nationalised industries. No private enterprise would have dared to act in such a high-handed fashion – but the absence of any competition and accountability turned the NCB into a lofty-minded, pretentious and literally lethal institution. In 1994 the NCB's government-owned successor, the British Coal Corporation, was dissolved and the country's 15 surviving collieries were handed back to private care and management.[420]

Today, thankfully, the majority of the waste coal tailings' tips in South Wales have been removed. Richard Llewellyn would be pleased to see how the valleys like Aberfan's are green again. But the outline of where the tips once rose above the village can still be clearly identified. There have been fervent and expert horticultural efforts to re-cultivate the sites, but the grass growing over those tips obstinately remains a different colour – a coarse and sickly shade of yellow.[421]

The captions at the end of the episode reflect how certain people close to the Queen have said that her delayed response to the disaster remains her 'biggest regret' as Sovereign – but this, of course, reflects other people speaking on her behalf. Aberfan was not the last time that Elizabeth II's response to tragedy would be critically examined by the media and the public – not least in 1997 following the death of Diana, Princess of Wales.

CHAPTER FOURTEEN

'BUBBIKINS'

APRIL 1967–NOVEMBER 1968

T HE ABERFAN DISASTER OF 1966 PROVED A TURNING POINT in Britain's attitude towards Queen Elizabeth II, souring the honeymoon that had started so brightly with her 1952 accession and the coronation of 1953. To some extent, this reflected the controversy over the monarch's delayed and stilted visit to the devastated village – but there was a deeper malaise, as Malcolm Muggeridge, the journalist and self-appointed gadfly of the Windsor clan had reflected in a 1964 US chat show. 'The English,' he declared, 'are getting bored with their monarchy.'[422] In fast-changing times, the values that the Crown was traditionally thought to represent – social distinction, respectability and deference – were coming to be seen as a joke: they were prime targets for the country's burgeoning satire industry. The values of the 'Swinging Sixties' were all about classlessness, novelty, equality – and, frankly, some colourful playing to the crowd.

Reflecting on these changes in 1968, the Buckingham Palace press office decided something must be done to portray Elizabeth personally – and the monarchy as a whole – in a more transparent and user-friendly light. The past year had seen the retirement of Elizabeth's long-serving and snobbish press secretary, Commander Richard Colville – fondly known in Fleet Street as the 'Anti-Press' Secretary,[423] on account of his determination to keep the media at arm's length. 'If there comes a time,' Colville once said, 'when the British Monarchy ever needs a "public relations officer", the institution of monarchy in this country will be in serious danger.'[424]

Colville's breezy Australian successor, William 'Bill' Heseltine, would adopt an altogether different approach – as he had shown in the summer of 1967 when he staged the televised knighting on the quay at Greenwich of the yachtsman Francis Chichester, the first sailor to circumnavigate the globe single-handed. Heseltine theatrically arranged for Elizabeth to knight Chichester with the same sword that Queen Elizabeth I had deployed in 1581 for the knighting of another maritime Francis, Sir Francis Drake.[425] Drake had been the first Englishman to sail around the world, bringing back enough treasure for the Queen's share of the loot to surpass the rest of her income for that entire year.

Treasure was the root of the problem for Queen Elizabeth II as the 1960s drew to an end. Harold Wilson had come to power in 1964 inheriting an annual balance of payments deficit from his Conservative predecessors of some £800 million, twice as high as the estimate Wilson himself had complained about in the general election campaign.[426] For three years he borrowed to try to stave off the inevitable, but in November

1967, having failed to secure a final, crucial bailout from either France or the US, he had to surrender to speculative pressures, announcing the devaluation of the pound sterling from US\$2.80 to US\$2.40.[427]

'Devaluation does not mean that the value of the pound in the pocket in the hands of the … British housewife … is cut correspondingly,'[428] the Prime Minister declared in a much-derided broadcast to the nation. The average British housewife knew very well that the value of the pound in her pocket had almost halved in spending power between 1950 and 1969 – 20 shillings were now worth little more than ten.[429] And even if the Queen herself did not need to carry around pounds in her pocket, the same remorseless economic pressures were coming to apply to herself and to the expenses of keeping her monarchy afloat.

Traditionally the Civil List, the annual government grant to cover the Sovereign's official duties as Head of State (including staff salaries, state visits, public engagements, and the upkeep of the various royal households), would be set at the beginning of the monarch's reign, and would then remain unchanged until that Sovereign's demise. But Elizabeth was a long way from 'demising' in 1962, when royal expenditure was found to have outrun income for the first time – and this was despite some highly creative accounting. The Royal Navy had loyally taken over the costs of the Royal Yacht *Britannia* to the tune of no less than £839,000 per year, with National Rail taking care of the £36,000 needed to keep the royal train on the tracks.[430]

As Edward Heath, Harold Wilson's successor as Prime Minister, would reveal in the Commons in December 1971, the salaries and expenses of the royal household had risen nearly

150 per cent since 1953 – just over £316,000 to £770,000. 'Over the same period,' he declared, 'the income of the average wage and salary earner has increased by over 200 percent, and the retirement pension by 260 percent.' The salaries of MPs, he pointed out, had actually trebled in the same period – 'by 350 percent'. So Elizabeth's request for a pay rise, he argued, did not seem so unreasonable in the circumstances.[431]

Not for the first time, however, Prince Philip had to have his say, and he got his chance when interviewed on the US TV programme *Meet the Press* in November 1969. 'Queen Elizabeth,' he was asked, 'has not had a pay rise for nearly 18 years, a situation that none of her subjects – her working-class subjects – would tolerate for a moment … Is that creating an awkward situation there?'

'Very,' replied Philip, jumping straight in. 'We go into the red, I think, next year. Which is not bad housekeeping when you come to think of it. I mean, we've kept the thing going on a budget which is based on costs from 18 years ago.'

So far, so reasonable … But then the Prince went on to venture a few jokes. 'The family,' he speculated, 'may have to move into smaller premises, who knows?' They had already had to sell a 'small yacht', and at this rate, he was wondering, he 'may have to give up polo'.[432]

Few laughed, or even chuckled. 'My heart bleeds,' responded the Labour MP Willie Hamilton, who spearheaded the Labour Party's republican movement.[433] The underwriting of 'the wealthy royal family – not only the Queen but her husband, mother, sister, daughter, and other assorted relatives' was not a popular cause in left-wing circles. The councillors of the London Borough of Lambeth took down their portrait of Elizabeth II, and hid it away under a sofa[434] – although a group of Bermondsey dockers did organise a collection to buy Prince Philip a new polo pony. 'When we were kids,' they said – with all seriousness, on the face of it – 'he did a lot for us with the playing fields and the boys' clubs ...'[435]

Enter breezy PR man Bill Heseltine with his plan for a large-scale television documentary that would follow the Queen and her family through a full year of activity to show how jolly hard they worked and how they were worth every penny that they consumed of taxpayers' money. As Philip put it privately, 'We are fighting an election every day of the week.'[436]

The forthcoming investiture of Charles as Prince of Wales offered a peg for the proposed film, along with some camouflage. The storyline would follow the young Prince as he prepared for this landmark event in his life, and would then branch out to survey the sort of activities to which Charles might look forward as his career developed.[437] ITV and the BBC agreed to sink their differences to collaborate on this unprecedented venture for which, in the event, they generated over 43 hours of filmed material[438] – at a cost, in 1969, of £150,000 (about £2.5 million today).[439] It was to be a high-security enterprise, all sides agreed, with the raw footage being stored in special vaults in cans labelled 'Religious Programming'.

Starting in the summer of 1968, the BBC/ITV film crew headed to Scotland to capture some Balmoral sequences that would live in the memory of all who saw the film – and which have been recreated in Episode 304 by the current cast of *The Crown*. Elizabeth and Prince Charles were shown chopping and preparing a salad, while Philip and Anne went to work barbecuing sausages and steak.

'Well,' the Queen reported, strolling over to her husband, 'the salad is finished!'

'Well done,' replied her husband sardonically, turning over a sausage on the griddle. 'This, as you will observe, is not.'[440]

Other 'private' glimpses of the family showed the Queen and the four-year-old Prince Edward visiting the Balmoral village shop in search of an ice cream. '*Cinema vérité!*' exulted Richard Cawston, the film's director and producer. Scarcely less pompous was President Richard Nixon's on-screen greeting to Prince Charles in the US-related sequences: 'I've seen you on television!'

'I've seen you, too!' was the Prince's snappy rejoinder.[441]

With regard to Prince Philip's startling use of nicknames for Elizabeth and Anne in this episode, there are reliable reports of him being heard to call the Queen 'Cabbage' (possibly an English variation of the French endearment 'mon petit chou'), but there is no solid evidence as to whether he ever called his daughter 'Sweetie'.

Royal Family proved a massive success, shown first in black and white on the BBC on 21 June 1969, then repeated the following week on ITV in colour. Over the years it would be seen in more than 125 countries and has been transmitted nearly a dozen times in Britain alone. 'There was no question of the Queen's censoring the film,' said Richard Cawston. 'I suppose I was much more stringent in my own cutting than they would ever have been.'[442]

The critics cheered. The film was praised by Stuart Hood, The *Spectator*'s TV critic, as the 'apotheosis of home movies'[443] – he predicted a British move towards a bicycle-riding, Scandinavian-style monarchy. Even the left-wing *New Statesman* felt compelled to suggest that Cawston and his co-producer Antony Jay should be given knighthoods: 'They'll certainly have added a decade or two to the life of the British Monarchy.'[444] In the event, Jay did receive a knighthood in 1988, though that was primarily for his work on the political satire *Yes Minister*.[445]

What the real *Royal Family* documentary did *not* include was the participation of Prince Philip's eccentric mother, Princess Alice of Greece, who was living in Buckingham Palace in these years, but was kept carefully away from the production. This, as Peter Morgan suggests in Episode 304, was a pity, since the Princess's life and character offered exactly the unsentimental element of reality that the programme makers were seeking. Though born royal, Alice of Battenberg, the elder sister of 'Dickie' Mountbatten, was congenitally deaf[446] and was diagnosed with schizophrenia while her son Philip was still a boy.[447]

The sources are not clear on the exact nature of the Princess's intonation and accent – despite her deafness she was able to lip-read and also to speak fluently. According to her grand-niece Lady Pamela Hicks, she could hear enough to converse on the phone from Greece. Born in England, raised in Germany and living most of her adult life in Greece, Alice could speak and understand all three national languages – though it is unclear whether her accent was more English, German or Greek.

Alice's deafness and other problems led to the breakdown of her already shaky marriage with Philip's father, Prince Andrew of Greece, and was followed by her confinement to a private sanitorium.[448] There the Princess found solace in religious mania, lying on the ground for hours on end in a trance-like state, seeking to develop what she described as 'the power conveyed to her from above'. Alice came to believe that she was literally the bride of Christ, and that she was physically involved not only with Jesus, but with other great spiritual figures like the Buddha.

The Princess's sexual fantasies attracted the attention of Sigmund Freud, who diagnosed Alice as suffering from a 'neurotic-pre-psychotic libidinous condition' – for which he prescribed radiation of her ovaries 'in order to accelerate the menopause'.[449] This brutal treatment was carried out on the great man's orders, with the Princess remaining locked up against her will in the sanitorium and seeing next to nothing of her son Philip for years. (Chapter Seventeen, 'Moondust' – Episode 307 – relates more of this traumatic episode in the young Philip's life.)

For 23 episodes of *The Crown* we have been observing Prince Philip's often unconventional behaviour. Now we have some clue to one major source of it – the psychosis of the mother who called him 'Bubbikins', but was separated from him for such long periods during his childhood. 'He just never had the love,' explained Michael Parker, his naval chum and later private secretary. 'There was no one really close – that day-to-day parental contact you need to smooth off the rough edges. That's where his apparent rudeness comes from – not enough slap-down when it mattered.'[450]

We have little idea, however, about how Prince Philip really felt about his mother's lengthy absences – which were hardly her fault. Indeed, the Prince had every reason to be proud of his unconventional parent, who made a comeback from her mental illness, moving to live in German-occupied Athens throughout the war, working for the Red Cross and helping to organise soup kitchens for the starving populace. She set up a sisterhood that operated as a convalescent home – part infirmary and part training school for nuns. She had neither an office nor a bedroom at the sisterhood, as depicted. But she certainly sold some of her family possessions in order to keep her sisterhood alive – the role of the pawnbroker and the subsequent police raid at the convent have been invented in order to dramatise this.

Sometime around 1943 the Princess secretly gave refuge to a Jewish friend, Rachel Cohen,[451] and two of her children, who were being sought by the Gestapo and would certainly have been deported to the death camps if Alice had not protected them – at considerable personal risk. To recognise this act of bravery, Yad Vashem, the Holocaust Memorial in Jerusalem, honoured Princess Alice as 'Righteous Among the Nations' in a ceremony on the Mount of Olives, which Prince Philip attended in October 1994.

'I suspect that it never occurred to her,' remarked Philip, 'that her action was in any way special. She was a person with

1960: Princess Alice of Greece and Denmark – and son

a deep religious faith, and she would have considered it to be a perfectly natural human reaction to fellow beings in distress.' In 2010 Princess Alice was posthumously named a 'Hero of the Holocaust' by the British government.[452]

Of all the royal grandchildren, Princess Anne was the closest to their remarkable Danish-Greek grandmother – hence the imagined sequence in this episode in the Palace gardens, where we see Anne pushing Alice into the path of the ITV/BBC cameras for an interview. This is surely the 'Stag Scene' of Season 3! Anne called Alice 'Yaya', the Greek word for grandmother,[453] and she enjoyed hearing the stories that her most unusual grandmother had to tell about Queen Victoria – who had actually been present at Alice's birth.

For both Charles and Anne, the connection with their grandmother went back to 1956, when 'Yaya' had joined the royal family on a cruise around the Outer Hebrides on *Britannia*, during which Anne's sixth birthday had been celebrated.[454] Revelling in her religious background, Alice had regaled her grandchildren with her favourite Bible stories – along with her 'little tales' of poor children in Greece whom she had fed bread and cabbages during the war while she was looking after orphans in Nazi-occupied Athens.

As a pupil at Benenden School, Anne was known for her frugality – fellow pupils noted how she always seemed to have something left over from her £2-a-term pocket money, and how she frequently attended practical lectures on subjects like nursing and social work. It seems reasonable to speculate that these traits reflected the influence of Anne's unique 'Yaya' – the remarkable princess-nun who tried to found an order of religious nurses in Greece.

CHAPTER FIFTEEN

'Coup'

May 1967–May 1968

―――――――

ONE OF THE MOST REGULAR VISITORS TO PRINCESS Alice of Greece and Denmark when she moved into Buckingham Palace in the late 1960s was her ever-busy younger brother 'Dickie', Earl Mountbatten of Burma. 'Dickie' loved dropping in on 'Alice-at-the-Palace', as he came to dub his sister – though Alice did develop some suspicions about the frequency of his visits: following her brother's departure, she could not help noticing how the stack of Buckingham Palace notepaper on her desk always seemed a little lower.[455]

There was no doubting that Lord Louis Mountbatten had a high opinion of himself – he had unquenchable ambition. That is the theme and question at the heart of Episode 305, 'Coup' – how far did Dickie's conceit and ambition extend? – since it is a matter of surprising but solid historical fact that on 8 May 1968, four eminent conspirators gathered in Lord Mountbatten's home in Kinnerton Street, a former mews in

Knightsbridge near the back of Buckingham Palace, to discuss the possibility of replacing Harold Wilson, the elected Prime Minister of the moment, with an unelected 'Government of National Unity'. They did not get very far with planning out the details of their deposition, but two of them, and maybe three, were quite clear on their main objective – that Prime Minister Wilson should be replaced by Lord Louis Mountbatten.

'Dickie,' noted one of the participants in his diary, 'is really intrigued by [the] suggestion that he should be the boss man of a "government"'.[456]

The moving spirit of this subversive gathering was Cecil Harmsworth King, the tall and bulky (6 foot 4 inches and 18 stone) press magnate who was chairman of the International Publishing Corporation (IPC), at that date the biggest publishing empire in the world, controlling the *Daily Mirror*, *The Sun*, the *Sunday Pictorial*, the *Daily Record* in Scotland, and some 200 other newspapers and magazines. In the run-up to the 1964 general election – which had proved surprisingly close – the *Daily Mirror* had conducted a brilliant campaign among its working-class readership to help deliver victory to Harold Wilson. King even drove around London with a red flag reading 'Vote Labour' fluttering from the bonnet of his Rolls-Royce.[457]

King had had high hopes for Wilson, rating him a canny improvement on his predecessor as leader of the Labour Party, Hugh Gaitskell, and hoping to play the role of Wilson's éminence grise. Wilson responded by offering King one of the recently invented life peerages, which King declined on the grounds that he wanted an *hereditary* peerage – ideally an earldom that would outrank his press baron uncles, Northcliffe and Rothermere. When Wilson explained his feeling that a socialist government had no business handing out hereditary privileges, King took offence and the two men's relationship never quite recovered.[458]

King's right-hand man – and another of the May 1968 players in Kinnerton Street – was Hubert 'Hugh' Cudlipp, the snappy, hands-on Welsh editor whose formula of gimmicks, stunts and punchy headlines was generally credited with the huge success of IPC and of the Mirror newspapers, in particular. Cudlipp had a fair claim to being the father of the modern tabloid 'rag'. He had deployed his graphic techniques during the Second World War in the creation of *Union Jack,* the morale-boosting British Forces, newspaper – and prior to that, as a 1942 participant in the first battle of El Alamein, he had developed his own stock of wartime anecdotes he could swap with 'Dickie' Mountbatten.[459]

1965 – Earl Mountbatten of Burma KG GCB
OM GCSI GCIE GCVO...

The fourth member of the Kinnerton quartet, the Russian-Jewish scientist Sir Solomon 'Solly' Zuckerman, also had a distinguished war record as designer of the lightweight steel 'Zuckerman' helmet used by civil defence organisations, and as a bombing consultant during the Normandy landings.[460] Zuckerman had been invited to the gathering as Mountbatten's friend and adviser, and, by his own subsequent account, it was just as well that he showed up.

All the participants left their own varying accounts of the meeting – after the event, these four powerful men became very well aware that they had been playing with fire in Kinnerton Street – and we know that Cecil King opened the agenda by recounting the catalogue of Wilsonian shortcomings that he would publish two days later in an editorial on the front of the *Daily Mirror* of 10 May. 'Enough is Enough' blared the headline above the name and photograph of Cecil H. King, chairman of the International Publishing Corporation, along with the list of the principal newspapers King controlled: 'Mr Wilson and his Government have lost all credibility: all authority,' complained King, his voice the more powerful for coming, apparently officially, from Britain's largest Labour-supporting newspaper group. 'The Government that was voted into office with so much good will only three and a half years ago has revealed itself as lacking in foresight, in administrative ability, in political sensitivity, and integrity. Mr Wilson is seen to be a brilliant Parliamentary tactician and nothing more.'[461]

King illustrated his complaint against Labour's parliamentary manoeuvring with photographs of the four ministers of education that Wilson had appointed in the last four years ('which means that effectively Mr Wilson has had no Minister of Education') – with education being just one by-product, in King's opinion, of a catalogue of disasters since 1964: the devastating strikes by the dockers and the National Union of Seamen, the doubling of unemployment within a year, the devaluation of the pound in November 1967 and the consequent loss of sterling reserves, rounded off by General de Gaulle's contemptuous refusal to let Britain join the Common Market – for a second time.

'We are now threatened with the greatest financial crisis in our history,' concluded King to his readers, and this was the message that he delivered verbally on 8 May to Cudlipp, Mountbatten and Zuckerman in Kinnerton Street. Britain's knife-edge national emergency, he would write two days later, 'is not to be removed by lies about our reserves, but only by a fresh start under a fresh leader'. And to make this fresh start, King made clear to his Kinnerton Street listeners that Lord 'Dickie' Mountbatten, the great war hero of the Burma campaign, was, in his opinion, the 'fresh leader' that Britain required at this perilous moment in its history.[462]

Episode 305 leaps off from this extraordinary proposal by setting the crucial meeting between King and Mountbatten in a boardroom at the Bank of England – which was not where it actually happened, but was certainly where King had developed the ideas that he presented that afternoon at Kinnerton Street. As the Queen Mother explains to 'Dickie' in this episode, while the two elder royals pore together over the *Mirror*'s angry 'Enough is Enough' editorial, Wilson had tried to pacify Cecil King by making him a director of the Bank of England. But that had only served to lock him in a room 'with Wilson's biggest enemies – financiers and bankers – who explained to King in graphic terms what a mess Wilson is making of the economy'.[463]

The Bank of England's 'big guns' were particularly angry about 'Operation Brutus', a Labour government plan to impose tighter regulations upon both the Bank and the City of London, and they had won King round to their view that 'Brutus' was an unconstitutional attack upon their traditional financial freedoms. As the Queen Mother puts it to 'Dickie', Wilson's too-ready endorsement of this left-wing project had 'scored something of an own goal'.[464]

We then see Mountbatten doing some research at Broadlands, his grand Hampshire home, into the practicalities of a coup with a large map on the wall. This scene is based on a subsequent allegation by Wilson's close ally and confidante Marcia Williams, who has to be viewed, of course, as a biased witness. Then the entire fantastic enterprise is brought to an end by the Queen herself, who rebukes 'Dickie' and defends Wilson's legitimacy in a confrontation in which, scripted by Peter Morgan, Her Majesty sets out the classic view of Britain's unwritten constitution. This is an 'invented' scene, but similar words could well have been uttered in May 1968, a few days after the Kinnerton Street gathering, when Elizabeth went to stay at Broadlands. That is when Uncle 'Dickie' is thought to have disclosed to her the details of his meeting with King, Cudlipp and Zuckerman:[465]

MOUNTBATTEN: 'Why would you protect a man like Wilson?

ELIZABETH: 'I'm protecting the *Prime Minister.* I'm

protecting the Constitution. I'm protecting Democracy.'

MOUNTBATTEN: 'But if the man at the heart of that democracy threatens to destroy it, are we supposed to stand by and do *nothing*?'

ELIZABETH: 'Yes. Doing nothing is EXACTLY what we do. And bide our time. And wait for the people who voted him in to vote him out again. *If*, indeed, that is what *they* decide to do ...'[466]

Cecil King's Bank of England colleagues had been correct in seeing Wilson's Operation Brutus as a limitation on their traditional financial freedoms. But as the Queen understood, and as Cecil King and Mountbatten did not – not, at least, when they conferred in Kinnerton Street – *any* control or limitation of any British freedom, no matter how apparently sacrosanct, is 100 per cent permissible so long as it has been supported by a democratic, voting majority in the British Houses of Parliament. The only way to change that is via the *voting* route. So it was for a general election and a subsequent parliamentary majority to depose and replace Harold Wilson – not Cecil Harmsworth King or 'Dickie' Mountbatten.

The directors of IPC and Mirror Newspapers grasped that quickly enough. Within a matter of days, they gathered to demand King's resignation for his wild and unauthorised 'Enough is Enough' editorial, and, when he refused, they sacked him ignominiously on 30 May 1968. King did not last out the year at the Bank of England, either.[467]

'Dickie' Mountbatten did survive into peaceful and dignified retirement, however, since the historical record showed that, whatever his private dreams and temptations, he knew how to hold them in check. He was certainly no right-wing conspirator. When Hugh Cudlipp had gone down to Broadlands early in May to set up the Kinnerton Street meeting and was cautiously probing Mountbatten's ideas as to which prominent public figure might best restore national morale, the name that 'Dickie' suggested was not his own but that of Barbara Castle, the fiery left-wing activist who had just become Secretary of State for Employment.[468]

At the crucial 8 May gathering, according to Philip Ziegler, Mountbatten's official biographer, Solly Zuckerman had stormed out of the house into Kinnerton Street protesting, 'This is rank treachery ... I am a public servant and will have nothing to do with it' – and Mountbatten had meekly followed his friend's lead. According to Ziegler, Mountbatten then informed Cecil King and Hugh Cudlipp 'courteously but firmly, that he could not even contemplate such a proposition'.[469] He then ushered both men to the door, and that was the end of the matter. 'Dangerous nonsense!' was his diary entry for the day.[470]

Zuckerman did remark later to Cudlipp, 'I wonder what Dickie would have said if I hadn't been there?'[471] But when Cecil King wrote to Mountbatten two years later suggesting the possibility of another get-together, he received a firm brush-off. 'I well recall our meeting,' wrote Mountbatten, 'but you will recall that at the end I came to the conclusion that there was nothing I could do to help in the matter. I am afraid my views are unaltered.'[472]

So in the end, and in reality, the Queen never had to intervene to save Harold Wilson and British democracy from Cecil King and her husband's uncle. In any case, Episode 305 portrays her as being more interested in her horse racing in May 1968 than in the processes of government, and while this certainly exaggerates her detachment from official business in these months – Elizabeth II has never been known to neglect her duties as Queen – it does fairly reflect the major changes she was making in the late 1960s to the horse breeding, training and racing operations that were such an important part of her life.

Elizabeth's love of horses went back to her very earliest years, when her grandfather, King George V, gave her a Shetland pony, Peggy, for Christmas – she was just four.[473] Her very first riding lessons were, in fact, on the broad back of the Sovereign, then in his mid-sixties, who loved to get down on all fours and shuffle around the Palace corridors with Lilibet digging her heels into his sides.[474] Once she was old enough, her grandfather would take her to the royal stud to explain the intricacies of breeding, and a few years after his death she was visiting the stud with her father the new King, George VI, when their guide apologised for forgetting the lineage of the mare that he was showing them, Bread Card – 'I can't remember her pedigree offhand, sir.' At which the 12-year-old Elizabeth instantly piped up: 'She is by the Derby winner Manna, out of Book Debt, by Buchan.'[475]

This encyclopaedic command of horse flesh was the basis of the expertise Elizabeth brought to a golden age of royal racing following her accession in 1952, when she steered her father's bloodstock and trainers to a sequence of victories unseen since the reign of Charles II. Thanks to horses like Aureole, whose 1954 successes were featured in Season 1 of *The Crown*,[476] Elizabeth twice came top of the fiercely competitive British horse-racing 'ladder', accumulating the prize money that made her the leading owner in Britain in both 1954 and 1957.

But this success did not outlast the 1950s. The 1960s crop of yearlings from the royal stud proved the worst for decades, with only three wins from eight foals, while Captain Cecil Boyd-Rochfort, her principal trainer at Newmarket, had 12 of her horses in training in 1960 without a single one winning a race.[477] Part of the trouble came from the sheer venerability which Boyd-Rochfort (80 years old in 1967) shared with the rest of the ageing royal racing team. But Elizabeth was honest and flexible enough to see that new thinking was required on her own part as well, and she decided to make changes.

The mid-1960s was a period of serious re-evaluation in British horse-racing circles when it came to the central question of how to breed, train up and put out a racing champion. Elizabeth herself had long subscribed to the old-school focus on a high-class pedigree that was almost noble or royal, with a principal emphasis on stamina. But by the mid-1960s racing experts were questioning this orthodoxy. The 'stayers' were losing out to horses who defied the 'science' of it all – apparent 'flukes' of breeding that seemed to find some extra sprinting capacity from somewhere unidentified, and Elizabeth decided that this was the direction into which she should shift her own bloodstock strategy.

'The emphasis *was* on "staying" blood,' she stated in a rare interview that she gave on the subject of her horses in the early 1970s, 'and recently I've been trying to inject a bit more speed.'[478]

The key to the Queen's new thinking was her old friend

'Porchey' – Henry Herbert, Lord Porchester, the future Earl of Carnarvon – whom we have met in earlier episodes.[479] A successful horse breeder and owner in his own right, 'Porchey' had been gently encouraging Elizabeth to push against the orthodoxies of the Boyd-Rochfort generation, notably in persuading her to take a lease in 1962 on the Polhampton Stud near his own HQ at Highclere Castle in Hampshire – familiar to modern television viewers as the setting for *Downton Abbey*. This had shifted Elizabeth's horse-racing centre of gravity down from East Anglia into her week-to-week Windsor routine, giving her more hands-on involvement with her equine team.

When those who know the Queen best try to define what makes her *really* tick, they begin and end with her horses. The first newspaper that she opens every morning is the *Racing Post* (*Sporting Life* prior to 1986), and her very first telephone calls, long before office hours, have always been to 'Porchey' (1924–2001) or to her trainers, early risers like herself. When she has no official business in Windsor, and especially at weekends, she goes out to check on her latest runners, visiting them in their stables to feed them clover and carrots, and always taking her camera to record their progress – like a parent on sports day.[480]

For the last three decades of the twentieth century 'Porchey' was Elizabeth's regular companion on these horsey outings, and they chatted about much more than horses together. With a strong instinct for public service, Lord Porchester (the seventh Earl of Carnarvon after 1987) served in the local Territorial Army, and successfully stood for election to the Hampshire County Council, of which he eventually became chairman. He also served as chairman of the South East Economic Planning Council.

Early in 1968, Elizabeth asked 'Porchey' to undertake a far-reaching enquiry into her future racing strategy, and this provides the basis for the foreign horse excursions in which we see her engaging in this episode. In May 1967 Elizabeth and 'Porchey' made a private visit to Normandy, to study the top studs in France and watch their leading stallions in action. She did not, in fact, visit America in 1968 as depicted, but since 1964 she had been flying some of the finest royal mares to Kentucky for the injection of speed that 'Porchey' had recommended.

Towards the end of Episode 305 a mildly jealous Prince Philip indecorously suggests that it was not just Her Majesty's racehorses that 'Porchey' was very keen on injecting – and the lifelong personal friendship that Elizabeth II enjoyed with Lord Porchester until his death aged 77 in 2001 has sometimes been a source of innuendo. But there is no historical basis for any suggestion of impropriety – and *The Crown* certainly has no truck with it. On their 1967 trip to Normandy, for example, Elizabeth and 'Porchey' were accompanied by his Anglo-American wife Jean Wallop, who remained one of the Queen's closest personal friends until her own death in April 2019.

The touching and unashamed intimacy enjoyed by Elizabeth II and Lord Porchester went back to the passion for horses they discovered they shared when they first got to know each other as teenagers. We have seen this relationship developing in previous episodes of *The Crown*, and 305 is the episode that makes it official. On 1 January 1970 Queen

Elizabeth II formally named Lord Porchester as her racing manager, completing her racing team on the same day with the recruitment of another fresh thinker, Michael Oswald, previously based at Newmarket, who was appointed Director of the Royal Studs. With Elizabeth and 'Porchey', Oswald completed the ambitious and open-minded 'triumvirate' that would run the royal racing stables for the rest of the twentieth century, re-establishing the Queen as a leading racehorse owner, not simply in Britain, but in the world.

'My philosophy about racing is simple,' said Elizabeth in her rare 1973 interview. 'I enjoy breeding a horse that is faster than other people's. I enjoy going racing, but basically I love horses. A Thoroughbred epitomises a really good horse to me, and my particular hope for the future, like all breeders of horses, is to breed the winner of the Derby.'[481]

The last time anyone checked the record – sometime around 2018 – racehorses owned by Queen Elizabeth II had won nearly 1,700 professional contests, including four of the five great British classics: the Oaks, the St Leger, the 1,000 Guineas and the 2,000 Guineas. In 1953, the year of her coronation, Elizabeth's much-cherished horse Aureole finished a close second in the Epsom Derby – but the Derby remains the one racing classic in which Her Majesty has yet to triumph.

CHAPTER SIXTEEN

'TYWYSOG CYMRU'
(PRINCE OF WALES)

FEBRUARY–OCTOBER 1969

ENTER PRINCE CHARLES, CENTRE STAGE – AT LAST. WE HAVE encountered the future Sovereign as a growing boy, notably in Episode 209 as he struggled through his unhappy schooldays at Gordonstoun in the shadow of his father. But now the Prince advances into the limelight – literally. As Episode 306 opens, we meet Charles at Cambridge, preparing to step onto the stage as *Richard II*, Shakespeare's lonely royal. In reality the Prince was never cast in such an elevated Shakespearean role. But he did participate actively in the university's Dryden Society, and, as a fan of Harry Secombe and *The Goon Show*, he participated in comedy sketches – most famously while sitting in a dustbin.

Charles had acted in both *Henry V* and *Macbeth* while he was at Gordonstoun, delivering performances that had provided rare high spots in his almost uniformly miserable Scottish education. So script writers Peter Morgan and James

193

Graham focus on the irony of a royal performer who truly loved acting – with the additional irony that Charles was incapable of acting in real life when it might well have suited him to strike a pose.

This became apparent in the spring of 1969 when the Prince gave his first radio interview – to the avuncular Jack de Manio on the BBC *Today* programme. Charles was about to head off to the west coast of Wales for a spell at Aberystwyth University prior to his investiture as Prince of Wales, and de Manio asked him his feelings about the Welsh Nationalists who were protesting against his arrival.

'I don't blame people demonstrating like that,' replied Charles quite openly. 'They've never seen me before. They

1969 – Prince Charles in a Footlights review
at Cambridge

don't know what I'm like. I've hardly been to Wales, and you can't really expect people to be over-zealous about the fact of having a so-called English Prince to come amongst them ...'[482]

The angry demonstrators were essentially the reason why Prince Charles was heading for Wales – and you did not need to be a Welsh Nationalist to feel that the whole idea of the heir to the British throne being called 'Prince of Wales' had something fishy and unconvincing about it. Why was the royal heir not Prince of Scotland – or Prince of Birmingham for that matter? The English status of the title went back to 1301 when King Edward I of England, having defeated the last Welsh Prince of Wales, Llywelyn ap Gruffudd, and paraded his severed head through the streets of London, invested his son and heir Edward, the future Edward II, with Llywelyn's same title as Prince of Wales, hoping that Welsh hearts would view England more fondly for the gesture.

As it happened, young Edward had been born in Caernarfon Castle while his father was campaigning there, and legend had it that Edward I proudly presented the infant to a crowd of discontented Welsh barons, promising them a prince 'born in Wales, who speaks not a word of English'. Being a baby, young Edward was at that point incapable of speaking any language at all – and when he was eventually proclaimed Prince of Wales at the age of 17 the investiture took place at a parliament in Lincoln.[483]

Such tokenism did not do much for Anglo-Welsh relations in 1301, and it did not seem to be making much difference six centuries later. In 1963 an underground organisation calling itself the Free Wales Army started performing military manoeuvres on remote Welsh mountainsides, where their clandestine radio transmitters called on Welsh patriots to rise up against their 'colonial' English oppressors.

The police laughed off their occasional thefts of gelignite – until 1968 when an RAF warrant officer was seriously injured by a bomb for which Welsh Nationalists claimed the credit. Shortly afterwards another bomb destroyed the Temple of Peace in Cardiff, and one more was found in the lost luggage department of Cardiff railway station. More respectably – and more worryingly – for the Labour government in London, a Welsh Nationalist, Gwynfor Evans, triumphed in the Carmarthen by-election of July 1966, ousting a Labour candidate and giving Plaid Cymru, 'The Party of Wales', its first ever seat at Westminster.

Separatist Celtic victories are never good news for London-based political parties. But the Labour Party has always had to view them with particular anxiety, given their electoral reliance upon the socialist voting traditions of the Welsh and Scottish heartlands. Hence the curious scene at the opening of this episode as Prime Minister Harold Wilson assembles the most radical socialist firebrands in his Labour cabinet – Tony Benn, Barbara Castle and Richard Crossman – to confer earnestly with the hereditary Earl Marshal, the Duke of Norfolk and his team of titled, old-school cohorts in order to make sure that the investiture of the latest Prince of Wales would go off with proper feudal dignity.

Until the Welsh Nationalist victory of 1966 Prince Charles had been heading for three uninterrupted years at Cambridge University studying Archaeology and Anthropology – his personal choice, on the basis of just two A level passes. Now Harold Wilson had a better plan. The wily Prime Minister proposed to the Queen, and Elizabeth accepted, that the Prince should interrupt his studies in England for a term at Aberystwyth University. There Charles could learn Welsh in a proper Welsh environment and prepare for the elaborate pageant at Caernarfon Castle that was intended to revive the memories of Edward I. Nineteen million viewers were expected to tune in for the ceremony in Britain – with a further 500 million watching worldwide.[484]

Much was made of the quasi-Arthurian origins of the spectacle, but this was a fraud. No such ceremony had been held for more than 250 years and the precedent on which Charles's ceremony was actually based was the investiture in July 1911 of George V's ill-fated son, King Edward VIII – known to his family, as it happened, by the Welsh name of 'David'. As with Prince Charles half a century later, the fundamental inspiration for the 1911 investiture was political. Britain's Welsh Chancellor of the Exchequer and future Prime Minister, David Lloyd George, wanted to shore up his Liberal vote in Wales, while also making much of the fact that he himself had been born in a humble cottage not far from Caernarfon Castle.

The consequence was that the young Prince Edward, just 17, had to dress up in what he later described as a 'preposterous rig' of white silk breeches and stockings, a purple velvet surcoat edged with ermine and white silk, and a gold coronet adorned with pearls and amethysts. Edward's scorn for the outfit did not prevent him, after he became the Duke of Windsor from taking the entire kit with him into exile following his abdication in 1936, along with his garter robes which he liked to try on from time to time in later life, whirling round the garden of Le

Moulin de la Tuilerie, his French country house, shouting out to his Duchess, 'Look, it still fits me like a glove!'[485]

It might have seemed sensible in 1969 to ask the Duke if he could hand back his 'preposterous rig' for the benefit of his successor. But since no one dared ask, an entirely new outfit had to be devised for Charles – with mixed results. Under the influence of Lord Snowdon who, as the only Welsh member of the family and a designer to boot, had been placed in charge of the general decor of the castle, Charles wore the elegant black and red uniform of the Colonel-in-Chief of the newly formed Royal Regiment of Wales, with a blue sash, his Order of the Garter and his Coronation Medal.

But the College of Arms vetoed Tony Snowdon's suggestion of a simple coronet for Charles along the lines of the elegant gold circlet worn by Laurence Olivier in the 1944 film *Henry V*. They insisted that the Worshipful Company of Goldsmiths should commission an elaborate Charles II-style coronet, with ermine and a cap of purple velvet. This complicated concoction featured 75 diamonds and 12 emeralds, topped off by a golden orb that resembled a painted ping-pong ball – inspiring newspapers to describe Charles's headgear as the 'Sputnik Crown' for the 'Space Age' Prince.

When it came to learning Welsh in 1911, the future Edward VIII had gone for lessons at 11 Downing Street, where he was instructed by the Welsh Chancellor of the Exchequer himself. This gave the Prince a smattering of Welsh expressions and the ability to stumble his way through the reading of a brief speech that Lloyd George composed for him. With Prince Charles it was decided to aim significantly higher – hence his eight weeks in Aberystwyth and his course of personal tuition with the university's top Welsh language lecturer, Edward 'Tedi' Millward.

Tedi Millward, 38 years old in the spring of 1969, who features as a major character in Episode 306, was a fervent Welsh Nationalist who had stood for Plaid Cymru in Montgomeryshire in the 1966 general election. He was vice-president of the independence party and a co-founder of the Welsh Language Society,[486] and he had no doubt at all that the investiture ceremony was a sordid political fix intended to shore up the Labour Party in Wales and knock back the movement for independence. When he heard that four Aberystwyth students were planning a week-long hunger strike in protest at Charles's imminent arrival at Aberystwyth, Millward congratulated them.[487] He was also married to a fellow nationalist, Silvia, who shared his fervour and felt strongly that Tedi should not get involved in teaching Charles.

'Many of my friends thought that I shouldn't teach him,' Millward later said. 'People's opinions were divided, for and against at that time. And one did feel that one was walking a knife's edge.'[488]

In the event, Millward accepted the university's challenge to become Charles's language tutor. This was partly for political reasons. 'Millward believed,' said Welsh Professor John Ellis, 'that direct access to the Prince gave Plaid an unprecedented opportunity to influence the thinking of Prince Charles and to turn the ceremony to the party's advantage.'[489]

Still more important, perhaps, Millward was passionate about the teaching of Welsh and especially the conversational style of instruction that he himself had developed in the Aberystwyth Language Laboratory. He had a lifelong dedication to arresting the language's decline and hoped that teaching the Prince of Wales would give Welsh a major popularity boost – which was precisely what happened. Then there was also an element of romance. How could a Welsh Nationalist, no matter how sceptical, turn his back on the chance to teach Welsh to a Prince of Wales?

So Charles and Millward started their lessons together, with Charles donning his headphones in the language laboratory's distinctive yellow booths. 'He had a one-on-one tutorial with me once a week,' Millward later recalled. 'He was eager, and did a lot of talking. By the end, his accent was quite good'.[490] Millward's daughter Llio later related how, towards the end of the term, Charles greeted one of the middle-aged Welsh ladies who stood outside the college every morning to cheer him on and keep protesters at bay: '*Bore da, shwd y'ch chi?*' ['Good morning, how are you?]'. To which she blushed and replied shyly, 'I'm sorry. I don't speak Welsh!'[491]

This was hardly surprising. A modern study by the Languageline translation service shows that barely a tenth of modern Wales's population of three million or so inhabitants speak fluent Welsh – some 310,600 people – and that the language is roughly twice as hard to learn as French or Portuguese, generally regarded as Europe's two 'easiest' languages. Welsh requires 1,040 hours of full-time tuition as compared to 550 hours for French.[492] Setting Charles's eight weekly sessions in the Aberystwyth language laboratory in this context, and assuming that the Prince allocated as many as five hours per working day to his linguistics, it seems likely that his Welsh language studies added up to 200 hours or more. Millward had pre-recorded language tapes for his royal student to practise, and residents in Charles's Neuadd Pantycelyn hall of residence later complained they became 'sick and tired' of hearing the tapes 'resounding through the darkness late at night' as the Prince rehearsed the latest phrases for his big speech.[493]

Going beyond linguistics, Tedi Millward engaged in fierce debates with Charles on Welsh issues. 'Not only did Millward get Charles's Welsh up to a standard which sounded brilliant,' wrote Charles's biographer Tim Heald, 'he also argued with him articulately and forcefully, never giving ground.'[494] In January 1969, Millward told *The Times*: 'There is an awakening in Wales and inevitably one would have to talk about this. The history of the language is an important facet and much of our life has been expressed through our language. It would be greatly to the Prince's benefit to hear all these things.'[495]

By the end of their eight weeks together Millward and Charles had grown genuinely fond and respectful of each other. While Millward had started by addressing Charles formally as 'Mr Windsor', which was how Charles had signed himself in at the university, they ended on mutually friendly, first name terms, with Millward judging the Prince to be 'sensitive, emotional, responsive and deeply thoughtful'.[496] When it came to the pay-off – how Charles delivered himself at the investiture on 1 July 1969 – the verdict was almost unanimously favourable. Charles had a Welsh accent to match that of many lifelong Welsh speakers, and the efforts that the Prince would make in later years to live up to his title have certainly borne Welsh fruit.

It cannot be confirmed whether Charles wrote the original version of his investiture speech, or if it was written for him.

But, given the significance of the event, it is likely that a combination of individuals had a hand in crafting his remarks: possibly Charles himself, along with his private secretary David Checketts with Elizabeth's private secretaries, and possibly the Palace press office as well.

Tedi Millward felt personally that his nationalist principles precluded him from accepting an invitation to the investiture ceremony itself, or to Charles's wedding in 1981. He was also disappointed, according to his family, that Charles did not keep up the Welsh language at which he had worked so hard, complaining that the Prince could have done more for Wales after he left Aberystwyth.[497] But in 1999, 30 years after the ceremony, a BBC Wales poll of Welsh speakers found that 73 per cent wanted the position of Prince of Wales to continue.[498] In July 2018 another poll showed a majority of Welsh people supporting the passing on of the title when the current Prince of Wales, Charles, becomes King, with only 27 per cent objecting to another investiture ceremony.[499]

So it would seem that Charles's son and heir, William (who went to university in Scotland), should be preparing himself for a good few months of language tuition and practice in Wales when the royal succession moves on. But whether he will then be required to dress himself in another 'preposterous rig' of white silk breeches and purple velvet remains to be seen.

In the aftermath of Charles's investiture, government documents show that the Labour Cabinet developed considerable anxieties about the free-thinking opinions on Welsh Nationalism that the Prince had brought back from Aberystwyth – and Welsh

Secretary George Thomas passed on his worries to Buckingham Palace. 'I am concerned by the speeches made by the Prince of Wales,' wrote Thomas to Harold Wilson on 22 July 1969, just three weeks after the investiture. 'I have no information about who his advisors are, but a dangerous situation is developing … In my presence in Cardiff he referred to the "cultural and political awakening in Wales". This is *most* useful for the Nationalists … The enthusiasm of youth is a marvellous spur, but it may lead to speeches that cause real difficulty… It has become quite evident to me that the Aberystwyth experience has influenced the Prince to a considerable extent.'[500]

Thomas requested that the Prime Minister should have 'a discreet word with the Queen'[501] on the subject, and this seems to have chimed with Palace anxieties – shared by both the Queen and Prince Philip – that the newly invested Prince was starting to develop a free-wheeling tendency to stray too far from the official script.

In the event, the political dividends to the Labour government from its initiative in sending Prince Charles to Wales could only be described as 'mixed'. In the 1970 election Labour regained the Carmarthen seat it had lost to Plaid Cymru – the original prompt for Charles being sent to Aberystwyth. On the other hand, the nationalists almost tripled their vote across Wales as a whole, from 61,000 in 1966 to 175,000 in 1970, and established themselves solidly as a permanent part of the Welsh political landscape. Plaid won two seats in the February 1974 election, and increased that to three in October 1974.

So it was arguable that the Welsh Nationalist cause was actually *strengthened* by the investiture pageant that was intended to reduce it. Analysts differ on the issue, with some suggesting that the much-publicised ceremony did indeed take the edge off extreme separatist sentiments, as Harold Wilson had hoped. Others see the investiture as simply reflecting the general nationalist tendencies in these years – in both Wales and Scotland – that put devolution on the table. Labour's October 1974 manifesto seemed to acknowledge this by pledging the creation of elected assemblies in Scotland and Wales.

Under James Callaghan's premiership of 1976–9 and the notorious 'Winter of Discontent', Labour by-election losses effectively destroyed Callaghan's Commons' majority – leaving the Labour Party dependent on the votes of Parliament's three Welsh Nationalist MPs to keep them in office. So, one way or another, Prince Charles's bravura acting performance in Caernarfon Castle helped keep socialist hands on the British helm as Harold Wilson had intended.

CHAPTER SEVENTEEN

'Moondust'

July–December 1969

A T THE END OF APRIL 1930 THE EIGHT-YEAR-OLD PRINCE Philip of Greece was invited to join his maternal grand-mother, Princess Victoria of Hesse and by Rhine (1863–1950), for a family holiday in Germany at the Neue Palais in Darmstadt, just south of Frankfurt. It was a wonderful chance for the boy to be reunited with his sisters and cousins, along with his fragile and deaf mother Princess Alice – especially since his father Andrew had, by this date, effectively deserted the family.[502]

But Grandmother Victoria had other plans. Deeply concerned about the mental wanderings of her daughter Alice, she had been consulting Professor Karl Wilmanns, a local expert on insanity,[503] and he had recommended some intensive, long-term treatment in a sanatorium. On 2 May 1930 Victoria arranged a day out for Philip and his sisters Cecilie and Theodora – who got back home to discover that their mother had vanished. In their absence, Professor Wilmanns had paid a visit, had restrained and sedated Alice with an injection of morphine and scopolamine, a nerve-paralysing agent,[504] and had then bundled her into a car to drive her down to the Bellevue sanitorium on the shores of Lake Constance over 200 miles away.[505] Philip would not see his mother again for years – and with his father moving to Monte Carlo around the same time, the boy was effectively an orphan.

Philip had already suffered a parentally solitary childhood. A major-general in the Greek army, his father Andrew was often away, making no contact with his only son for months on end. 'When he needed a father,' recalled Mike Parker, Philip's Australian naval pal who became his first private secretary, 'there just wasn't anybody there.'[506]

Far younger than his four elder sisters, Philip had little in common with any of them, so he was pretty much an only child, with sibling relationships that were fond and loving, but inevitably remote. The boy would withdraw into himself, as Uncle 'Dickie' Mountbatten, Alice's younger brother, would later recall. 'Dickie' described how at the age of four, his nephew loved to squirrel himself away for hours under the vast bed at the Mountbattens' London residence, quite alone and refusing to leave. The boy would scream in fury if anyone ventured to drag him out of his private refuge.[507]

There was, above all, the issue of Philip's remoteness from his mother, who was sincere and devoted but unable to listen in any real sense to anything her son wanted to tell or ask her. When these emotional gaps were compounded by the trauma of his mother's dramatic disappearance in May 1930

– Darmstadt was the last occasion on which the 'family' could be said to have been together in any meaningful sense – it was hardly surprising that Philip should start to exhibit signs of what psychologists describe as 'avoidant behaviour'. The 'avoidant' child declines to reveal their personal feelings to those close to them in later life, according to this diagnosis, in order to avoid triggering further rejection.[508]

In Philip's case, this 'avoidance' came to manifest itself in a 'toughness' that was amplified by his boarding school education. Weeks after the disappearance of his mother, the nine-year-old was packed off for three years to the austere surroundings of Cheam, a religiously-based boarding school near Sutton in Surrey that dated back to the 1640s.[509] He was then sent to Germany to board for two terms at Schule Schloss Salem – to 'save on the school fees', as he later put it dismissively, because the school was owned by the family of his brother-in-law[510] – followed by Gordonstoun, whose Highland harshness we tasted in Chapter Nine (Episode 209). In all these formative years, Philip had minimal contact with either his father or his mother – and it is known that he neither saw nor heard anything at all from Alice in particular between the ages of 11 and 16 (1932–7), while she was suffering the worst horrors of her manic depression.[511]

Kurt Hahn, who never married, saw no need to instruct his Gordonstoun boys on the importance and functioning of emotional relationships. All discussion of sex was forbidden.[512] One Gordonstoun schoolmaster recalls sixth-form boys coming to him as they were leaving school to ask him about the facts of life. 'I suppose the truth is,' he said, '[that] Hahn was a repressed homosexual. Certainly, we all thought so.'[513]

Hahn himself suffered from mental problems which he both hid from the world and bizarrely revealed in the floppy straw hat that he wore so frequently – the hat concealed a large metal plate that was the consequence of an operation to relieve blinding headaches from the pressure of cerebro-spinal fluid on the brain. He was also hospitalised twice in his life for manic depression – in the late 1930s as he was getting the school established (while Philip was a pupil), and then again in the 1950s.[514] The second hospitalisation led to his retirement as headmaster in 1953.

Philip left Gordonstoun in 1939 to train as an officer at Dartmouth Naval College – where, as we saw in Episode 1 (Chapter One of *The Crown*, Volume 1), the Prince was introduced to the young Elizabeth on her visit with her father George VI that July.[515] Apart from occasional visits by 13-year-old princesses, Dartmouth was another exclusively masculine environment, so after all his years of high-pressure training it was hardly surprising that Philip should confess in an early interview that he would be ashamed of admitting to crying. As we noted in Chapter Nine, the Prince's upbringing endowed him with highly defended 'survival' mechanisms.[516] Asked in an early interview what language he had spoken at home, he replied sharply with a question of his own: 'What do you mean, "at home"?'[517]

Philip's aggressive 'survival' mechanisms were defiantly on display over Easter 1964 in the Chapel Royal at Windsor during Prince Charles's service of confirmation into the Church of England. Philip had been strongly opposed to his son receiving confirmation at such an early age. Charles was only 16 – too young, in his father's opinion, to make such a serious personal commitment. But his objections had been overruled by the Queen, the Archbishop of Canterbury, Michael Ramsey, and by Prince Charles himself, and Philip showed his feelings by ostentatiously reading a book throughout the service, holding the volume noticeably high during the Archbishop's sermon.

'Bloody rude!' complained Ramsey afterwards to the Dean of Windsor, Robin Woods, who was a friend of Philip's but had to agree. In mitigation of Philip's behaviour, some said that the book he was reading had been the Bible, but if anything that made it worse. Philip had not only been rude to the Archbishop and to the Anglican Church as a whole – but most of all to his own son, whose special day it was, and who had approached the occasion with genuine religious feeling.[518]

The dynamic Robin Woods – a major character in this episode – had been brought in to shake up the royal parish, or 'Deanery' of Windsor, two years earlier. Himself the son of a vicar who rose to be a bishop, Woods had served as an army chaplain during the Second World War, earning mention in dispatches for his gallantry during the Italian campaign. He had ministered in Leicester, Singapore and Sheffield, as well as serving as Secretary of SCM, Britain's Student Christian Movement, before coming to Windsor in 1962 as Domestic Chaplain to the Queen. But the new Dean soon discovered that his spiritual services were less urgently required by Her Majesty than by her spouse, and it was fortunate that Woods had arrived in Windsor with an idea that appealed to Prince Philip's practical turn of mind.

'St George's House' was a long-nurtured dream of Woods that the Church needed some sort of refuge and revival centre where priests who were burned out could renew their sense of mission. This would be achieved through discussion and study with each other, but also with outsiders – scientists, trades unionists, politicians, town planners, doctors, arts representatives and military folk. The secular world would be invited in, helping the ministers to get back their mojo by contact with the reality and rapidity of twentieth-century change, while also identifying new channels that could seek to mingle spiritual elements into the material life of the country.[519]

Philip liked the idea. It sounded to him like the clerical equivalent of the staff colleges that pepped up serving officers in the armed forces, and he immediately identified a physical home for Woods' proposed study centre. Less than 20 years after the Second World War, there were still dilapidated corners of the Windsor compound with rundown houses dating back to the sixteenth, seventeenth and eighteenth centuries – the long disused residences of royal retainers and minor canons. Few causes could be better calculated to inspire the hands-on Duke of Edinburgh than repair and renovation, and he soon put together a restoration plan to create 15 modernised bedrooms in these old buildings, with new bathrooms and an adequate kitchen, along with study and meeting rooms – a modern conference centre behind Windsor's Georgian façades, with space for further extension into the nearby Canons' Cloister.

It was an expensive project – £350,000 in 1960s prices, the equivalent of some £6,000,000 today – and Philip responded to that challenge as well. He shamelessly exploited his status to raise the money via Knights of the Garter drawn to the idea of rebuilding Windsor in the name of their own – and England's –

patron saint. They brought in banks, international companies and such philanthropists as Lord Iveagh of the Guinness family, the property developer Max Rayne and Edward Lewis, the chairman of Decca, the hot UK record company of the moment, who had famously turned down The Beatles, but had managed to sign up The Rolling Stones.

Fully funded, St George's House opened on time on Sunday 23 October 1966 – two days, by sad happenstance, after the tragedy of Aberfan. Regular updates from the Welsh mining village disaster were fed into the gathering over the weekend, injecting sadness into the deliberations of the 35 'diverse and distinguished' guests invited to the centre's first residential consultation. But Prince Philip matched the gravity of the moment with the speech with which he opened the Saturday evening discussion, 'What does the Nation expect of the Churches?'[520]

Robin Woods later said that the Duke spoke 'quite brilliantly' on his theme for 40 minutes,[521] stimulating a provocative debate which the Prince himself moderated. St George's House clearly provided the long-needed dimension for which Philip had been searching in his spiritual life. We have seen how Elizabeth II was helped to find her spiritual path through the evangelistic teachings of the American Dr Billy Graham (in Chapter Six, 'Vergangenheit'). Now Philip found guidance via a practically based strand of the Anglican faith.

The Prince had found the challenge he had been seeking, coaxing him out from behind his hard-built psychological defences. In the months that followed, he gave further talks and led St George's House discussions on topics that ranged from human conflict to 'Truth', moving onwards over the years into his ecological interests and his campaigning for the conservation of nature. In 1982 the Prince published a collection of his lectures in a book, *A Question of Balance*, and two more volumes would follow.[522] In 1986 he invited religious representatives of Buddhism, Christianity, Hinduism, Islam and Judaism to come to Assisi, northern Italy, to discuss faith and the environment – in the footsteps of St Francis.[523]

It was Peter Morgan's inspiration to set Prince Philip's relatively late-life religious awakening – sometime in his mid-to-late forties – into the context of men landing on the Moon. In Episode 307, 'Moondust', we watch the Prince eagerly tracing every detail of the US Apollo 11 mission – displaying a fascination with space travel that followed a family tradition. Back in February 1962 Prime Minister Harold Macmillan had arrived at Buckingham Palace for his regular Tuesday night audience to find the Queen engrossed in the BBC radio commentary of US astronaut John Glenn's historic first circling of the Earth. The retro-rockets had just been fired and, after a perfunctory greeting, Elizabeth turned her attention back to the radio. Macmillan made an attempt to revert to business, but soon realised that the cause was hopeless. 'I think we might as well listen, Ma'am,' said the Prime Minister – and his Sovereign smiled. They happily agreed to skip the audience.[524]

Peter Morgan depicts Prince Philip making heroes of the US astronauts Armstrong, Aldrin and Collins – until he meets the trio and discovers that they are, in reality, quite ordinary, stolidly Earth-bound human beings. There was nothing wrong with them, but they had no particularly profound or dazzling vision to offer on life's mysteries. So, in Morgan's dramatic narrative, this inspires the Duke to move on to the spiritual insights available on his doorstep through Robin Woods and St George's House.

This scenario actually reverses the true chronology of events – St George's House opened three years *before* man landed on the Moon. But the invented truth remains – that Prince Philip spent many years searching for fulfilment in secular and especially scientific directions, only to locate his spirit in the old-fashioned Church that he had spurned. And when it comes to the history of the astronauts – Neil Armstrong (commander), Edwin 'Buzz' Aldrin Jr (lunar module pilot), and Michael Collins (command module pilot) – it turns out that they *did*, in fact, inject a religious dimension into the great lunar achievement that some people considered to have heralded the death of religion.

1969 – Astronaut Neil Armstrong, 39, meets
Prince Edward, 5

Buzz Aldrin, the second man on the Moon, who stepped down from the lunar module in the wake of Neil Armstrong, was a fervently practising Christian. He served as an elder at the Webster Presbyterian Church in Houston, Texas, which packed him up a 'Holy Communion kit' to take on his adventure – miniature plastic containers of bread and wine. He intended to open these in the Sea of Tranquility, planning to take his holy communion while reading aloud words on a card from the Bible, and broadcasting the service back to Earth: '*When I look at Your heavens, the work of Your fingers, the moon and the stars that You have established; what are human beings that You are mindful of them, mortals that You care for them?*' (Psalms 8:3–4).[525]

At the last moment NASA asked Aldrin not to broadcast. The Agency was embroiled in a tricky legal battle with Madalyn Murray O'Hair, the celebrated atheist and campaigner for the separation of Church and state, who had already lodged a complaint against the Apollo 8 crew who had read from the Book of Genesis while circling the Moon the previous Christmas.[526] So Aldrin agreed not to broadcast – 'reluctantly', as he later wrote – but he did make his personal sacrament just the same, sitting inside the lunar module on the surface of the Moon.

'*Eagle*'s metal body creaked,' he recalled. 'I ate the tiny Host and swallowed the wine. I gave thanks for the intelligence and spirit that had brought two young pilots to the Sea of Tranquility. It was interesting for me to think the very first liquid ever poured on the Moon, and the very first food eaten there, were the communion elements.'[527]

Before the radio blackout ended, and with the wine still

curling languidly in the cup in the one-sixth gravity of the
Moon, Aldrin concluded with the New Testament words from
the Gospel of St John used in the traditional communion
ceremony: '*I am the vine, you are the branches. Whosoever abides
in me will bring forth much fruit*' (John 15:5). Every year since
1969, Webster Presbyterian has held a Lunar Communion
service in Houston to commemorate Buzz Aldrin's celebration
on the Moon.[528]

His companion Neil Armstrong, meanwhile, was a believer
of another stripe – in the late 1950s Armstrong had inscribed
'Deist' as his personal 'Belief' definition on an application
form when seeking to lead a local Boy Scout troop in Southern
California.[529] Founding his personal credo on the precepts
of reason rather than revelation, Armstrong was in the great
American tradition of 'Deist' Founding Fathers and Mothers
like Thomas Paine, Abigail Adams and Benjamin Franklin,
who believed that God had created the world, but had since
declined to get involved with humankind – and was certainly
not to be discovered inside the sectarian belief systems of any
of the Earth-bound Christian churches.[530]

In 1994 the celebrated astronaut, by then 64, was on a visit
to Israel touring the Old City of Jerusalem, when he asked
Meir Ben-Dov, his host and noted archaeologist, if Jesus
himself might actually have walked on the spot where they
were walking.

'I told him,' recalled Ben-Dov, '"Look, Jesus was a Jew.
These are the steps that lead to the Temple, so he must have
walked here many times".'

Armstrong asked Ben-Dov if these particular old stone steps
were the original steps dating back through all the centuries

to the very time of Christ, and his guide informed him that they were.

'So Jesus stepped right here?' asked Armstrong.

'That's right,' answered Ben-Dov.

'I have to tell you,' Armstrong then replied to the Israeli archaeologist, 'I am more excited stepping on these stones than I was stepping on the Moon.'[531]

So, like Prince Philip, the great astronaut put all his science, deism and rationality aside when he came face to face with the appeal of old-time religion and the basic Christian message.

Olivia Colman takes over as Queen Elizabeth II for Seasons 3 and 4 of *The Crown* – with corgi actors Lily (left) and Prince (centre). © Sophie Mutevelian / Netflix, Inc.

Tobias Menzies plays
Prince Philip (left) in
Season 3 with Jason
Watkins (below) as
Prime Minister Harold
Wilson. Erin Doherty
(facing page right) takes on
the role of Princess Anne.

All © Des Willie / Netflix, Inc.

Helena Bonham Carter and
Ben Daniels portray Princess
Margaret and Lord Snowdon in
Los Angeles for a cocktail party in
November 1965 – Episode 302,
'Margaretology'. © Des Willie / Netflix. Inc.

Emerald Fennell plays Camilla
Parker Bowles, pictured (left)
on her wedding day in 1973.
Camilla's marriage would not
discourage the attentions of
Prince Charles (below left)
played by Josh O'Connor.

Derek Jacobi and Geraldine Chaplin play the Duke and Duchess of Windsor at their
French home-in-exile, where Prince Charles visited the Duke before his death.

Top © Colin Hutton / Netflix, Inc. Bottom © Des Willie / Netflix, Inc.

May 1968: Elizabeth II contemplates the news that her Uncle 'Dickie' Mountbatten has been flirting with conspiracy against her Prime Minister Harold Wilson. © Sophie Mutevelian / Netflix, Inc.

CHAPTER EIGHTEEN

'DANGLING MAN'

JUNE 1970–MAY 1972

---

*D*ANGLING MAN WAS THE FIRST NOVEL PUBLISHED BY THE Pulitzer Prize-winning author Saul Bellow, in which he imagined the daily journal of Joseph, an unemployed history graduate in Chicago in 1941. Joseph patriotically enlists for the American war effort – only to be told that his services will not be required for another 12 months. So what does Joseph do for a year? He 'dangles' …

Joseph's dilemma struck writers David Hancock and Peter Morgan as neatly expressing the quandary of Prince Charles throughout his life. 'Prince of Wales?' he complains in Episode 308 of *The Crown*. 'It's not so much an existence as a predicament. I am both free and imprisoned, utterly superfluous and quite indispensable. One can never fully invest in one thing or another, because at any moment it could all change …'

The Prince is confiding these thoughts to Camilla Parker

Bowles – Camilla Shand before her marriage to Andrew Parker Bowles in 1973 – whom Charles has just met and has invited to Buckingham Palace for dinner.

'Until she dies,' he remarks morosely of his mother the Queen, 'I am not fully alive. Nor can I be the thing for which I have been born. So one is condemned to this frightful business of waiting … existing in a timeless, slightly ridiculous abyss.'[532]

Camilla cheerfully admits she has no idea who Saul Bellow is or was, but when Charles explains Joseph's 1941 conundrum she gets the point immediately. So this Joseph character wants to go to war, she muses, because it would give his life meaning? But then he could easily be killed …

'Yes,' responds Charles gravely. 'That's how much humans need meaning.'

'Golly,' says Camilla gloomily, catching his mood. 'People just see the prince in the palace. But all that weight … It's crushing you.'

'It is quite a lot to bear,' agrees Charles mournfully – at which point a footman arrives bearing a tray on which is an envelope addressed to 'CAMILLA'.

'Oh!' says Camilla with some surprise and pleasure. 'For me? …' eagerly taking the envelope and turning it over to open it. 'TWANG!' A rubber band flies out of the envelope to hit her directly in the face – and Charles shrieks with delight: 'Ha! Gotcha!'

Camilla is roaring with laughter as well. 'I wasn't expecting THAT, sir! You GOT me!'

The couple – who are on their very first dinner date – collapse into giggles. 'All that dreadful waffle about "dangling"?' laughs

Charles. 'And "the abyss"? ... Mummy kicking the bucket at long last? ... then GOTCHA!'

'Brilliant!' agrees Camilla. The couple have tears running down their cheeks.[533]

This scene, entirely invented, typifies the dramatic technique of *The Crown*. Prince Charles never once 'twanged' a girlfriend with a rubber band so far as anyone can discover. This whole imagined scenario springs from the vision of screenwriters Hancock and Morgan – and some critics might judge their fabricated jape to be over-lengthy and less than funny.

But those very shortcomings are part of the objective – to illustrate the clowning and the sheer daft sense of silliness that has proved such a powerful element (some would say the crucial and enduring glue) in the 48-year-long relationship between Prince Charles and Camilla Parker Bowles. Their perplexing love affair would consume and, in some senses, traumatise the British monarchy for more than a quarter of a century – and the trauma starts in this episode. Love it or loathe it, the complex drama between Camilla and the 'dangling man' now becomes central to the storyline of *The Crown*.

There are two versions of how this historic and much written about relationship began. Prince Charles has always insisted that they were first introduced by the beautiful and brainy Lucia Santa Cruz, the daughter of a Chilean diplomat who had been his first serious girlfriend at Cambridge. Lucia had come up to London after graduating and moved into the Cundy Street flats near Victoria Station where Camilla happened to have a flat on another floor. The two women became friends, so when Charles came for a drink with Lucia one evening in

1970/71 she told him she had found 'just the girl' for him and invited Camilla to join them.[534]

Santa Cruz has confirmed this story, but the more widespread version centres on a rainy afternoon at Smith's Lawn, Windsor Great Park, in the summer of 1971, after Charles has finished playing polo. As he strokes one of his ponies, Camilla approaches him to praise the beast. 'That's a fine animal, sir,' she says. 'I'm Camilla Shand.'

'Pleased to meet you,' responds Charles – to which Camilla, in a reference to her ancestor, King Edward VII's mistress, Alice Keppel, then opens up: 'You know, sir, my great-grandmother was the mistress of your great-great-grandfather – so how about it?' The couple then talk animatedly for more than an hour …[535]

One of the several well-informed chroniclers of the romance, Gyles Brandreth, considers it highly unlikely that Camilla would have marched up to Prince Charles and introduced herself out of the blue.[536] But another, Caroline Graham, quotes an onlooker as saying that Camilla 'saw the Prince standing alone on the other side of the field. Cool as you like, she walked across and started talking to him. To be honest, no-one thought it surprising or strange. She was part of the inner circle. She'd been at social functions with the royal family before.'[537]

Camilla's father, Major Bruce Shand, was certainly a close friend of the Queen Mother, and the striking portrait of Alice Keppel hanging in Cundy Street bore witness to Camilla's keen interest in her great-grandmother. Like Alice, Camilla had bright blue eyes, was humorous, kindly and vivacious – and she had no objection at all to becoming a royal mistress.

'It took no more than a glance,' reported another chronicler, 'to see that something was going to happen. There was an electric magnetism between them … You could tell from the intensity of their conversation and the way they looked at each other what the upshot would be.'[538]

Camilla was in no way conventionally attractive – earthy-looking, with apple-red cheeks. She was not into designer clothes, she bit her nails and her hair was consistently unkempt. But she had presence. As Lady Annabel Goldsmith described Camilla's magnetism: 'You could see what a man could see: an intensely warm, maternal, laughing creature, with enormous sex-appeal.'[539] Camilla was awash with energy, along with a bright and easy sense of fun. Lord Patrick Beresford, a close friend, described the feeling of Camilla walking into a room: 'Your spirits rise, because you know you are going to have a laugh.'[540]

1975 – Prince Charles and the married
Camilla Parker Bowles

A laugh was just what Prince Charles needed at the start of the 1970s. His emotional life remained complicated by the approval he vainly sought from his father and the lack of overt affection expressed by his mother. Searching for love and reassurance, he was dogged by a sense of worthlessness – his romantic liaisons seemed to be leading him nowhere. He felt both energised and relaxed in Camilla's company, with their shared love of hunting, horses and country pursuits – along with their zany sense of humour which extended to Bluebottle (Peter Sellers), Eccles (Spike Milligan) and their greatest hero of all, Neddie Seagoon (Harry Secombe). The couple were dedicated fans of *The Goon Show*, BBC radio's 1950s predecessor to – and, indeed, the original inspiration of – *Monty Python's Flying Circus*.[541] The couple gave each other Goon nicknames, 'Fred' and 'Gladys' – which, say friends, the future King and his Consort cheerfully call each other to this day.[542]

The problem was that Camilla already had a boyfriend with whom she was obsessed – the dashing Household Cavalry officer Major Andrew Parker Bowles. Parker Bowles treated Camilla with abominable infidelity, picking her up and dropping her as he pleased, and running her against his other on-off consort, Lady Caroline Percy – who later described how Camilla eventually struck back by bedding the banking heir Rupert Hambro.

'Rupert knew the affair was futile because of Camilla's obsession with Andrew,' Lady Caroline told the writer Christopher Wilson. 'But he liked her and knew they would always be friends … He still remembers the masochistic glee she took in telling him about tricky situations Andrew's unfaithfulness caused.'[543]

Parker Bowles's adventuring rose to fresh heights in the summer of 1970, when the 30-year-old set his cap at the 19-year-old Princess Anne whom he encountered at Windsor, where his father Derek was staying as a guest of the Queen Mother. The Princess and the galloping major were said to have enjoyed a full-blown affair during Ascot week that year – and there is one school of thought that believes Camilla was only driven to seduce Charles because Andrew had previously seduced Anne.

'She was determined to show [Andrew],' recalled one of the polo community, 'that she could do as well in the royal pulling stakes as he had done. There was always that element of pursuit by her, the feeling that she was determined to show him that she was as good as him, in no matter what.'[544]

There could be no future, however, for Parker Bowles's romance with Anne. The Princess would have had to renounce her succession rights if she had married him – Andrew was a Catholic – and, anyway, by the autumn of 1970 her friendship was deepening with her fellow equestrian Captain Mark Phillips, whom she would marry in 1973. Parker Bowles's relationship with Camilla was further complicated by his military duties that took him out of the country to Germany, Cyprus and Northern Ireland – which gave Camilla the chance to get started seriously on her relationship with Prince Charles.

In 1972 the couple spent time with friends at Annabel's nightclub in Berkeley Square and were seen dancing together at the Argentine Embassy. Charles was a regular visitor to Cundy Street, and he loved the weekends he spent in Sussex with Camilla's family, where he got on famously with her father Major Bruce Shand. Warm and welcoming, the Shands were not stuffy in the slightest, and they made Charles feel very much part of the family – giving him the chance, for the first time, to experience a relatively normal, relaxed and intimate family life.[545]

The approval of 'Dickie' Mountbatten, Charles's 'honorary grandfather', was a crucial step in the right direction. During Charles's naval courses at Portsmouth the Prince was permitted to stay at 'Dickie's' nearby Hampshire home, Broadlands, instead of bunking at the officers' mess, and Uncle 'Dickie' was delighted for Camilla to join the party. To keep up appearances, she was allotted the Portico Room, the same room in which Elizabeth and Philip had consummated their marriage on their honeymoon in 1947. Charles was assigned the suite next door, with an interconnecting door, and at Broadlands the couple – still not on the press radar – could go fishing, riding and on long walks around the estate, openly holding hands, laughing and joking.

'When Uncle Dickie approved of Camilla, that was the final seal of approval as far as Charles was concerned,' explained John Barratt, Mountbatten's private secretary for many years. But there was a catch involving Amanda Knatchbull, Mountbatten's 14-year-old granddaughter, for whom the old man had long-term plans. 'Mountbatten knew Camilla would make a perfect mistress for Charles until Amanda was of marriageable age,' says Barratt. 'So he gave the blossoming love affair his full blessing.'[546]

In this episode the writers depict Prince Charles confiding his feelings about Camilla to his Great Uncle David, the former Prince of Wales, whose royal destiny was to be so complicated by love. It is certainly true that Charles did correspond with his great uncle over the years, but it is not known if he ever mentioned Camilla to him, and the Duke certainly never passed on such correspondence to Charles's mother, as shown in the final scenes. The role of the dying ex-king at this point in the drama is to provide historical context to these early months of the relationship between Charles and Camilla, setting the couple's romance into the wider dynastic framework.

Despite the fun of her visits to Broadlands in 1972 and her growing love for Charles, Camilla's emotions remained complicated, since she still carried a torch for Andrew. She was torn. 'I love Charles very much,' she told a friend, 'but I simply cannot forget about Andrew. I often wonder where he is or what he's doing. I think of him all the time. Is it possible to love two men at the same time?'[547]

Camilla could not believe that she could possibly marry Charles – let alone ride in the Gold State Coach to Westminster Abbey one day. Having grown up around the royal family, she knew what royal marriage involved and required, and as quite a shy woman in some respects, living in the public eye did not appeal to her. Then there was another issue that mattered more in the early 1970s than it would today. As Patricia, Lord Mountbatten's elder daughter, and the mother of Amanda Knatchbull, disdainfully put it, the problem with Camilla was that she had quite a spicy 'history' that everyone knew about: 'You didn't want a past that "hung about". And she was a subject ... *Nobody* marries a subject.'[548]

When Andrew Parker Bowles returned from his posting in Germany, he was flattered to discover that Camilla had been having a fling with Charles. It lent him extra status – but it also meant that Camilla could play a stronger hand. If Andrew wanted her now, he would have to do the decent thing – and Camilla took some pleasure in playing a delicate juggling game between her two beaux. Mountbatten started to worry that his honorary grandson was getting too serious with his 'mistress material', and, according to author Sarah Bradford, he arranged a distant naval posting to help things cool down. Towards the end of 1972 it was announced that the Prince would be joining HMS *Minerva* on a six- to eight-month commission in the West Indies.

On the weekend of 9/10 December 1972 Charles went to stay with Mountbatten at Broadlands – and Camilla was invited as well. Charles took them both down to Portsmouth for a tour of *Minerva* and went back to Broadlands again the following weekend, again with Camilla. Both knew this was the last time they would see each other before Charles's eight months at sea, and the Prince declared his love, but not his full hand. He offered no long-term commitment to Camilla – and he certainly did not propose marriage or anything like it.

'Sometimes,' wrote Gyles Brandreth, Charles's biographer, 'the actions we do not take are indeed more significant than those we do.'[549]

CHAPTER NINETEEN

'IMBROGLIO'

JUNE 1972–JULY 1973

———

'IMBROGLIO' IS A LONG-WINDED NOUN OF ITALIAN ORIGIN meaning 'muck-up', 'muddle' or quite simply 'mess' – and this episode centres on two major British messes of the early 1970s: the ongoing drama of Prince Charles's tangled relationship with Camilla Shand (still not yet 'Parker Bowles'), and Prime Minister Edward Heath's tragic *lack* of relationship with the National Union of Mineworkers that led to the power cuts and national chaos of 1974's notorious 'Three-Day Week'.

In retrospect, it is easy to see that Prince Charles committed a fatal romantic error when he failed to offer a solid emotional commitment to Camilla Shand before he set off for the West Indies on HMS *Minerva* early in 1973. 'This is the last time I shall see her for eight months,' he wrote longingly to 'Dickie' Mountbatten.[550]

But the Prince had not conveyed his longing to Camilla

in any concrete terms, and he is not known to have written longingly to *her* from *Minerva*. Charles might, for example, have hinted that he would hope to make some sort of engagement proposal to her on his return in the summer, since, coming up to her twenty-sixth birthday in July, Camilla was entering the 'engagement' stage of life. Her flatmate Virginia Carrington got married that January of 1973, and most of Camilla's contemporaries from her debutante season were already married with children. She needed to catch up.

Subsequent history has shown that, through all their ups and downs, Charles and Camilla were clearly soul mates. But this was not the message left in Camilla's heart and head as Charles went to sea in 1973 – while Andrew Parker Bowles was right beside her in London, moving ahead with his British Army career. Camilla's father, Major Bruce Shand, was becoming irritated by Andrew's dithering. He had been delighted at his daughter's relationship with the Prince of Wales, but, like Camilla herself, he did not believe it could possibly lead to a top-level royal marriage and all that entailed. Now was the time, in Charles's absence, to exert some pressure, and according to John Bowes-Lyon (Andrew's cousin) Camilla's family decided to force Andrew's hand by publishing an engagement notice in *The Times* in the middle of March 1973.[551]

That spring Charles had a week's break from *Minerva*, but he did not fly home to Camilla. Instead he accepted Uncle 'Dickie's' invitation to join him and his daughter Patricia Knatchbull's family on the island of Eleuthera in the Bahamas. Staying in the maid's room at the back of the house, Charles spent happy days skinny dipping and painting seascapes, and he began to take notice, as Mountbatten had long plotted, of Patricia's 15-year-old daughter, Amanda.

'I must say,' he wrote to her grandfather, who was also his own, thoroughly delighted great-uncle, 'Amanda really has grown up into a very good-looking girl – most disturbing.'[552]

Charles and Amanda began writing to each other, and Mountbatten noted frankly in a letter to Charles that he hoped something 'permanent' would come of it.[553] Reporting back for duty to *Minerva*, Charles felt desperately lonely, describing to the Knatchbulls a 'ghastly feeling of empty desperation and apparent hopelessness … so utterly similar to going back to school that it frightened me'.[554] It was in this mood, while docked in English Harbour in Antigua, that he heard of Camilla's engagement, and he could not believe that 'such a blissful, peaceful and mutually happy relationship' could have lasted only six months.[555] If the story was true that the Shands had published the engagement notice to force the hand of the galloping major, Andrew 'Poker' Bowles evidently did not mind getting cornered.

Out in the Bahamas the Prince locked himself in his cabin when he heard the news, emerging three hours later with red-rimmed eyes to join his fellow officers for dinner, mourning that he would have 'no one' to go back to and forlornly hoping 'I suppose the feeling of emptiness will pass eventually'.[556] Then early in May, Charles received another blow with the news that his sister Anne had become engaged to her fellow equestrian Captain Mark Phillips. Within a matter of months, Charles had lost two of his closest female companions.

As the Queen's two elder children grew up together, Anne had become quite a close element in her brother's life, a straight-talking companion in whom he could confide naturally. Now Anne would belong to someone else, with whom Charles also happened to feel that she was badly mismatched[557] – and he finally began to worry about his own marriage prospects. 'I can see I shall have to find myself a wife pretty rapidly,' he fretted, 'otherwise I shall get left behind and feel very miserable!'[558]

Meanwhile Camilla and Andrew Parker Bowles were enjoying all the fun of preparing for their wedding, which they celebrated on 4 July 1973 at the Guards Chapel at Wellington Barracks in London. Their guests included the Queen Mother and Princess Anne – proof of how well liked and well connected the Parker Bowles and Shand families were.

Charles was invited, but he did not attend on grounds of 'duty', as he was the official representative for the Queen in Nassau, where the Bahamas were about to celebrate their independence. He sent a telegram to explain his absence, but no one bought his excuse. The Prince simply could not face seeing Camilla getting married, and his personal frustrations began to boil over into trivial matters. During a polo match in which he played poorly he stormed off the field after the American polo player/commentator twice called him 'Prince Philip' accidentally-on-purpose, and sarcastically shouted out 'Great shot!' after Charles missed the ball.

'I was forced, in a rage, to stump up to the top of the commentary box,' recorded Charles in his diary, 'and ask him to stop making pathetic remarks.'[559] As one of the Prince's aides later confided to biographer Sally Bedell Smith, this 'irritability and blackness' was very much part of Charles's nature.[560]

'Irritability and blackness' were two equally key words at

the heart of Episode 309's other great mess, the Conservative premiership of Edward Heath from June 1970 to March 1974, and particularly the disaster of the Three-Day Week. The stiff and humourless personality of Heath, aged 53 when he came to power, did not make for easy or genial royal audiences, and it did not help that the very unmarried Prime Minister was indifferent to – and even sometimes contemptuous of – women.

'Harold [Wilson] was fine, because he loved her [the Queen] and treated her marvellously,' confided one courtier to biographer Ben Pimlott. 'But Ted was tricky   she was never comfortable with him.'[561] According to another account, Private Secretary Michael Adeane soon found himself preparing detailed agendas for Elizabeth's audiences with Heath to help push through the awkward silences.[562]

Paradoxically, Heath enjoyed a very warm relationship with the Queen Mother. In 1962 she had danced the twist with the young Lord Privy Seal – then an up-and-coming Tory-hopeful leading Britain's first attempt to join the European Common Market – at a dinner party held by the still-respectable John Profumo. In June 1970 Heath attended the senior Queen Elizabeth's seventieth birthday party, held the night after he entered No. 10, and whenever he was up at Balmoral he would escape for drinks with her at nearby Birkhall. Their friendship was based on their shared love of music – whatever his shortcomings, Heath holds the undisputed claim to have been the finest concert-grade pianist ever to occupy Downing Street. In March 1972, he sat down at the keyboard to provide musical entertainment for the Queen Mother at a seventieth birthday party for the composer William Walton, with her friend Benjamin Britten among the guests.

Unlike Harold Wilson, Edward Heath had an 'undisguised dis-respect' for the British Commonwealth,[563] and he liked to downplay its importance to his Common Market pals like France's President Pompidou in order to demonstrate that Britain's modern spirit was truly European. This set the new Prime Minister at odds with the Queen, for whom the Commonwealth mattered deeply – and in 1971 matters rapidly came to a head over CHOGM, the Commonwealth Heads of Government Meeting, which was due to be held that year in Singapore.

On becoming Prime Minister, Heath had controversially jettisoned Harold Wilson's arms embargo against white-ruled apartheid South Africa. This British move was vehemently opposed by all the other 47 Commonwealth members, except for the maverick regime in Malawi, with two nations threatening to leave the organisation. Several African leaders spoke of expelling Britain, and in the hopes of avoiding a confrontation Heath prevented Elizabeth from going to Singapore, a ban that she found deeply upsetting. Had she been allowed to attend, Martin Charteris later commented, it would have actually diminished the chances of bad temper and conflict.

'If she's there, you see, they behave,' explained Adeane's 1972 successor as private secretary. 'It's like Nanny being there. Or perhaps it's Mummy. Anyway she demands that they behave properly in her presence. Never by *saying* anything, but by *looking* like a Queen – "and no bloody nonsense from you!" It also works because she knows them all, and they like her.'[564]

As it turned out, the Singapore CHOGM proved particularly

sour, and Elizabeth was determined that it would not happen again. In December 1972 she exploited the fact that she was Head of State in Canada, (as she was and is Head of State of Australia, New Zealand and a total of 16 Commonwealth countries) to accept a formal invitation directly from Canadian Prime Minister Pierre Trudeau (1919–2000, the father of Canada's current Prime Minister Justin Trudeau) to the 1973 CHOGM in Ottawa without deigning to consult No. 10.

Edward Heath's Europhilia was never especially popular in Britain, but EEC membership came to be the central feature of his legacy. In 1971 French President Pompidou ignored de Gaulle's 1967 veto to approve Britain's application, and in January 1972 Heath signed the Accession Treaty. In July 1972 Parliament passed the European Communities Act after a free vote, and on 1 January 1973 Britain entered officially.

'The new links with Europe will not replace those with the Commonwealth,' Elizabeth was careful to say in her Christmas speech for 1972. 'They cannot alter our historical and personal attachments with kinsmen and friends overseas. Old friends will not be lost.'[565]

So the Queen and Philip were shocked in January 1973 when they attended the opening gala of the Fanfare for Europe intended to celebrate EEC entry. As they arrived at the Royal Opera House with Edward Heath, several hundred anti-marketeers booed and chanted '*Sieg Heil!*' It was the beginning of Brexit. *The Guardian* described the royal couple as 'momentarily shaken by the size and noise of the demonstration – the largest involving members of the Royal Family seen in London'.[566]

The most lethal and bloody issue of these years was the

growth of Anglo-Irish conflict that came to be known as 'The Troubles'. In February 1971 the first British soldier was killed in Ulster, and in August Home Secretary Reginald Maudling introduced the controversial policy of internment without trial. With the confinement and torture of Irish Republican Army internees in barbed wire complexes like Long Kesh, Heath's Ulster policy soon became internationally contentious. The shooting of 28 unarmed civilians (14 died) by British soldiers on Bloody Sunday, 13 January 1972, raised tensions still further, and 'Operation Motorman', the capture of IRA 'no-go areas' in July 1972, proved to be the biggest deployment of British troops since Suez. As for the IRA, they soon brought their campaign to the British mainland, with a bomb going off every day in London over Christmas 1973.[567]

'The Queen received me at one of my regular audiences,' Edward Heath later recalled, 'after she had been watching coverage of riots in Belfast on the television, and was obviously shaken by the ferocity of the events in a part of her Kingdom. In particular, she was horrified by the film of women's faces contorted with hate as they clung to the high-wired fences protecting British troops. Whenever the Queen is accused of remoteness or indifference towards the tribulations of her subjects, I think back to that moment.'[568]

The backdrop to all these dark events was a crumbling British economy which was becoming increasingly uncompetitive, with unemployment rising at the same time that global commodity prices – and oil prices, in particular – were pushing up inflation. In January 1972 the number of Britons out of work and claiming benefits rose to over a million for the first time since the Great Depression of the 1930s – and when the news was announced, parliamentary uproar was so great that Prime Minister's Questions were suspended for the first time in the twentieth century.

'You ought to be ashamed of yourself,' shouted Labour MP Dennis Skinner as he shook his fist at Edward Heath. 'You're better fitted to cross the Channel and suck President Pompidou's backside!'[569]

Threatened simultaneously by unemployment, taxation and a fall in the value of the pound in their pocket, British workers turned increasingly to trades union protection and solidarity. In 1968, 43 per cent of the national workforce were union members. By 1978 this figure had risen to 54 per cent,[570] and in the three years 1969–72 there were more strikes than at any time since 1919. In 1970, 11 million working days were lost to industrial action, the highest since the General Strike of 1926, and in 1972 this figure more than doubled to 24 million days – ten million of which were due to the first ever national strike by the National Union of Mineworkers.

The chaos started even as Heath entered No. 10. By the autumn of 1970, a 'dirty jobs' strike by local council workers was paralysing London. Strikes by pumping station staff caused sewage to fill up the Thames, killing thousands of fish, and school days were lost when caretakers walked out. As rubbish piled up in Leicester Square, Heath moved to invoke the first of five national 'states of emergency' that his government would call in their three and a half years in power. Through the Depression and the Second World War British governments had only resorted to such measures, created in 1920, some 12 times – increasing the impression that Heath's Britain was ungovernable.[571] Constitutionally, the calling of a state of emergency is a matter for the monarch's prerogative, so Elizabeth had to summon four Councils of State during Heath's premiership – with the fifth, on 9 February 1972, being presided over by her mother, since Elizabeth herself was then touring in the Far East.

In January 1972, the seven-week miners' strike brought Britain to the very brink, plunging the country into unpredictable power cuts. Conventional wisdom was that the miners could not win. 'Rarely have strikers advanced to the barricades with less enthusiasm or hope of success,' wrote Woodrow Wyatt, the former Labour MP, in the *Daily Mirror*. 'Miners have more stacked against them than the Light Brigade in their famous charge.'[572]

But early in February 1972 mass pickets gathered round a fuel storage depot at Nechells near Birmingham which was crucial to industry in the West Midlands – up to 700 vehicles a day collected coke there for neighbouring factories. As the queues of lorries built up for miles, Birmingham police sent hundreds of officers to keep the depot gates open. The miners responded by themselves travelling from all over the country, along with other unionised workers, so that by 10 February there were upwards of 15,000 pickets around the plant, as well as the nearby Saltley Gas Works.

In the interests of public safety, Sir Derrick Capper, the local Chief Constable, ordered the depot to close its gates and keep them closed – a massive victory for the strikers that became known as the Battle of Saltley Gate. Heath had no choice but to surrender to the wage demands of the NUM following a cabinet meeting held by candlelight thanks to a power cut.

Matters got even worse. On 6 October 1973 – Yom Kippur, the holiest day in Judaism, which happened also to fall that year during the Muslim holy month of Ramadan – a coalition of Arab states launched an attack against Israel in Sinai and the Golan Heights. Though taken by surprise, Israel fought back with remarkable success, marching to within 60 miles of Cairo and 20 miles of Damascus, before being persuaded to halt at the behest of the United Nations. Blaming their defeat on the West's massive military and financial support to Israel, OAPEC, the Organization of Arab Petroleum Exporting Countries, imposed an oil embargo on the United States, Canada, Japan, the Netherlands and the United Kingdom. As a result, the price of crude oil rose in a matter of weeks from $2 to $7 a barrel in December 1973, with Britain's rate of inflation increasing consequently to over 9 per cent.[573]

On 12 November 1973, with their recently improved pay packets having fallen right back to where they had started the year, the mineworkers and electricity Workers began an overtime ban in support of another significant pay increase, and Edward Heath felt he had to invoke his fifth national state of emergency. On 13 November, the day before Princess Anne's wedding, he announced a programme of daily power cuts, with street lighting to be reduced by half, along with a 10.30pm curfew on TV programming – after which all screens were to go blank.

'SOS – Switch Off Something now,' read government advertisements in the newspapers, with the atmosphere of economic apocalypse made worse by the continual IRA bomb scares. The much-ridiculed President Idi Amin of Uganda took the chance to get his own back by announcing a Save Britain Fund 'to assist our former colonial masters'.[574] Then on 13 December Edward Heath went on television (before the 10.30pm shutdown) to announce that, starting on 2 January next year, all industry would be restricted to working a three-day week.

Horrified by this succession of disasters, Elizabeth felt that she had to inject some note of sympathy for ordinary Britons' plight into her Christmas message that year – so she asked Martin Charteris to notify Heath that she planned to conclude her broadcast with an acknowledgement of the 'difficulties … of deep concern to all of us as individuals and as a nation', together with a reminder and plea that 'what we have in common is more important than what divides us'.[575]

The words were hardly inflammatory, but at her audience the next day Heath bluntly instructed the Queen not to mention the crisis at all. Undaunted, Charteris came back later with a shortened version which he had worked out with the Queen – only for Heath to baulk again. The Prime Minister instructed Robert Armstrong, his private secretary, firmly to 'dissuade' Her Majesty, and Elizabeth finally felt she had no choice but to comply.

The remorseless succession of domestic and foreign crises in the years 1970–74 finally broke Edward Heath – both physically and mentally. When the Prime Minister delivered his notorious televised address to announce the Three-Day Week, he had barely slept for four days, and it showed. 'Ted Heath seemed to match his anagram – "the death",' remarked the broadcaster Michael Cockerell.[576] Putting on weight from a thyroid condition that was only diagnosed later, Heath was growing increasingly tired and indecisive, given to long, morose silences in cabinet, and in February 1974 he decided to call a general election using the challenging slogan, 'Who governs Britain?'

The answer to his challenge came on 28 February as a clear 'Not you, mate!'. Labour had won marginally more seats than the Conservatives around the country, and after the failure of some inconclusive attempts to create a coalition government with Jeremy Thorpe and the Liberal Party, Heath resigned on 4 March, to be replaced by a minority Labour government. As we shall see in the next chapter, Harold Wilson made his way back to the Palace ...

The 1970–74 'Imbroglio' of Edward Heath turned out to be a double-edged sword for the British monarchy. On the one hand, the unforgiving and almost continuous atmosphere

December 1973 – Edward Heath announces the
Three-Day Week

of political crisis reinforced the crown's position as a symbol of stability. Celebrations like Elizabeth and Philip's silver wedding anniversary in November 1972, and Princess Anne's marriage to Mark Phillips the following November, helped to generate a certain up-tick in public morale – and they certainly promoted a sense of national unity.

On the other hand, widespread economic hardship placed royal rank and privilege under fiercer scrutiny than ever before. May 1971 saw the first ever deliberations of parliament's 'Select Committee on the Civil List' which initiated open public debate about the monarchy's value for money – with Princess Margaret, and to some extent the Queen Mother, facing criticism for their extravagant lifestyles and lack of work ethic. In December 1971 *The Sun* devoted a two-page spread to royal finances, claiming that four out of five readers opposed a 'royal pay rise'.[577] The cost of Anne's 1973 wedding to Mark Phillips raised further concerns, with widespread criticism that the newlyweds should be given the use of the Royal Yacht *Britannia* with its crew of 21 officers and 250 sailors for their honeymoon.[578]

Throughout the crisis of the power cuts and the Three-Day Week, no one doubted that the Queen herself was personally frugal, with apocryphal stories circulating of how she would stalk the Palace corridors at night switching off superfluous electric lights – and at the end of 1973 it emerged that she would be digging into her private funds to find the £200,000 needed to carry out modernisations on her Norfolk estate at Sandringham.

That Christmas Her Majesty made a point of cancelling the usual showy procession of royal limousines to the parish church. Instead she travelled with her guests in a single minibus from Sandringham House in order to provide an example of petrol-saving – only to find assembled a record post-war crowd of 10,000 people, virtually all of whom had driven to the village in their petrol-powered cars.[579]

The crowds had come to see Prince Charles stepping out with his first major post-Camilla girlfriend, Lady Jane Wellesley, the daughter of the Duke of Wellington. For some British motorists, it seemed, the monarchy remained as popular as ever – and certainly when it came to the latest details of the family's love life.

CHAPTER TWENTY

'CRI DE COEUR'

AUGUST 1973–JUNE 1977

'In days of disillusion,
However low we've been,
To fire us and inspire us,
God gave to us our Queen …'

POET LAUREATE SIR JOHN BETJEMAN'S SILVER JUBILEE HYMN
was greeted with derision when it was published in February
1977 to celebrate the twenty-fifth anniversary of Queen
Elizabeth II's accession to the throne. 'Worse than this we
cannot go,' complained *The Guardian* – never a fervently
royalist voice, of course. The normally loyalist (and wine-
loving) Conservative MP Sir Nicholas Fairbairn sniffed at
Betjeman's couplets as 'crude, *vin ordinaire* "plonk"', while
the Poetry Society dared to denounce their Laureate for
propagating 'nursery-rhyme gibberish'.[580]

Humbler critics, however, rather appreciated the sentiment.

'Days of disillusion? Right on, Sir John!' Most ordinary Britons had suffered more than a few 'days' of disillusion in their recent lives, and for all Elizabeth's caution and conservatism (with a small 'c'), their monarch had manifestly stood by her bench. 'It's only fallen apart,' comments Princess Margaret towards the end of this episode, 'if we say it has.' That summer of 1977 millions of loyal 'subjects' trooped out into the streets of London, and all over Britain, to acknowledge the Queen as someone who had both fired them and inspired them – a stubborn and defiant cry from the heart.

Peter Morgan's title for Episode 310, *Cri de Coeur*, has several connotations – starting with Harold Wilson's resumption of power and his two-year premiership from 1974 to 1976. It was quite a triumph for the Labour leader to step in and make a success of the minority government situation created by Edward Heath's 'Who Rules Britain?' campaign of 28 February 1974. Wilson himself had no majority, holding just 301 seats out of 635 – 17 votes shy of security, in the only stalemated House of Commons since 1929. That summer Simon Hoggart of *The Guardian* described the Westminster situation as a 'Hung Parliament' – coining the phrase for the first time on the basis of the American expression 'hung jury'.[581]

In these precarious circumstances the Labour leader relied on the fact that neither of the other main parties – Tory or Liberal – wished to fight another election, nor had the funds to do so. For the moment Wilson carefully postponed controversial issues and rolled out a succession of calming policies to undo the damage of Heath's 'Three-Day Week'. Then he called an election at a time of his choosing – on

10 October 1974 – and secured 319 seats, giving him a bare working majority of three.

In right-wing eyes, however, Labour's 'calming' policies were simply a surrender to the subversive left-wing forces that Edward Heath had vainly tried to combat. Wilson's remedy to end the power cuts of the Three-Day Week, for example, was essentially to pay the mineworkers whatever they would settle for. 'For some Establishment cold warriors,' wrote the Scottish anarchist Stuart Christie, 'Wilson back in Downing Street was like having Stalin back in the Kremlin.'[582]

Chapter Eleven, 'Olding', laid out many of the ambivalent Soviet suspicions that had hung around Harold Wilson since the 1950s. Across the Atlantic, the CIA's spy-hunting Director of Counterintelligence, James Jesus Angleton, had absolutely no doubt that Wilson took his orders from Moscow, and his suspicions were echoed in Britain by the equally obsessive Peter Wright, an assistant director of MI5. Wright ran his counter-espionage team on the assumption that his ultimate boss, Harold Wilson, was a Soviet spy – even believing that the KGB had contrived the death of Labour's previous leader Hugh Gaitskell to get their own man into power.

In the mid-1970s the journalist Chapman Pincher, whose expertise lay in espionage, was leaked a copy of an extraordinary MI5 surveillance report showing how Harold Wilson had been the object of 'active surveillance' by British intelligence while he was leader of the opposition early in 1974. 'Several pages long,' wrote Pincher, 'it listed details of how he had been watched and followed, with the times in and times out of places he had visited and names of people he had contacted.'[583]

Moving on to Downing Street, the report expressed concern

that Wilson's new socialist government 'might increase trade with Russia, leading to greater opportunities for KGB activity in Britain'. Evidence for this was that 'Wilson had previously refused to reduce the number of KGB agents posing as diplomats and had criticized the Heath government for expelling 105 of them'.[584] From Wright's perspective, Wilson could also be seen as pro-Soviet because he was planning reductions in the Secret Service as part of his government's programme of spending cuts.

It must be emphasised that the embittered and unstable Peter Wright, later the author of the bestselling *Spycatcher*, was very much a lone wolf. Anxious MI5 enquiries subsequently made clear that Wright's search-and-smear campaign, with which he hoped eventually to blackmail Wilson into resigning, was essentially a freelance operation. Once Wright's activities were discovered, they were shut down immediately.

But Wright – and Angleton in America, who was forced out of the CIA in 1975 when his own excesses came to light – were not the only enemies with motives for undermining the Labour Prime Minister. Wilson's steadfast opposition to apartheid and his support for sanctions against the white government of South Africa had aroused the animosity of BOSS, the South African Bureau for State Security. And then there was the suspicion that Wilson's sympathy for the Palestinian cause had earned him the enmity of Israel's counterintelligence service, Mossad.

Mossad? MI5? The CIA? BOSS? Take your pick to explain what happened next. Between the two elections of 1974, in February and October, a burglary at Wilson's home in Lord North Street saw the loss of his personal tax papers, copies of which later turned up in the hands of the satirical magazine *Private Eye* – who, to their credit, declined to publish them. Somehow other thieves (or the same thieves?) then discovered that the Prime Minister stored some of his personal papers in a room in Buckingham Palace Road and these were also burgled – specifically tax documents, personal letters, along with photographs and tape recordings of his dealings with President Nixon and the Rhodesian premier, Ian Smith. In that same year Bernard Donoughue, Wilson's chief policy adviser, was burgled three times, and there were two further break-ins at the offices of Wilson's friend, adviser and lawyer, Lord Goodman. Later, Goodman stated that the intruders had been searching particularly 'for documents that might in some way incriminate Harold Wilson'.[585]

The catalogue continues ... Early in 1974 there was a burglary at the home of Marcia Williams, the head of Wilson's political office, along with two break-ins at her country home at Great Missenden, Buckinghamshire. In the same period, there was a break-in at the offices of Joseph Kagan, Wilson's Lithuanian-born friend who manufactured the famous Gannex raincoats so favoured by the Prime Minister. Nothing was stolen, but documents relating to Wilson were photocopied – while there were also burglaries at the home of Labour Environment Secretary Tony Crosland, Wilson's late personal private secretary Michael Halls, Labour Deputy Leader Edward Short and Labour aide John Allen, who said that he experienced several break-ins.[586] As Geoffrey Goodman, head of Downing Street's Counter Inflation Unit, put it to Tony Benn after suffering three burglaries himself in 1976, 'Something strange is going on'.[587]

In the absence of definitively proved conclusions from the multitude of investigative articles and books inspired by this curious sequence of events, one can only explain the mystery in terms of Cold War fever. In the early seventies James Angleton was believed by many in the CIA when he maintained that Lester Pearson and Willy Brandt, respectively the democratically elected leaders of Canada and West Germany, were Soviet agents like Wilson.[588] Angleton was an extreme example of the paranoia that the Cold War produced at its height, so extreme that it would have been almost laughable – if in Britain, at least, its real-life consequence had not been to inspire disturbing paranoia in its victim ...

'Look! *That's* where they'll come,' a senior civil servant recalls Wilson suddenly exclaiming during a briefing in the Cabinet Room, pointing at the French doors leading to the garden of No. 10. '*They'll* come through *there*.'

'Who, Prime Minister?' asked the civil servant.

'*Them*,' replied Wilson. 'When they come to take over the government.'[589]

Talking to the thrice-burgled Bernard Donoughue, Joe Haines, Wilson's press secretary, recalled how one day he had been discussing strategy with the Prime Minister when Wilson silenced him with a finger to his lips. 'He walked over to the portrait of [William] Gladstone [Prime Minister for 12 years under Queen Victoria], raised it and pointed to the wall behind. He was clearly indicating that the room was bugged. He whispered ... "We will have to go for a walk in the open".'[590]

Wilson's suspicions of the Gladstone portrait in his Downing Street study became legendary. Not trusting MI5, he sent for outside engineers who confirmed that there was indeed a hole in the plaster behind the painting, but insisted it had accommodated nothing more sinister than a power point for an earlier picture light.[591] The Prime Minister was not convinced, however, about the portrait in his study – nor about anywhere else in the second grandest address in the land. 'During his last few months in office,' wrote Christopher Andrew, the official historian of MI5, 'Wilson appears rarely to have said anything in the lavatory without first turning on all the taps and gesturing at imaginary bugs in the ceiling.'[592]

To allay the British Prime Minister's suspicions about CIA involvement, US Vice-President Hubert Humphrey sent the CIA's reforming new director George H. W. Bush (the future President) to London to reassure Wilson in person – only for Bush to emerge from the meeting perplexed. 'Is that man mad?' he asked. 'He did nothing but complain about being spied on!'[593]

The medical and psychological factors underlying Harold Wilson's premature mental decline – he was 57 in February 1974 when he became Prime Minister for his second spell in office – were complex. Wilson himself would murmur poignantly to confidants, 'My mother died of premature senility, you know'.[594] When feeling less straightforward he would indulge in 'confabulation' – the making up of details to cover gaps in the memory, which doctors now recognise as an early symptom of Alzheimer's disease. In 2008 neurologist Dr Peter Garrard published an analysis of Wilson's speech patterns at the dispatch box from 1974 to 1976 showing how they deteriorated markedly during his second term of office. 'Language is known to be vulnerable to the earliest stages of Alzheimer's disease ...' explained Dr Garrard. 'Linguistic changes can appear even before the symptoms are recognized by either the patient or their closest associates.'[595]

As early as 1974 on his way to see French President Giscard d'Estaing, Wilson suffered 'heart racing' when his plane landed unevenly in Paris, and his doctor had to intervene.[596] Then a Northern Ireland Office official was amazed to be instructed by Wilson to 'ring the number of a callbox in the Mile End Road at a certain time when a certain person would be waiting to give him information he might need to hear'. The official made the call, and nothing transpired.[597] Another civil servant was asked by Wilson (always kindly and concerned in personnel matters) why he, the official, had not sought Wilson's help on a particular career issue.

'I didn't think it an appropriate thing to bother you with as Prime Minister,' the official replied.

'Not even a part-time Prime Minister like me?' asked Wilson, his eyes filling with tears.[598]

Medically speaking, the factors undermining Harold Wilson's wellbeing in the early to mid-1970s were insomnia, gastrointestinal problems, proneness to eye infections and decades of heavy drinking – as early as 1964, when he first became Prime Minister, Wilson was already notorious as a 'vigorous toper' who filled his glass with brandy 'and quaffed it as though it were ale'.[599] This had no apparent impact during his first term of office, but in 1974–6 his control of cabinet meetings became notably muddled, and he was also seen to develop high anxiety which he sought to allay by resorting to a glass or two of cognac before tackling Prime Minister's Questions in the House of Commons.[600]

This episode's scenes showing Wilson's incoherence and inability to memorise speeches have been enhanced in certain details – in fact, he always delivered his speeches from notes. But anticipatory worry was now preying on the Prime Minister as it had never done before, and the many political problems that once inspired him now filled him with embittered despair.[601]

There was no shortage of problems. In 1974 the British rate of inflation was moving towards its highest level in history – 26.5 per cent.[602] This reflected OPEC's ongoing oil embargo, together with the accompanying domestic strikes as workers desperately sought to keep their wages in line with the rising cost of living. One of Wilson's prized economic remedies, membership of the European Common Market, provoked additional conflict starting in his own cabinet. The year 1974 was also a tragic high point in the Irish 'Troubles', with the IRA bombings of pubs in Guildford, Woolwich and Birmingham killing 28 and injuring 266. The Houses of Parliament themselves were bombed that June – mercifully with no loss of life, but injuring 17 and leaving extensive damage. On the foreign scene, there were the ongoing problems with South Africa, and the enduring aftermath of Ian Smith's UDI (Unilateral Declaration of Independence) in Rhodesia.[603] It was hardly surprising that, in the eyes of many observers, Harold Wilson should have 'no sparkle left'.[604]

As early as 1972, two years before he returned to power, Wilson had confided to Denis Healey, one of his most trusted Labour allies, that if ever he got back into Downing Street he did not plan to serve for more than three years.[605] A few years later, he recounted to Barbara Castle, another favoured colleague, that when he went to the Palace to take up office in

March 1974, he had actually informed the Queen of the date when he would retire. 'She's got the record of it,' he said, 'so no one will be able to say afterwards that I was pushed out.'[606]

Then at the Labour Party annual conference in the autumn of 1975 he shared his plans – which were now imminent because he was hoping to leave before his sixtieth birthday the following spring – with his press secretary Joe Haines. 'Harold Wilson asked me to draw up the timetable for his resignation the following year,' recalled Haines, 'which was to be announced at the end of February, indeed, the afternoon of the last Wednesday in February.'[607]

Wilson's to-the-day precision was obviously an attempt to assert his control over a process that cruelly demonstrated his loss of control over so many other aspects of his life and faculties. His principal private secretary Robert Armstrong remembers how Wilson remained as sharp as ever with economic statistics – always the basis of his intellectual pre-eminence. Armstrong also recalls being asked by Wilson to accompany him on the Downing Street piano at what proved to be his last Christmas party, as the Prime Minister regaled the assembled staff and ministers with his robust rendition of the Yorkshire folk anthem 'On Ilkla Moor Baht 'At' (translating as 'On Ilkley Moor without a hat') – singing every one of the nine verses word for word by memory, without a mistake.[608]

Reflecting later on Wilson's surprise resignation announcement – which occurred finally on Friday 19 March 1976 – Armstrong always wondered why Wilson, the devoted royalist so proud of his closeness to the Queen, as we saw in Chapter Eleven, did not extend his premiership by just a year and a half so that he could enjoy the celebrations of the

1977 Jubilee, in whose planning he had played an active role. It was the measure of the honesty – and probably too of the fear – with which the Prime Minister confronted the reality of his mental frailties that he decided to step down when he did.

But there was a royal twist in the tale – which might have perplexed James Angleton and Peter Wright had they known about the true priorities of their perfidious Soviet agent in Downing Street. In March 1976 Buckingham Palace was confronted by the embarrassing necessity of announcing the breakdown of the marriage between Princess Margaret and Lord Snowdon – and Wilson thought he saw a way that his retirement could help.

The complexities of Princess Margaret's love life have been a running theme in *The Crown* from her romance with Peter Townsend (Episode 106, 'Gelignite'), to her meeting with Antony Armstrong-Jones (Episode 204, 'Beryl') and their marriage adventures in the early-to mid-1960s (Episode 302, 'Margaretology'). Now we confront their respective *cris de coeur* as their dreams turn sour. By 1973 Tony, aged 43, was deeply involved with Lucy Lindsay-Hogg, 32, the intelligent and attractive TV production assistant whom he would marry in 1978. In retaliation – yet with a deep affection that her friends say she had never quite achieved with anyone else – Princess Margaret, also 43, had turned to the shy and disarming young landscape gardener Roderic 'Roddy' Llewellyn, 17 years her junior at the age of 26, who bore an astonishing physical resemblance to her alienated husband, by whom she now had two children, Sarah and David.

This private mess became dramatically public in February

1976 when the *News of the World* published a shocking front-page photograph of Margaret and Roddy, semi-naked together in swimming costumes, on the Caribbean island of Mustique. The next day Margaret's private secretary, Lord Napier, called to tell her that her husband had announced his intention of moving out of their Kensington Palace apartment that very week. 'Thank you, Nigel,' replied the delighted Princess. 'I think that's the best news you've ever given me.'[609] But Tony Snowdon was also insisting that the news of the couple's legal separation should be made public – and quickly, too.

Enter the retiring Prime Minister, whose not-so-slow mind worked out and suggested to the Queen that the announcement of his own retirement could be timed to coincide with the Snowdons' bad news.

'He came back from the Palace with some glee,' recalled Joe Haines. 'He said he made this arrangement with the Queen to blank out the separation by announcing his resignation on the same day. Having worked on popular newspapers, I was doubtful.'[610]

Haines's doubts proved justified. Wilson's resignation was announced at 11.30 on the Friday morning, with the news of Princess Margaret's separation being disclosed at 5.00pm the same day. 'The papers went for the later, sexier story,' remembered Haines. The ever-troublesome Princess pushed the loyal Prime Minister right off the front page.

On Tuesday 7 June 1977 Prince Philip joined the Queen and sat beside her in the Golden State Coach for the Silver Jubilee procession to St Paul's Cathedral and the Guildhall, then back to Buckingham Palace. The event proved an immense success – with more than a million spectators cheering so loudly that the coachmen could not hear their horses' hooves hitting the pavement. Shops overflowed with Jubilee ashtrays, thermometers and egg timers, and a chain of hilltop beacons was lit across Britain. Locally organised street parties were tokens of the authentic grass-roots enthusiasm that the Jubilee inspired in communities around the country, with more than 4,000 held in London alone. In one sense, the most telling tributes were the rejoicings reported by the usually subversive *Private Eye* in Colonel 'Buffy' Cohen's Neasden launderette – an invented scenario, like so many in *The Crown*.

The full text of the Poet Laureate John Betjeman's Silver Jubilee Hymn heard over this episode's final processional sequence (and also starting this chapter) ran:

In days of disillusion,
However low we've been,
To fire us and inspire us,
God gave to us our Queen.

She acceded, young and dutiful,
To a much-loved father's throne:
Serene and kind and beautiful
She holds us as her own.

And twenty-five years later,
So sure her reign has been,
That our great events are greater
For the presence of our Queen.

Hers the grace the Church has prayed for,
Ours the Joy that she is here.
Let the bells do what they're made for,
Ring our thanks, both loud and clear.

From that look of dedication
In those eyes profoundly blue,
We know her coronation
As a sacrament and true.

Chorus: For our Monarch and her people,
United yet and free,
Let the bells ring from every steeple —
Ring out the Jubilee.

April 6, 1977 – *Punch*, Silver Jubilee cartoon by Trog

ENDNOTES

CHAPTER ONE

1   *The Crown* Broadcast Script, Episode 201 NETFLIX, 'Misadventure' by Peter Morgan, 00:00:50.

2   Ibid., 00:00:34.

3   Joan Graham, *The Baltimore Sun*, 8 February 1957.

4   *The Crown* Broadcast Script, Episode 201 NETFLIX, 'Misadventure' by Peter Morgan, 00:00:50.

5   Ibid.

6   Profile – Ulanova, *Observer*, 7 October 1956.

7   'Duke leaves to-day on world tour', *Manchester Guardian*, 15 October 1956.

8   Seward, *My Husband and I*, pp. 135–6.

9   Baron, *Baron*, pp. 129–31, 135.

10   Parker, *Step Aside for Royalty*, p. 179.

11   'Queen sees Ulanova "Giselle" ballet', *Manchester Guardian*, 26 October 1956.

12   Cited in *Detroit Free Press*, 27 November 1956.

13   Louis, *Ends of British Imperialism*, p. 635.

14   Colville, *The Churchillians*, p. 171.

15 Thorpe, *Eden*, p. 25.

16 Cosgrave, *R. A. Butler*, p. 12.

17 Vickers, *Loving Garbo*, p. 235.

18 Frankland, *Documents on International Affairs, 1956*, pp. 108–9.

19 'Middle East war threat eases', *Edmonton Journal*, 9 August 1956.

20 'U.K. ponders moves as Suez Canal seized', *Edmonton Journal*, 27 July 1956.

21 *The Crown* Broadcast Script, Episode 201 NETFLIX, 'Misadventure' by Peter Morgan, 00:27:40.

22 *The Crown* Broadcast Script, Episode 201 NETFLIX, 'Misadventure' by Peter Morgan, Ibid., 00:49:22.

23 Ibid., 00:27:40.

24 Ibid., 00:45:46.

25 Bernard Levin, 'Lord Mountbatten and the Suez fiasco: how the truth was nearly suppressed', *The Times*, London, 5 November 1980.

26 *The Crown* Broadcast Script, Episode 201 NETFLIX, 'Misadventure' by Peter Morgan, 00:45:46

27 Ibid., 00:47:52.

CHAPTER TWO

28 Robert Jobson, *Evening Standard*, London, 17 January 2019.

29 Jack Hardy, *The Daily Telegraph*, 19 January 2019.

30 Brandreth, *Philip and Elizabeth*, p. 251.

31 Stephanie Koscak, The 18th-Century Common, 10 January 2018.

32 *The Crown* Broadcast Script, Episode 202 NETFLIX, 'A Company of Men' by Peter Morgan, 00:01:32 – 00:02:44.

33 Miles Kington, *The Independent*, London, 16 January 1996.

34 Ibid.

35 Ibid.

36 Parker, *Step Aside for Royalty*, p. 178.

37 Ibid., p. 179.

38 Joan Graham, *The Baltimore Sun*, 8 February 1957.

39 'New King starts Empire wondering', *The Baltimore Sun*, 22 January 1936.

40 'Palace rumours "are untrue"', *Daily Herald*, 11 February 1957.

41 Seward, *My Husband and I*, p. 134.

42 Court Circular, *The Times*, 20 November 1947.

43 Whitehall, *London Gazette*, 22 February 1957.

44 Paul Taylor, *Manchester Evening News*, 6 April 2013.

45 'Wrath at the helm?' *The Times*, 26 May 1956.

46 'Duke enters battle over Teddy Boys', *Des Moines Tribune*, 16 June 1955.

47 'Ibid.

48 'Duke of Edinburgh Award Scheme', *The Times*, 27 June 1956.

49 Hannah Furness, *The Daily Telegraph*, 12 March 2019.

50 'Queen's Awards?', *Birmingham Daily Post*, 2 November 1957.

51 'Duke: "I know I couldn't win one"', *Birmingham Daily Post*, 4 November 1959.

52 Becker et al., *The Changing World of Outdoor Learning in Europe*, p. 190.

CHAPTER THREE

53 'Wrath at the helm?', *The Times*, 26 May 1956.

54 Heilpern, *John Osborne*, pp. 66–8.

55 Denison, *John Osborne*, p. xxvii.

56 Osborne, *Look Back in Anger*, pp. 10–11.

57 Michael Billington, *Guardian*, 30 March 2015.

58 Shellard, *Kenneth Tynan*, pp. 161–2.

59 Beckett, *Olivier*, pp. 95, 97.

60 Osborne, *Look Back in Anger*, p. 22.

61 Ibid., p. 75.

62 *The Crown* Broadcast Script, Episode 203 NETFLIX, 'Lisbon' by Peter Morgan, 00:14:46, 00:15:44.

63 Borhi, *Hungary in the Cold War, 1945–1956*, p. 301.

64 *The Crown* Broadcast Script, Episode 203 NETFLIX, 'Lisbon' by Peter Morgan, 00:09:47.

65 James Blitz, *Financial Times*, 24 May 2019.

66 Jago, *Rab Butler*, p. 380.

67 Beckett, *Macmillan*, p. 67.

68 Campbell, *Pistols at Dawn*, p. 270.

69 Peter Jenkins, *The New York Times*, 5 March 1989.

70 D. R. Thorpe, *Spectator*, 21 October 2013.

71 Ibid.

72 Ibid.

73 Thorpe, *Supermac*, p. xii.

74 'On this day', *BBC News*, 20 July 1957.

75 J. Y. Smith, *The Washington Post*, 30 December 1986.

76 D. R. Thorpe, *Spectator*, 21 October 2013.

77 D. R. Thorpe, 'Leadership and Change: Prime Ministers in the Post-War World – Macmillan.' Lecture at Gresham College, 30 November 2005.

78 Ibid.

79 Charles Moore, *The Daily Telegraph*, 8 May 2011.

80 D. R. Thorpe, Gresham College, 30 November 2005.

CHAPTER FOUR

81 Cathcart, *Princess Margaret*, p. 81.

82 Fraser, *Marie Antoinette*, p. 135.

83 Charles Nevin, *The Guardian*, 10 February 2002.

84 Payn and Morley, *The Noël Coward Diaries*, p. 289.

85 Payne, *My Life with Princess Margaret*, p. 90.

86 Brown, *Ma'am Darling*, p. 148.

87 'Socialite rolls himself "out"', *Palm Beach Post*, 25 September 1956.

88 'Film rocks, rolls today', *Los Angeles Times*, 19 December 1956.

89 Kynaston, *Modernity Britain*, p. 14.

90 Ibid.

91 Payne, *My Life with Princess Margaret*, p. 65.

92 Ibid., p. 66.

93 'Restraint order on ex-footman', *Manchester Guardian*, 11 November 1960.

94 Payne, *My Life with Princess Margaret*, p. 66.

95 Warwick, *Princess Margaret*, p. 80.

96 McIlvaine and Sherby, *P. G. Woodhouse*, p. xv.

97 Dempster, *Princess Margaret*, p. 43.

98 Ibid., pp. 32–3.

99   Aronson, *Princess Margaret*, p. 155.

100 Mark Olden, *The Independent*, 29 August 2008.

101 Alan Travis, *The Guardian*, 24 August 2002.

102 Linda Pressly, *BBC News*, 21 May 2007.

103 Alan Travis, *The Guardian*, 24 August 2002.

104 Newton, *Paving the Empire Road*, p. 87.

105 Mark Olden, *The Independent*, 29 August 2008.

106 'Why 492 West Indians came to Britain', *Manchester Guardian*, 23 June 1948.

107 Schofield, *Enoch Powell and the Making of Postcolonial Britain*, p. 235.

108 Christmas 1961 Broadcast Script by Queen Elizabeth II.

109 Anthony Bevins, *The Independent*, 7 July 1997.

110 Janice Williams, *Newsweek*, 20 April 2018.

111 Audrey Woods, *Everett Herald*, 9 February 2002.

112 'Leslie Arthur Julien "Hutch" Hutchinson', *Harlem World Magazine*, 28 September 2017.

113 Keith Dovkants, *Evening Standard*, 11 February 2002.

114 Michael Thornton, *Daily Mail*, 14 November 2008.

CHAPTER FIVE

115 Malcolm Muggeridge, 'Royal Soap Opera', *New Statesman*, 22 October 1955.

116 Ibid.

117 'Press criticizes royal house for silence over Margaret', *The San Francisco Examiner*, 21 October 1955.

118 Ward, *Britishness Since 1870*, p. 28.

119 Lord Altrincham, 'The Monarchy Today', *National and English Review*, August 1957.

120 Ward, *British Culture and the End of Empire*, p. 40.

121 Rafael Epstein, *The World Today*, 19 April 2006.

122 Humphry Berkeley, 'The Finances of the Monarchy', *National and English Review*, August 1957.

123 B. A. Young, 'Foundation-Stones and Things', *National and English Review*, August 1957.

124 Ibid.

125 Lord Altrincham, 'The Monarchy Today', *National and English Review*, August 1957.

126 Ibid.

127 Ibid.

128 Ibid.

129 Ibid.

130 'Lord Altrincham hits back', *Manchester Guardian*, 31 August 1957.

131 *The Crown* Broadcast Script, Episode 205 NETFLIX, 'Marionettes' by Peter Morgan, 00:01:33.

132 'Lord Altrincham's assailant fined', *The Times*, 8 August 1957.

133 Ziegler, *Crown and People*, p. 131.

134 John Grigg, 'Punched, Abused, Challenged', *Spectator*, 16 August 1997.

135 Altrincham et al., *Is the Monarchy Perfect?*, pp. 93–6.

136 Ibid., p. 57.

137 'The Last Debutantes', *Country Life*, 17 July 2008.

138 Pimlott, *The Queen*, p. 283.

139 'Peerage Act of 1963', UK Parliamentary Archives, 2019.

140 Pilkington, *The Politics Today Companion to the British Constitution*, p. 117.

141 Wrigley, *Winston Churchill*, p. 54.

142 Ibid.

143 Lord Altrincham, 'A Word in Edgeways: Goodbye to the gallows', *Manchester Guardian*, 25 January 1962.

144 Altrincham and Gilmour, *The Case of Timothy Evans*, p. 4.

145 Ibid., p. 3.

146 'United Kingdom marks 50th anniversary of death penalty abolition', Death Penalty Information Center, 2015.

147 Ibid.

148 Block and Hostettler, *Hanging in the Balance*, p. 196.

149 Ibid., p. 249.

150 John Grigg, 'A Second Opinion', *Manchester Guardian*, 13 October 1966.

151 John Grigg, '"Look" & the Kennedys', *Manchester Guardian*, 20 October 1966.

152 Ibid.

153 John Grigg, 'Punched, Abused, Challenged', *Spectator*, 16 August 1997.

CHAPTER SIX

154 Lambert, *Documents of German Foreign Policy*, Series D, Volume X, title page.

155 Ibid., p. 2.

156 Ibid., p. 187.

157 Robert Pear, 'U.S. Says 1939 German-Soviet Treaties Are Real', *The New York Times*, 5 June 1989.

158 'GFM 35: German War Documents Project', UK National Archives, 2019.

159 Windsor, *The Heart Has Its Reasons*, p. 332.

160 Sontag and Beddie, *Nazi-Soviet Relations, 1939–1941*, p. 157.

161 Donaldson, *Edward VIII*, p. 359.

162 King, *The Duchess of Windsor*, p. 330.

163 Frederick Birchall, 'Windsor Received Warmly by Nazis; Sees Model Plant', *The New York Times*, 12 October 1937.

164 Andrew Morton. *17 Carnations: The Windsors, the Nazis and the Cover-Up*, London, Michael O'Mara Books, 2015, p.55.

165 Rory Tingle, 'When Edward VIII went to see Hitler: Never-before-seen photos emerge for sale of Duke of Windsor's infamous trip to Nazi Germany in 1937', *Daily Mail*, 8 October 2018.

166 Lambert, *Documents of German Foreign Policy*, Series D, Volume X, p. 97.

167 Ibid., p. 187.

168 Ibid.

169 Ibid., p. 68.

170 Ibid., p. 290.

171 Ibid.

172 'Not the truth, says Duke', *Manchester Guardian*, 1 August 1957.

173 Ziegler, *King Edward VIII*, pp. 366–7.

174 Dahl, *Quisling*, p. 186.

175 'War Situation', House of Commons Debate, 4 June 1940.

176 Lambert, *Documents of German Foreign Policy, Series D*, Volume X, p. 377.

177 Ibid.

178 Ibid., p. 398.

179 Ibid.

180 St John, *William Heinemann*, p. 275.

181 Paul Sweet, 'The Windsor File', *The Historian*, Winter 1997.

182 Payn and Morley, *The Noël Coward Diaries*, p. 520.

183 Colville, *The Fringes of Power*, p. 197.

184 Gilbert, *Winston S. Churchill*, Volume 6, p. 703.

185 Bloch, *Operation Willi*, p. 122

186 December 11, 2017. *Just As I Am*, by Billy Graham quoted in 'Billy Graham Reflects on His Friendship with Queen Elizabeth II'. https://billygraham.org/story/billy-graham-and-the-queen/

187 Holy Bible, New Testament, Gospel of St. John, chapter 5, verse 8.

188 Graham, *Just As I Am*, p.698

CHAPTER SEVEN

189 de Lisle, *The Sisters Who Would Be Queen*, p. 4.

190 Warnicke, *The Marrying of Anne of Cleves*, p. 138.

191 'Statement by Princess', *The Times*, 1 November 1955.

192 Kynaston, *Modernity Britain*, p. 14.

193 de Courcy, *Snowdon*, p. 9.

194 de la Haye et al., *A Family of Fashion*, p. 95.

195 de Courcy, *Snowdon*, p. 10.

196 Author interview with Francis Wyndham, 1976.

197 de Courcy, *Snowdon*, pp. 9–10.

198 Smallman-Raynor and Cliff, *Poliomyelitis*, p. 318.

199 'The International Year of Disabled People', House of Lords Debate, 14 January 1981.

200 Tony Jones, *Independent*, 13 January 2017.

201 Simon Hattenstone, *The Guardian*, 30 May 2005.

202 Elizabeth Grice, *The Daily Telegraph*, 5 March 2010.

203 Ibid.

204 Nan Robertson, *The New York Times*, 10 November 1979.

205 de Courcy, *Snowdon*, p. 29.

206 Lord Snowdon interview, *British Journal of Photography*, January 14, 2017.

207 Ibid.

208 Ibid.

209 'Our London Correspondence', *The Guardian*, 26 June 1957.

210 de Courcy, *Snowdon*, p. 52.

211 Geoffrey Levy, *Daily Mail*, 20 September 2009.

212 de Courcy, *Snowdon*, p. 37.

213 Haslam, *Redeeming Features*, p. 103.

214 Warwick, *Princess Margaret*, p. 215.

215 'Why Margaret's smile is rare these days', *The Des Moines Register*, 24 April 1960.

216 *The Crown* Broadcast Script, Episode 207 NETFLIX, 'Matrimonium' by Peter Morgan, 00:13:26.

217 de Courcy, *Snowdon*, p. 37.

218 Tony Allen-Mills, *The Times*, 26 November 2017.

219 Off-the-record interview.

220 Ibid.

221 Tim Heald, *Evening Standard*, 3 July 2007.

222 de Courcy, *Snowdon*, pp. 80–81.

223 Tony Allen-Mills, *The Times*, 26 November 2017.

224 de Courcy, *Snowdon*, p. 81.

225 Tim Heald, *Evening Standard*, 3 July 2007.

226 Andrew Alderson, *The Daily Telegraph*, 31 May 2008.

CHAPTER EIGHT

227 Myers, 'Harold Macmillan's '"Winds of Change" Speech: A Case Study in the Rhetoric of Policy Change', *Rhetoric and Public Affairs*, 2000.

228 Butler and Stockwell, *The Wind of Change*, p. 31.

229 'Ghana's "National Welcome" to Duchess of Kent', *Manchester Guardian*, 5 March 1957.

230 Pimlott, *The Queen*, p. 305.

231 Ibid.

232 Beeston, *Looking for Trouble*, p. 74.

233 Longford, *Elizabeth R*, p. 255.

234 Murphy, *Monarchy & the End of Empire*, p. 77.

235 Catherine Armecin, '"Elizabeth: Our Queen": Queen Has "Heart And Stomach Of A Man"', *International Business Times*, 22 February 2018.

236 Cathcart, *The Queen Herself*, p. 178.

237 Marr, *The Diamond Queen*, p. 233.

238 'The Queen at Accra Ball', *The Times*, 20 November 1961.

239 'Queen mobbed by Ghanaians', *The Canberra Times*, 20 November 1961.

240 'African shuffle enjoyed by Queen', *Fort Myers News-Press*, 20 November 1961.

241 'Disgusted with Queen', *Lethbridge Herald*, Alberta, 25 November 1961.

242 'The Queen's dance with Dr. Nkrumah', *The Times*, 26 November 1961.

243 Caroline Howe, 'Sammy Davis Jr. endured being called 'boy, 'c**n' and the N-word', *Daily Mail*, 18 April 2014.

244 Lacey, *Monarch*, p. 260.

245 Lacey, *God Bless Her!*, p. 112.

246 Botwe-Asamoah, *Kwame Nkrumah's Politico-Cultural Thought and Politics*, p. 128.

247 Greene and Butcher, *The Servant Queen and the King She Serves*, p. 1.

248 Colquhoun, *Harringay Story*, p. vii.

249 Graham, *Just As I Am*, p. 426.

250 Gilbreath, 'Level Ground at the Cross', *Christianity Today* Billy Graham Commemorative Issue, pp. 80–81.

251 Christmas 2004 Broadcast Script by Queen Elizabeth II.

252 Ibid.

CHAPTER NINE

253 Fiammetta Rocco, 'A Strange Life: Profile of Prince Philip',
   The Independent, 13 December 1992.

254 Eilish O'Gara, 'Prince Philip: Married to the Monarchy', *Newsweek*,
   12 June 2015.

255 Ken Purdy, 'Prince Philip: England's Most Understood Man', *LOOK*,
   7 April 1964.

256 Vickers, *Alice*, p. 148.

257 'King Paul Gained Wide Popularity', *The New York Times*, 7 March
   1964.

258 Seward, *My Husband and I*, p. 34.

259 'How a Prince was saved', *Launceston Daily Telegraph*, 21 March 1923.

260 'The Greek War in Asia Minor: Prince Andrew's History', *The Times*,
   1 July 1930.

261 Alexandra, *Prince Philip*, p. 14.

262 Heald, *Philip*, p. 22.

263 Alexandra, *Prince Philip*, p. 41.

264 'About', Kurt Hahn, 2019.

265 Lacey, *Majesty*, p. 102.

266 *The Crown* Broadcast Script, Episode 209 NETFLIX, 'Paterfamilias'
   by Tom Edge and Peter Morgan, 00:19:14.

267 Bradford, *Queen Elizabeth II*, p. 54.

268 Marina Ewald cited in Veevers and Allison, *Kurt Hahn*, p. 11.

269 Chatfield and Glenn, *Leadership the Outward Bound Way*, pp. 30–31.

270 '"If" by Rudyard Kipling', Poetry Foundation, 2019.

271 Stewart and McCann, *The Educational Innovators*, p. 192.

272 Emily Hanford, 'Kurt Hahn and the roots of Expeditionary Learning',
   American RadioWorks, 10 September 2015.

273 Veevers and Allison, *Kurt Hahn*, p. 70.

274 Prince Charles's confidential letter of 8 February 1964, cited in
   Dimbleby, *The Prince of Wales*, p. 65.

275 Bedell Smith, *Prince Charles*, p. 296.

276 Wilson, *The Windsor Knot*, p. 48.

277 Emily Hanford, 'Kurt Hahn and the roots of Expeditionary Learning',
   American RadioWorks, 10 September 2015.

278 Ibid.

279 Ibid.

280 Patrick Jones, 'My Schooldays with Prince Charles', *The Sydney Morning Herald*, 30 June 1963.

281 Eade, *Young Prince Philip*, pp. 67–8.

282 Seidler, *Remembering Diana*, pp. 64–5.

283 Heald, Philip, p. 45.

284 Kurt Hahn, 'Prince Philip Was My Pupil', *Maclean's*, 15 August 1947.

285 Bedell Smith, *Elizabeth the Queen*, p. 27.

286 Alexandra, *Prince Philip*, p. 66.

287 Georgian, 'This is the Man', *Woman's Journal*, June 1953.

CHAPTER TEN

288 Riginos, *Platonica*, p. 177.

289 Eldridge, *The Oxford Handbook of Philosophy and Literature*, p. 144.

290 Programme for *Beyond the Fringe* by Bennett, Cook, Miller and Moore at the Fortune Theatre, London. Playbill, 1961.

291 *The Crown*, Episode 210, 'Mystery Man' by Peter Morgan, 00:21:53.

292 Turnock, *Television and Consumer Culture*, p. 72.

293 Levin, *The Pendulum Years*, pp. 49–50.

294 Davenport-Hines, *An English Affair*, pp. 290–91.

295 Pimlott, *The Queen*, p. 325.

296 Ibid., p. 344.

297 Ibid., pp. 263–4.

298 Ibid., p. 324.

299 'Prince Philip and the Profumo Scandal', *Daily Mirror*, 24 June 1963.

300 Eade, *Young Prince Philip*, p. 217.

301 Thompson, *Stephen Ward*, p. 131.

302 'His Royal Highness Prince Philip, Duke of Edinburgh: A Portrait from the Life', *Illustrated London News*, 24 June 1963.

303 Summers and Dorrill, *The Secret Worlds of Stephen Ward*, p. 292.

304 'Prince Philip and the Profumo Scandal', *Daily Mirror*, 24 June 1963.

305 Donald Macintyre, 'The 1963 Cabinet Papers / The Leadership Crisis: The Queen sent "reviver" to sick Macmillan', *The Independent*, 1 January 1994.

306 Thorpe, *Supermac*, p. xii.

307 Pimlott, *The Queen*, p. 324.

308 Horne, *Macmillan 1957–1986*, p. 533.

309 Beckett, *Macmillan*, p. 67.

310 Iain Macleod, 'Tory Leadership', *Spectator*, 17 January 1954.

311 Campbell, *Pistols at Dawn*, p. 259.

312 Horne, *Macmillan 1957–1986*, p. 540.

313 'Peerage Act of 1963', UK Parliamentary Archives, 2019.

314 Bedell Smith, *Elizabeth the Queen*, pp. 163–4.

315 Horne, *Macmillan 1957–1986*, p. 555.

316 Bedell Smith, *Elizabeth the Queen*, p. 165.

317 Pimlott, *The Queen*, p. 331.

318 Horne, *Macmillan 1957–1986*, p. 566.

319 Pimlott, *The Queen*, p. 329.

320 Ibid., p. 332.

321 Ibid., p. 335.

322 Butler and King, *The British General Election of 1964*, p. 294.

CHAPTER ELEVEN

323 *The Crown*, Episode 301, 'Olding' by Peter Morgan, Scene 19.

324 Pimlott, *Harold Wilson*, p. 3.

325 Butler and King, *The British General Election of 1964*, p. 294.

326 Cannadine and Quinault, *Winston Churchill in the Twenty-First Century*, p. 111.

327 Wilson, *The Labour Government 1964–70*, p. 22.

328 Crines and Hickson, *Harold Wilson*, p. 23.

329 Wilson, *The Labour Government 1964–70*, p. 22.

330 Roth, *Sir Harold Wilson*, p. 309.

331 Philip Ziegler, 'Prime Ministers in the Post-War World.' Lecture at Gresham College, 21 February 2006.

332 Morrison, *Essential Public Affairs for Journalists*, p. 20.

333 Jackson, *Women Leaders of Europe and the Western Hemisphere*, p. 82.

334 Bedell Smith, *Elizabeth the Queen*, p. 165.

335 Shawcross, *Queen and Country*, p. 99.

336 Vickers, *Elizabeth*, p. 409.

337 Ramsden, *Man of the Century*, p. 26.

338 Ibid.

339 Christopher Lehmann-Haupt, 'Michael Straight, Who Wrote of Connection to Spy Ring, Is Dead at 87', *The New York Times*, 5 January 2004.

340 Lucy Clarke-Billings, 'Top secret report on Cambridge spies Burgess and Maclean emerges from Foreign Office', *The Daily Telegraph*, 16 October 2015.

341 'Former Foreign Office Officials (Disappearance)', House of Commons Debate, 7 November 1955.

342 'Mr. Harold Philby', House of Commons Debate, 1 July 1963.

343 Riordan, *Comrade Jim*, p. 168.

344 'Renegade British Diplomats Deny Being Communist Agents', *Ottawa Journal*, 13 February 1956.

345 Lubenow, *The Cambridge Apostles*, p. xii.

346 Christopher Lehmann-Haupt, 'Michael Straight, Who Wrote of Connection to Spy Ring, Is Dead at 87', *The New York Times*, 5 January 2004.

347 Ibid.

348 Ibid.

349 'Obituary: Michael Straight', *The Daily Telegraph*, 17 January 2004.

350 Richard Norton-Taylor, 'Michael Straight', *The Guardian*, 8 January 2004.

351 Christopher Lehmann-Haupt, 'Michael Straight, Who Wrote of Connection to Spy Ring, Is Dead at 87', *The New York Times*, 5 January 2004.

352 'Mr. Anthony Blunt', House of Commons Debate, 21 November 1979.

353 Pimlott, *The Queen*, p. 337.

354 'Mr. Anthony Blunt', House of Commons Debate, 21 November 1979.

355 Andrew and Mitrokhin, *The Mitrokhin Archive*, p. 528.

356 Ellis, *Britain, America and the Vietnam War*, p. 40.

357 Ben Macintyre, 'Operation Labour: how Soviet spooks infiltrated the left', *The Times*, 24 February 2018.

358 Roy Jenkins, 'Wilson, (James) Harold', *Oxford Dictionary of National Biography*, 7 January 2016.

359 Bewes, *Swiss Watching*, p. 108.

360 Andrew and Mitrokhin, *The Mitrokhin Archive*, p. 528.

361 Malcolm Gladwell, 'Trust No One: Kim Philby and the hazards of mistrust,' *New Yorker*, 20 July 2014.

362 Ben Macintyre, 'Operation Labour: how Soviet spooks infiltrated the left', *The Times*, 24 February 2018.

363 'Lord George Brown is dead at 70', *The New York Times*, 4 June 1985.

364 John Kelly, 'The 10 most scandalous euphemisms', *BBC News Magazine*, 15 May 2013.

CHAPTER TWELVE

365 Adam Helliker and Jane Slade, *The Daily Telegraph*, 10 February 2002.

366 Milligan, *The Whistling Spy Enigma*, 28 September 1954.

367 'From a royal family album', *Detroit Free Press, 26 October 1965.*

368 Tim Heald, *Evening Standard*, 3 July 2007.

369 Elizabeth Grice, *The Daily Telegraph*, 5 May 2010.

370 de Courcy, *Snowdon*, pp. 102, 114–15.

371 Ibid., p. 131.

372 Ibid., p. 136.

373 Ibid., p. 139.

374 Hutchinson and Kahn, *A Family Affair*, p. 101.

375 'July 20, 1957,' *BBC: On This Day*, 2008.

376 *The Economist* cited in Dorey, *The Labour Governments 1964–70*, p. 67.

377 Dan Rather, The Dolph Briscoe Center for American History, 2019.

378 Beinart, *The Icarus Syndrome*, p. 161.

379 Dallek, *Flawed Giant*, p. 491.

380 Fredrik Logevall, *The New York Times*, 24 March 2018.

381 Smith, *The Wilson–Johnson Correspondence*, p. 5.

382 Paul Montgomery, *The New York Times*, 20 November 1965.

383 de Courcy, *Snowdon*, p. 104.

384 *The Crown*, Episode 302, 'Margaretology' by Peter Morgan, Scene 95.

385 Ibid.

386 Ibid., Scene 97.

387 Ibid., Scene 102.

388 Scott, *Royal Betrayal*, p. 11.

389 David Traynor, *Daily Star*, 26 February 2016.

390 Ziegler, *King Edward VIII*, p. 333.

391 Hart-Davis, *King's Counsellor: Abdication and War*, p. 417.

392 Mitchell, *Daily Life in Victorian England*, p. xiii.

393 Rose, *King George V*, p. 42.

394 Wheeler-Bennett, *King George VI*, p. 27.

395 *The Crown*, Episode 302, 'Margaretology' by Peter Morgan, Scene 103.

CHAPTER THIRTEEN

396 Richard Llewellyn's *How Green Was My Valley* was first published by Michael Joseph in 1939.

397 Ceri Jackson, 'The mistake that cost Aberfan its children', *BBC News*, 21 October, 2016.

398 Jenny Johnston, 'Mothers bound by grief', *Daily Mail*, 11 October 2016.

399 Ibid.

400 Ibid.

401 Ceri Jackson, 'The mistake that cost Aberfan its children', *BBC News*, 21 October 2016.

402 Ibid.

403 Roy Greenslade, 'Aberfan: a reporter's letter home reveals the true horror of the tragedy', *The Guardian*, 20 October 2016.

404 Ibid.

405 de Courcy, *Snowdon*, p. 149.

406 Bedell Smith, *Elizabeth the Queen*, pp. 198–9.

407 Lacey, *Monarch*, p. 223.

408 'The Queen at 90: Memories from people around Wales', *BBC News*, 21 April 2016.

409 Austin, *Aberfan*, p. 230.

410 Ibid., p. 9.

411 Miller, *Aberfan*, pp. 24–5.

412 'NC-bloody-B', National Museum Wales, 25 February 2008.

413 Ceri Jackson, 'The mistake that cost Aberfan its children', *BBC News*, 21 October 2016.

414 Dominic Midgely, 'EXPOSED: The full scale of the negligence that led to Aberfan disaster', *Daily Express*, 20 June 2016.

415 Gwilym, 'Today We Mourn As a Nation', *Ein Gwlad News*, 21 October 2018.

416 Dominic Midgely, 'EXPOSED: The full scale of the negligence that led to Aberfan disaster', *Daily Express*, 20 June 2016.

417 Ian McLean, 'Aberfan: no end of a lesson', *History & Policy*, 5 February 2007.

418 *Aberfan: The Untold Story* by Jonathan Jones, *BBC*, 2006, 00:43.

419 Ian McLean, 'Aberfan: no end of a lesson', *History & Policy*, 5 February 2007.

420 'The Coal Industry Act 1994', UK National Archives, 2019.

421 Thomas, *Coal in Our Veins*, pp. 15–16.

CHAPTER FOURTEEN
422 Paterson, *A Brief History of the Private Life of Elizabeth II*, p. 97.

423 Pimlott, *The Queen*, p. 377.

424 John Parker, 'Prince Harming', *Chicago Tribune*, 25 August 1991.

425 Pimlott, *The Queen*, p. 378.

426 Pimlott, *Harold Wilson*, p. 350.

427 Healey, *The Time of My Life*, p. 333.

428 Pimlott, *Harold Wilson*, pp. 483–4.

429 Ibid.

430 Lacey, *Monarch*, p. 239

431 'Civil List', House of Commons Debate, 14 December 1971.

432 Duncan, *The Queen's Year*, pp. 171–3.

433 Lacey, *Monarch*, p. 236.

434 Sandbrook, *Seasons in the Sun*, p. 625.

435 Lacey, *Monarch*, p. 236.

436 Pimlott, *The Queen*, p. 380.

437 BBC Television and Independent Television, *Royal Family*, p. ROYAL FAMILY.

438 Rosenthal, *The New Documentary in Action*, p. 208.

439 David Wilsworth, 'Behind the Pomp with the Royal Family', *The Times*, 20 June 1969.

440 Kelly, *The Royals*, p. 211.

441 BBC Television and Independent Television, *Royal Family*, p. SPRING.

442 'Royal Family: An intimate look at the monarchy', *Annapolis Capital*, 23 August 1969.

443 Marr, *Diamond Queen*, p. 198.

444 Ibid.

445 'Sir Antony Jay, co-author of *Yes Minister* – obituary', *The Daily Telegraph*, 23 August 2016.

446 Alexandra, *Prince Philip*, p. 16.

447 Vickers, *Alice*, p. 205.

448 Ibid., pp. 57–8.

449 Ibid., p. 205.

450 Commander Michael Parker CVO interview with author, Australia, 2000.

451 'Righteous Among the Nations', Yad Vashem, 2019.

452 'Britons Honoured for Holocaust Heroism', *The Daily Telegraph*, 9 March 2010.

453 Vickers, *Alice*, p. 360.

454 Cathcart, *Anne and the Princesses Royal*, p. 143.

CHAPTER FIFTEEN

455 Barratt and Ritchie, *With the Greatest Respect*, p. 146.

456 Zuckerman's diary cited in Ziegler, *Mountbatten*, p. 660.

457 Sandbrook, *White Heat*, p. 650.

458 Edwards, *Newspapermen*, p. 340.

459 John Beavan, 'Obituary: Lord Cudlipp', *The Independent*, 18 May 1998.

460 Bruce Lambert, 'Lord Zuckerman, 88, a Scientist of Scope Who Guided Churchill', *The New York Times*, 2 April 1993.

461 'Enough is Enough', *Daily Mirror*, 10 May 1968, p. 1.

462 Ziegler, *Mountbatten*, p. 659.

463 *The Crown*, Episode 305, 'Coup' by Peter Morgan, Scene 42.

464 Ibid.

465 Lownie, *The Mountbattens*, pp. 317–24.

466 *The Crown*, Episode 305, 'Coup' by Peter Morgan, Scene 75.

467 'Cecil King, 86, dies in Dublin', *The New York Times*, 19 April 1987.

468 Ziegler, *Mountbatten*, p. 659.

469 Ibid.

470 Ibid., p. 660.

471 Ziegler, author interview with Lord Cudlipp, *Mountbatten*, p. 660.

472 Ziegler, *Mountbatten*, p. 660.

473 Murray, *All the King's Horses*, p. 217.

474 Ibid.

475 André Laguerre, 'The Queen who loves the sport of kings', *Sports Illustrated*, 18 October 1954.

476 Lacey, *The Crown*, pp. 317.

477 Murray, *All the King's Horses*, p. 258.

478 Ibid., p. 166.

479 Lacey, *The Crown*, Volume 1, pp. 314, 315.

480 Muscat, *Her Majesty's Pleasure*, pp. 23–4.

481 Ibid., p. 74.

CHAPTER SIXTEEN

482 Dimbleby, *The Prince of Wales*, p. 118.

483 Fisher, *Princes of Wales*, p. vii.

484 Bedell Smith, *Elizabeth the* Queen, p. 222.

485 Menkes, *The Windsor Style*, p. 16.

486 Philip, *The Welsh Question*, p. 112.

487 Holden, *Charles, Prince of Wales*, p. 184.

488 Edward Millward, interviewed in *The Real Prince Charles* TV documentary (2001).

489 Ellis, *Investiture*, p. 197.

490 Hannah Booth, 'Dr Tedi Millward, at the first Welsh language protest, 2 Feb 1963', *The Guardian*, 30 October 2015.

491 *The Crown* research team interviews with Llio, Tedi Millward's daughter, 13 August and 28 September 2018.

492 Adam Aspinall, 'Time it takes to become fluent in another language revealed', *Daily Mirror*, 20 November 2016.

493 Millward, *Taith Rhyw Gymro*. From the chapter 'Royal Student'.

494 Heald and Mohs, *HRH: The Man Who Will Be King*, p. 91.

495 Ellis, *Investiture*, p. 269.

496 *The Crown* research team interviews with Llio, Tedi Millward's daughter, 13 August and 28 September 2018.

497 Ibid.

498 'Wales backs Charles for King', *BBC News*, 25 June 1999.

499 Zara Whelan, *North Wales Live*, 18 November 2018.

500 George Thomas to Harold Wilson, 22 July 1969, PREM 13/2907, cited in Ellis, *Investiture*, p. 269.

501 Ibid.

CHAPTER SEVENTEEN

502 Seward, *My Husband and I*, p. 50.

503 Vickers, *Alice*, pp. 207–8.

504 Interview, Dr John Stephens, August 2019.

505 Ibid., pp. 209–10.

506 Fiammetta Rocco , 'A Strange Life: Profile of Prince Philip', *The Independent*, 13 December 1992.

507 Alexandra, *Prince Philip*, p. 37.

508 Vickers, *Alice*, p. 210.

509 A History of Cheam School, Cheam School website, 2019.

510 Brandreth, *Philip and Elizabeth*, p. 72.

511 Eade, *Young Prince Philip*, p. 67.

512 Fiammetta Rocco , 'A Strange Life: Profile of Prince Philip', *Independent*, 13 December 1992.

513 Ibid.

514 'Kurt Hahn and the Pursuit of Genius'. Lecture by Jocelin Winthrop-Young, 28 September 2001, at the Round Square Conference at St Philip's College, Alice Springs, Australia. Quelle: *Outward Bound International*, Volume 10, Number 2, December 2003.

515 Ziegler, *Mountbatten*, p. 102.

516 Oliver James interview cited in Eade, *Young Prince Philip*, p. 68.

517 Stephen Bates, 'Prince Philip at 90: still sees no need to apologise, or explain, or emote', *The Guardian*, 9 June 2011.

518 Bradford, *Elizabeth*, p. 333.

519 Woods, *Robin Woods*, pp. 172–3.

520 Ibid., p. 168.

521 Ibid., pp. 167–8.

522 *A Question of Balance*, 1982, Royal Collection Trust, 2019.

523 Interview with Prince Philip, Alliance of Religions and Conservation, July 2003.

524 'Macmillan talk with Queen upset by Glenn flight', 23 February 1962, *St Louis Post Dispatch*.

525 The Spiritual Side of Apollo 11, St Peter's Episcopal Church, 2017.

526 Matthew Cresswell, 'How Buzz Aldrin's communion on the moon was hushed up', *The Guardian*, 13 September 2012.

527 The Spiritual Side of Apollo 11, St Peter's Episcopal Church, 2017.

528 Ibid.

529 Hansen, *First* Man, p. 33.

530 Holmes, *The Faiths of the Founding Fathers*, pp. 39–52.

531 Feldstein, Jonathan. www.townhall.com, 17 July 2018.

CHAPTER EIGHTEEN

532   *The Crown* Episode 308, Scene 40, 'Dangling Man' by David Hancock and Peter Morgan. Left Bank Pictures 2019.

533   Ibid.

534   Bedell Smith, *Prince Charles*, p. 68.

535   Graham, *Camilla and Charles*, p. 26.

536   Brandreth, *Charles & Camilla*, p. 178.

537   Graham, *Camilla and Charles*, p. 26.

538   Wilson, *A Greater Love*, p. 59.

539   Bedell Smith, *Prince Charles*, p. 67.

540   Ibid.

541   http://www.thegoonshow.net/tributes/terry_gilliam.asp.

542   Bradford, *Elizabeth*, p. 425.

543   Wilson, *A Greater Love*, p. 59.

544   Ibid., p.62.

545   Bedell Smith, *Prince Charles*, p. 74.

546   Graham, *Camilla and Charles*, p. 31.

547   Ibid., p. 33.

548   Brandreth, *Charles & Camilla*, p. 184.

549   Ibid.

CHAPTER NINETEEN

550   Dimbleby, , *The Prince of Wales*, p. 184.

551   Bedell Smith, *Prince Charles*, p. 78.

552   Dimbleby, *The Prince of Wales*, p. 230.

553   Brandreth, *Charles & Camilla*, p. 200.

554   Dimbleby, *The Prince of Wales*, p. 231.

555   Ibid., p. 232.

556   Confidential letter quoted in ibid., p. 232.

557   Dimbleby, *The Prince of Wales*, p. 232.

558   Ibid.

559   Ibid., p. 235.

560   Bedell Smith, *Prince Charles*, p. 147.

561 Pimlott, *The Queen*, pp. 398–9.

562 Ziegler, *Edward Heath*, p. 319.

563 Lloyd, *Diplomacy with a Difference*, p. 231.

564 Lacey, *Monarch*, p. 260.

565 Shawcross, *Queen and Country*, p. 107.

566 *The Guardian*, 4 January 1973, quoted in Beckett, *When the Lights Went Out*, p. 9.

567 'Watch for bombers at Tubes, Yard says', *The Times*, 28 December 1973.

568 Shawcross, *Queen and Country*, p. 108.

569 Turner, *Crisis, What Crisis?*, p. 18.

570 Beckett, *When the Lights Went Out*, p. 54.

571 Sandbrook, *State of Emergency*, p. 126.

572 Ibid., p. 115.

573 UK inflation rate in 1973: 9.10 per cent, Official Data Foundation, 2019.

574 Turner, *Crisis, What Crisis?*, p. 23.

575 Ziegler, *Edward Heath*, p. 319.

576 Bradford, *Queen Elizabeth II*, p. 175.

577 Pimlott, *The Queen*, p. 406.

578 Paterson, *A Brief History of the Private Life of Elizabeth II*, p. 131.

579 Follain, *Jackal: The Complete Story of the Legendary Terrorist*, p. xvii.

CHAPTER TWENTY

580 Fred Hauptfuhrer, 'Much of Britain is NOT Amused by Poet John Betjeman's Tribute to the Queen', *PEOPLE*, 21 February 1977.

581 Simon Hoggart, 'Tories set sail for early poll', *Guardian*, 22 June 1974 .

582 Christie, *Granny Made Me an Anarchist*, p. 404.

583 Pincher, *Inside Story*, p. 30.

584 Ibid., p. 30.

585 Dorril and Ramsay, *Smear!*, p. 292.

586 Ibid.

587 Ibid., p. 293.

588 Harold Jackson, 'David Blee: CIA chief who rescued the agency from paranoia', *The Guardian*, 21 August 2000.

589 Hennessy, *The Prime* Minister, pp. 372, 373.

590 Donoughue, *Downing Street Diary*, p. 656.

591 Andrew, *The Defence of the Realm*, p. 637.

592 Ibid.

593 Ibid., p. 639.

594 Off-the-record interview.

595 'Wilson "had Alzheimer's when PM"', BBC News Channel, 10 November 2008.

596 Donoughue, *Downing Street Diary*, p. 260.

597 Hennessy, *The Prime* Minister, p. 372.

598 Pimlott, *Harold Wilson*, p. 341.

599 Davidson, *Downing Street Blues*, p. 157.

600 Off-the-record interview.

601 Ziegler, *Wilson*, pp. 467, 468.

602 Hennessy, *The Prime Minister*, p. 360.

603 Smith, *Bitter Harvest*, p. 146.

604 Pimlott, *Harold Wilson*, pp. 674–5.

605 Hennessy, *Cabinet*, p. 149.

606 Castle, *The Castle Diaries, 1964–76*, pp. 671–2.

607 Peter Hennessy, *Muddling Through*, p. 265.

608 Author interview with Robert Armstrong, July 2019.

609 Heald, *Princess Margaret*, p. 197.

610 Author interview with Joe Haines, January 2001.

BIBLIOGRAPHY

BOOKS

Alexandra, Queen of Yugoslavia. *Prince Philip: A Family Portrait*. Indianapolis: The Bobbs-Merrill Company, Inc., 1959.

Altrincham, Lord and Ian Gilmour. *The Case of Timothy Evans: An Appeal to Reason*. London: Spectator Limited, 1956.

Altrincham, Lord et al. *Is the Monarchy Perfect?* London: John Calder Publishers, 1958.

Andrew, Christopher. *The Defence of the Realm: The Authorized History of MI5*. London: Penguin Books, 2009.

— and Vasili Mitrokhin. *The Mitrokhin Archive: The KGB in Europe and the West*. London: Allen Lane, 1999.

Aronson, Theo. *Princess Margaret: A Biography*. Washington, DC: Regnery Publishing, Inc., 1997.

Austin, Tony. *Aberfan: The Story of a Disaster*. London: Hutchinson & Co., 1967.

Baron, Henry Nahum. *Baron*. London: Frederick Muller Ltd, 1957.

Barratt, John and Jean Ritchie. *With the Greatest Respect: The Private Lives of Earl Mountbatten and Prince and Princess Michael of Kent*. London: Sidgwick & Jackson, 1991.

BBC Television and Independent Television. *Royal Family: A Filmed Portrait of Queen Elizabeth II and Her Family – On and Off Duty*. Feltham: The Hamlyn Group, 1969.

Becker, Peter, et al., eds. *The Changing World of Outdoor Learning in Europe*. Abingdon: Routledge, 2018.

Beckett, Andy. *When the Lights Went Out: Britain in the Seventies*. London: Faber and Faber, 2009.

Beckett, Francis. *Olivier*. London: Haus Publishing, 2005.

—. *Macmillan*. London: Haus Publishing, 2006.

Bedell Smith, Sally. *Elizabeth the Queen: The Life of a Modern Monarch*. New York: Random House Trade Paperbacks, 2012.

—. *Prince Charles: The Passions and Paradoxes of an Improbable Life*. New York: Random House, 2017.

Beeston, Richard. *Looking for Trouble: The Life and Times of a Foreign Correspondent*. London: Brassey's, 1997.

Beinart, Peter. *The Icarus Syndrome: A History of American Hubris*. New York: HarperCollins, 2010.

Bewes, Diccon. *Swiss Watching: Inside the Land of Milk and Money*. London: Nicholas Brealey Publishing, 2012.

Bloch, Michael. *Operation Willi: The Nazi Plot to Kidnap the Duke of Windsor, July 1940*. London: Weidenfeld & Nicolson, 1984.

Block, Brian and John Hostettler. *Hanging in the Balance: A History of the Abolition of Capital Punishment in Britain*. Sherfield-on-Loddon: Waterside Press, 1997.

Borhi, László. *Hungary in the Cold War, 1945–1956: Between the United States and the Soviet Union*. Budapest: Central European University Press, 2004.

Botwe-Asamoah, Kwame. *Kwame Nkrumah's Politico-Cultural Thought and Politics: An African-Centered Paradigm for the Second Phase of the African Revolution*. Abingdon: Routledge, 2005.

Bradford, Sarah. *Elizabeth: A Biography of Her Majesty the Queen*. London: Mandarin, 1997.

—. *Queen Elizabeth II: Her Life in Our Times*. London: Viking, 2012.

Brandreth, Gyles. *Philip and Elizabeth: Portrait of a Royal Marriage*. New York: W. W. Norton & Company, 2004.

—. *Charles & Camilla: Portrait of a Love Affair*. London: Century, 2005.

Brown, Craig. *Ma'am Darling: 99 Glimpses of Princess Margaret*. London: 4th Estate, 2017.

Buckle, Richard, ed., *Self-Portrait with Friends: The Selected Diaries of Cecil Beaton 1922–1974*. New York: Times Books, 1979.

Butler, David and Anthony King. *The British General Election of 1964*. London: Macmillan, 1965.

Butler, L. J. and Sarah Stockwell, eds. *The Wind of Change: Harold Macmillan and British Decolonization*. Basingstoke: Palgrave Macmillan, 2013.

Campbell, John. *Pistols at Dawn: Two Hundred Years of Political Rivalry from Pitt and Fox to Blair and Brown*. London: Jonathan Cape, 2009.

Cannadine, David and Roland Quinault. *Winston Churchill in the Twenty-First Century*. Cambridge: Cambridge University Press, 2005.

Castle, Barbara. *The Castle Diaries, 1964–76*. London: Weidenfeld & Nicolson, 1984.

Cathcart, Helen. *Anne and the Princesses Royal*. London: W. H. Allen, 1973.

—. *Princess Margaret*, London: W. H. Allen, 1974.

—. *The Queen Herself: In Celebration of the First Thirty Years of Her Majesty's Reign*. London: W. H. Allen, 1982.

Chatfield, Rob and Lewis Glenn, eds. *Leadership the Outward Bound Way: Becoming a Better Leader in the Workplace, in the Wilderness, and in Your Community*. Seattle: Mountaineers Books, 2007.

Christie, Stuart. *Granny Made Me an Anarchist: General Franco, The Angry Brigade and Me*. Edinburgh: AK Press, 2007.

Colquhoun, Frank. *Harringay Story: The Official Record of the Billy Graham Greater London Crusade 1954*. London: Hodder & Stoughton, 1955.

Colville, John. *The Churchillians*. London: Weidenfeld & Nicholson, 1981.

BIBLIOGRAPHY

—. *The Fringes of Power: Downing Street Diaries, 1939–55*, London: Hodder & Stoughton, 1985.

Cosgrave, Patrick. *R. A. Butler: An English Life*. London: Quartet Books, 1981.

Crines, Andrew and Kevin Hickson, eds. *Harold Wilson: The Unprincipled Prime Minister?* London: Biteback Publishing, 2016.

Dahl, Hans Fredrik. *Quisling: A Study in Treachery*. Cambridge: Cambridge University Press, 1999.

Dallek, Robert. *Flawed Giant: Lyndon Johnson and His Times, 1961–1973*. Oxford: Oxford University Press, 1998.

Davenport-Hines, Richard. *An English Affair: Sex, Class and Power in the Age of Profumo*. London: HarperPress, 2013.

Davidson, Jonathan. *Downing Street Blues: A History of Depression and Other Mental Afflictions in British Prime Ministers*. Jefferson, North Carolina: McFarland & Company, 2010.

Davies, Nicholas. *Elizabeth: Behind Palace Doors*. Edinburgh: Mainstream Publishing Projects, 2000.

de Courcy, Anne. *Snowdon: The Biography*. London: Weidenfeld & Nicolson, 2008.

de la Haye, Amy et al. *A Family of Fashion: The Messel Dress Collection, 1865–2005*. London: Philip Wilson Publishers, 2006.

de Lisle, Leanda. *The Sisters Who Would Be Queen: Mary, Katherine, and Lady Jane Grey: A Tudor Tragedy*. New York: Ballantine Books, 2009.

Dempster, Nigel. *Princess Margaret: A Life Unfulfilled*. London: Macmillan, 1982.

Denison, Patricia, ed. *John Osborne: A Casebook*. New York: Garland Publishing, 1977.

Dimbleby, Jonathan. *The Prince of Wales: A Biography*. London: Little, Brown, 1994.

Donaldson, Frances. *Edward VIII*. London: Weidenfeld & Nicolson, 1974.

Donoughue, Bernard. *Downing Street Diary: With Harold Wilson in No. 10*. London: Random House, 2005.

Dorey, Peter, ed. *The Labour Governments 1964–70*. Abingdon: Routledge, 2006.

Dorril, Stephen and Robin Ramsay. *Smear! Wilson and the Secret State*. London: Grafton, 1992.

Duncan, Andrew. *The Queen's Year: The Reality of Monarchy*. London: Doubleday, 1970.

Eade, Philip. *Young Prince Philip: His Turbulent Early Life*. London: HarperPress, 2011.

Edwards, Ruth Dudley. *Newspapermen: Hugh Cudlipp, Cecil Harmsworth King and the Glory Days of Fleet Street*. London: Secker & Warburg, 2003.

Eldridge, Richard, ed. *The Oxford Handbook of Philosophy and Literature*, New York: Oxford University Press Inc., 2009.

Ellis, John. *Investiture: Royal Ceremony and National Identity in Wales, 1911–1969*. Cardiff: University of Wales Press, 2008.

Ellis, Sylvia. *Britain, America, and the Vietnam War*. Westport, California: Praeger Publishers, 2004.

Fisher, Deborah. *Princes of Wales*. Cardiff: University of Wales Press, 2006.

Follain, John. *Jackal: The Complete Story of the Legendary Terrorist, Carlos The Jackal*. New York: Arcade Publishing, 1998.

Frankland, Noble, ed. *Documents on International Affairs, 1956*. London: Oxford University Press, 1959.

Fraser, Antonia. *Marie Antoinette: The Journey*. London: Weidenfeld & Nicolson, 2001.

Gilbert, Martin. *Winston S. Churchill*, Vol. 6: *Finest Hour, 1939–1941*. London: William Heinemann, 1983.

Graham, Billy. *Just As I Am: The Autobiography of Billy Graham*, rev. edn. New York: HarperCollins, 2007.

Graham, Caroline. *Camilla and Charles: The Love Story*. London: John Blake Publishing, 2005.

Greene, Mark and Catherine Butcher. *The Servant Queen and the King She Serves*. UK: Bible Society, HOPE & LICC, 2016.

Hansen, James. *First Man: The Life of Neil A. Armstrong*. New York: Simon & Schuster, 2005.

Hardman, Robert. *Queen of the World*. London: Century, 2018.

Hart-Davis, Duff, ed. *King's Counsellor: Abdication and War – The Diaries of Sir Alan Lascelles*. London: Weidenfeld & Nicolson, 2006.

Haslam, Nicholas. *Redeeming Features: A Memoir*. New York: Alfred A. Knopf, 2009.

Heald, Tim. *Philip: A Portrait of the Duke of Edinburgh*. New York: William Morrow & Co., 1991.

—. *Princess Margaret: A Life Unravelled*. London: Orion, 2007.

— and Mayo Mohs. *HRH: The Man Who Will Be King*. New York: Arbor House Publishing Company, 1979.

Healey, Denis, *The Time of My Life*. London: Penguin Books, 1990.

Heilpern, John. *John Osborne: The Many Lives of the Angry Young Man*. London: Chatto & Windus, 2006.

Hennessy, Peter. *Cabinet*. Oxford: Blackwell, 1986.

—. *Muddling Through: Power, Politics and the Quality of Government in Post-War Britain*. London: Weidenfeld & Nicolson, 1996.

—. *The Prime Minister: The Office and Its Holders Since 1945*. London: The Penguin Press, 2000.

Holden, Anthony. *Charles: Prince of Wales*. London: Weidenfeld & Nicolson, 1979.

Holmes, David. *The Faiths of the Founding Fathers*. New York: Oxford University Press, Inc., 2006.

Horne, Alistair. *Macmillan 1957–1986*, Vol. II: *1957–86*. Cheltenham: Membury Press, 1989.

Hutchinson, Roger and Gary Kahn. *A Family Affair: The Margaret and Tony Story*. New York: Two Continents Publishing Group, 1977.

Jackson, Guida. *Women Leaders of Europe and the Western Hemisphere: A Biographical Reference*. Bloomington: Xlibris, 2009.

Jago, Michael. *Rab Butler: The Best Prime Minister We Never Had?* London: Biteback Publishing, 2015.

Kelly, Kitty. *The Royals*. New York: Warner Books, 1997.

King, Greg. *The Duchess of Windsor: The Uncommon Life of Wallis Simpson*. New York: Citadel Press, 2000.

Kynaston, David. *Modernity Britain: Opening the Box, 1957–1959*. London: Bloomsbury Publishing, 2013.

Lacey, Robert. *Majesty: Elizabeth II and the House of Windsor*. New York: Harcourt Brace Jovanovich, 1977.

—. *God Bless Her! Queen Elizabeth the Queen Mother*. London: Century, 1987.

Bibliography

—. *Monarch: The Life and Reign of Elizabeth II*. New York: Free Press, 2003.

Lambert, The Honourable Margaret, et al. *Documents of German Foreign Policy: 1918–1945, Series D (1937–1945)*, Vol. X: *The War Years, June 23–August 11, 1940*. London: Her Majesty's Stationery Office, 1957.

Levin, Bernard. *The Pendulum Years: Britain in the Sixties*. London: Jonathan Cape, 1970.

Lloyd, Lorna. *Diplomacy with a Difference: The Commonwealth Office of High Commissioner, 1880–2006*. Leiden: Brill, 2007.

Longford, Elizabeth. *Elizabeth R: A Biography*. London: Weidenfeld & Nicolson, 1983.

Louis, Wm. Roger. *Ends of British Imperialism: The Scramble for Empire, Suez, and Decolonization*. London: I. B. Tauris, 2006.

Lownie, Andrew. *The Mountbattens: Their Lives and Loves*. London: Blink Publishing, 2019.

Lubenow. W. C. *The Cambridge Apostles, 1820–1914: Liberalism, Imagination, and Friendship in British Intellectual and Professional Life*. Cambridge: Cambridge University Press, 1998.

Marr, Andrew. *The Diamond Queen: Elizabeth II and Her People*. London: Macmillan, 2012.

McIlvaine, Eileen and Louise Sherby. *P. G. Wodehouse: A Comprehensive Bibliography and Checklist*. New York: James H. Heineman, 1990.

Menkes, Suzy, *The Windsor Style*. London: Grafton Books, 1987.

Miller, Joan. *Aberfan: A Disaster and Its Aftermath*. Edinburgh: Constable, 1974.

Millward, Edward. *Taith Rhyw Gymro*. Llandysul: Gwasg Gomer, 2015.

Mitchell, Sally. *Daily Life in Victorian England*. Westport: Greenwood Press, 1996.

Morrison, James. *Essential Public Affairs for Journalists*. Oxford: Oxford University Press, 2009.

Morton, Andrew. *17 Carnations: The Windsors, the Nazis and the Cover-Up*. London: Michael O'Mara Books, 2015.

Murphy, Philip. *Monarchy & the End of Empire: The House of Windsor, The British Government and the Postwar Commonwealth*. Oxford: Oxford University Press, 2013.

Murray, Amanda. *All the Kings' Horses: Royalty and their Equestrian Passions from 1066 to the Present Day*. London: Robson Books, 2006.

Muscat, Julian. *Her Majesty's Pleasure: How Horseracing Enthrals the Queen*. Newbury: Racing Post, 2012.

Newton, Darrell. *Paving the Empire Road: BBC Television and Black Britons*. Manchester: Manchester University Press, 2011.

Parker, Eileen. *Step Aside for Royalty: A Personal Experience*. Maidstone: Bachman & Turner, 1982.

Paterson, Michael. *A Brief History of the Private Life of Elizabeth II*. London: Constable & Robinson, 2019.

Payn, Graham and Sheridan Morley, eds. *The Noël Coward Diaries*. London: Little, Brown, 1982.

Payne, David John. *My Life with Princess Margaret*. Greenwich, Minnesota: Fawcett Publications, Inc., 1961.

Philip, Alan Butt. *The Welsh Question: Nationalism in Welsh Politics 1945–1970*. Cardiff: University of Wales Press, 1975.

Pilkington, Colin. *The Politics Today Companion to the British Constitution*. Manchester: Manchester University Press, 1999.

Pimlott, Ben. *Harold Wilson*. London: HarperCollins, 1992.

—. *The Queen: Elizabeth II and the Monarchy*. London: HarperPress, 2012.

Pincher, Chapman. *Inside Story: A Documentary on the Pursuit of Power*. New York: Stein & Day Inc., 1979.

Programme for *Beyond the Fringe* by Bennett, Cook, Miller and Moore at the Fortune Theatre, London. Playbill, 1961.

Ramsden, John. *Man of the Century: Winston Churchill and His Legend Since 1945*. New York: Columbia University Press, 2002.

Riginos, A. S. *Platonica: The Anecdotes Concerning the Life and Writings of Plato*, Leiden: Brill, 1976.

Riordan, Jim. *Comrade Jim: The Spy Who Played for Spartak*. New York: Harper Perennial, 2009.

Rose, Kenneth. *King George V*. New York: Alfred A. Knopf, 1983.

Rosen, Andrew. *The Transformation of British Life, 1950–2000: A Social History*. Manchester: Manchester University Press, 2003.

Rosenthal, Alan. *The New Documentary in Action: A Casebook in Film Making*. Berkeley: University of California Press, 1971.

Roth, Andrew. *Sir Harold Wilson: Yorkshire Walter Mitty*. London: Macdonald and Jane's, 1977.

Sandbrook, Dominic. *White Heat: A History of Britain in the Swinging Sixties*. London: Little, Brown, 2006.

—. *State of Emergency: The Way We Were: Britain, 1970–1974*. London: Allen Lane, 2010.

—. *Seasons in the Sun: The Battle for Britain, 1974–1979*. London: Allen Lane, 2012.

Schofield, Camilla. *Enoch Powell and the Making of Postcolonial Britain*. Cambridge: Cambridge University Press, 2013.

Scott, Michael. *Royal Betrayal: The Great Baccarat Scandal of 1890*. London: Endeavour Press, 2017.

Seidler, Victor. *Remembering Diana: Cultural Memory and the Reinvention of Authority*. Basingstoke: Palgrave Macmillan, 2013.

Seward, Ingrid. *My Husband and I: The Inside Story of 70 Years of the Royal Marriage*. London: Simon & Schuster, 2017.

Shawcross, William. *Queen and Country: The Fifty-Year Reign of Elizabeth II*. New York: Simon & Schuster, 2002.

Shellard, Dominic. *Kenneth Tynan: A Life*. New Haven, Connecticut: Yale University Press, 2003.

Smallman-Raynor, Matthew and Andrew Cliff. *Poliomyelitis: A World Geography: Emergence to Eradication*. Oxford: Oxford University Press, 2006.

Smith, Anthony. *Sex, Genes and All That: The New Facts of Life*. London: Macmillan, 1997.

Smith, Ian. *Bitter Harvest: The Great Betrayal and the Dreadful Aftermath*. London: Blake Publishing, 2001.

Smith, Simon, ed. *The Wilson–Johnson Correspondence, 1964–69*. Abingdon: Routledge, 2016.

Sontag, Raymond and James Beddie, eds. *Nazi-Soviet Relations, 1939–1941: Documents from the Archives of the German Foreign Office*. Washington, DC: United States Department of State, 1948.

St John, John. *William Heinemann: A Century of Publishing 1890–1990*. London: Arrow Books, 1990.

Stewart, W. C. and W. P. McCann. *The Educational Innovators*, Vol. II: *Progressive Schools 1881–1967*. London: Macmillan, 1968.

Summers, Anthony and Stephen Dorrill. *The Secret Worlds of Stephen Ward: Sex, Scandal, and Deadly Secrets in the Profumo Affair*. London: Weidenfeld & Nicolson, 1987.

Taraborrelli, J. Randy. *Jackie, Janet & Lee: The Secret Lives of Janet Auchincloss and Her Daughters Jacqueline Kennedy Onassis and Lee Radziwill*. New York: St Martin's Press, 2018.

Thomas, Erin Ann. *Coal in Our Veins: A Personal Journey*. Logan: Utah State University Press, 2012.

Thompson, Douglas. *Stephen Ward: Scapegoat*. London: John Blake Publishing, 2014.

Thorpe, D. R. *Eden: The Life and Times of Anthony Eden First Earl of Avon, 1897–1977*. London: Chatto & Windus, 2003.

—. *Supermac: The Life of Harold Macmillan*. London: Random House, 2010.

Turner, Alwyn. *Crisis? What Crisis?: Britain in the 1970s*. London: Aurum Press, 2007.

Turnock, Rob. *Television and Consumer Culture: Britain and the Transformation of Modernity*. London: I. B. Tauris, 2007.

Veevers, Nick and Pete Alllson. *Kurt Hahn. Inspirational, Visionary, Outdoor and Experiential Educator*. Rotterdam: Sense Publishers, 2011.

Vickers, Hugo. *Loving Garbo: The Story of Greta Garbo, Cecil Beaton, and Mercedes de Acosta*. New York: Random House, 1994.

—. *Alice: Princess Andrew of Greece*. New York: St Martin's Press, 2000.

—. *Elizabeth: The Queen Mother*. London: Hutchinson, 2005.

Vidal, Gore, *Palimpsest: A Memoir*. New York: Random House, 1995.

Ward, Paul. *Britishness Since 1870*. London: Routledge, 2004.

Ward, Stuart. *British Culture and the End of Empire*. Manchester: Manchester University Press, 2002.

Warnicke, Retha. *The Marrying of Anne of Cleves: Royal Protocol in Early Modern England*. Cambridge: Cambridge University Press, 2000.

Warwick, Christopher. *Princess Margaret: A Life in Contrasts*. London: André Deutsch, 2000.

Wheeler-Bennett, John. *King George VI: His Life and Reign*. New York: St Martin's Press, 1958.

Wilson, Christopher. *A Greater Love: Prince Charles's Twenty-Year Affair with Camilla Parker Bowles*. New York: William Morrow and Company, 1994.

—. *The Windsor Knot: Charles, Camilla and the Legacy of Diana*. New York: Citadel Press Books, 2002.

Wilson, Harold. *The Labour Government 1964–70: A Personal Record by Sir Harold Wilson*. London: Weidenfeld & Nicolson, 1971.

Windsor, Wallis, Duchess of. *The Heart Has Its Reasons: The Memoirs of the Duchess of Windsor*. London: Michael Joseph, 1956.

Woods, Robin. *Robin Woods: An Autobiography*. London: SCM Press, 1986.

Wrigley, Chris. *Winston Churchill: A Biographical Companion*. Santa Barbara California: ABC-CLIO, 2002.

Ziegler, Philip. *Crown and People*. New York: Alfred A. Knopf, 1978.

—. *King Edward VIII: The Definitive Portrait of the Duke of Windsor*. London: William Collins, 1990.

—. *Wilson: The Authorised Life*. London: Weidenfeld & Nicolson, 1993.

—. *Mountbatten: The Official Biography.* London: Phoenix Press, 2001.

—. *Edward Heath: The Authorised Biography.* London: HarperPress, 2010.

ARTICLES AND PROCEEDINGS

A History of Cheam School. Cheam School, 2019. Retrieved from https://www.cheamschool.com/528/about-cheam/history

A Political Yardstick: How the British Measure America (27 November 1956). *Detroit Free Press*, p. 8.

A Question of Balance 1982. Royal Collection Trust, 2019. Retrieved from https://www.rct.uk/collection/1006555/a-question-of-balance

About. Kurt Hahn, 2019. Retrieved from http://www.kurthahn.org/about/

African shuffle enjoyed by Queen (20 November 1961). *Fort Myers News-Press*, p. 10.

Alderson, Andrew. 'Lord Snowdon, his women, and his love child.' *The Daily Telegraph*, 31 May 2008. Retrieved from http://www.telegraph.co.uk/news/uknews/theroyalfamily/2059552/Lord-Snowdon-his-women-and-his-love-child.html

Allen-Mills, Tony. 'Margaret and Snowdon — the princess and the playboy.' *The Times*, 26 November 2017. Retrieved from https://www.thetimes.co.uk/article/margaret-and-snowdon-the-princess-and-the-playboy-7gh3xhnnr

Altrincham, Lord. 'The Monarchy Today.' *The National and English Review*, Vol. 149, No. 894, August 1957, p. 60.

—. 'A Word in Edgeways: Goodbye to the gallows.' *The Manchester Guardian*, 25 January 1962, p. 22.

An interview with Lord Snowdon from the BJP archives (14 January 2017). *British Journal of Photography*. Retrieved from https://www.bjp-online.com/2017/01/lord-snowdon-bjp-archives/

Armecin, Catherine. '"Elizabeth: Our Queen": Queen Has "Heart And Stomach Of A Man"' *International Business Times*, 22 February 2018. Retrieved from https://www.ibtimes.com/elizabeth-our-queen-queen-has-heart-stomach-man-2656201

Bates, Stephen. 'Prince Philip at 90: still sees no need to apologise, or explain, or emote.' *The Guardian*, 9 June 2011. Retrieved from https://www.theguardian.com/uk/2011/jun/09/prince-philip-at-90

Beavan, John. 'Obituary: Lord Cudlipp.' *The Independent*, 18 May 1998. Retrieved from https://www.independent.co.uk/news/obituaries/obituary-lord-cudlipp-1158344.html

Berkeley, Humphry. 'The Finances of the Monarchy.' *The National and English Review*, Vol. 149, No. 894, August 1957, pp. 73–6.

Bevins, Anthony. 'The Queen fails in duty to minorities.' *Independent*, 7 July 1997. Retrieved from https://www.independent.co.uk/news/the-queen-fails-in-duty-to-minorities-1249486.html

Billington, Michael. 'Look Back in Anger: how John Osborne liberated theatrical language.' *The Guardian*, 30 March 2015. Retrieved from https://www.theguardian.com/stage/2015/mar/30/how-look-back-in-anger-john-osborne

Birchall, Frederick. 'Windsor Received Warmly by Nazis; Sees Model Plant.' *The New York Times*, 12 October 1937. Retrieved from https://timesmachine.nytimes.com timesmachine/1937/10/12/94437502.html?action=click&contentCollection=Archives&module=LedeAsset&region=ArchiveBody&pgtype=article&pageNumber=1

Bibliography

Blitz, James. 'Theresa May in numbers: defeats, resignations and Brexit.' *Financial Times*, 24 May 2019. Retrieved from https://www.ft.com/content/617f3318-7e24-11e9-81d2-f785092ab560

Booth, Hannah. 'Dr. Tedi Millward, at the first Welsh language protest, 2 Feb 1963.' *Guardian*, 30 October 2015. Retrieved from https://www.theguardian.com/artanddesign/2015/oct/30/dr-tedi-millward-welsh-language-protest-aberystwyth

Cecil King, 86, Dies in Dublin; A British Newspaper Leader (19 April 1987). *New York Times*. Retrieved from https://www.nytimes.com/1987/04/19/obituaries/cecil-king-86-dies-in-dublin-a-british-newspaper-leader.html

Civil List (14 December 1971). House of Commons Debate, Vol. 828, Columns 278–400.

Clarke-Billings, Lucy. 'Top secret report on Cambridge spies Burgess and Maclean emerges from Foreign Office.' *The Daily Telegraph*, 16 October 2015. Retrieved from https://www.telegraph.co.uk/news/uknews/11937454/Top-secret-report-on-Cambridge-spies-Burgess-and-Maclean-emerges-from-Foreign-Office.html

Court Circular: Buckingham Palace, Nov. 19 (20 November 1947). *The Times*, p. 7.

Cresswell, Matthew. 'How Buzz Aldrin's communion on the moon was hushed up.' *The Guardian*, 13 September 2012. Retrieved from https://www.theguardian.com/commentisfree/belief/2012/sep/13/buzz-aldrin-communion-moon

Disgusted with Queen: Newspaper raps black dancing partners (25 November 1961). *Lethbridge Herald*, p. 1.

Dovkants, Keith. 'Marriage and Indiscretion.' *London Evening Standard*, 11 February 2002. Retrieved from https://www.standard.co.uk/news/marriage-and-indiscretion-6308276.html

Duke enters battle over Teddy Boys (16 June 1955). *Des Moines Tribune*, p. 21.

Duke: 'I know I couldn't win one' (4 November 1959). *Birmingham Daily Post*, p. 25.

Duke Leaves To-Day On World Tour (15 October 1956). *The Manchester Guardian*, p. 1.

Duke of Edinburgh Award scheme (27 June 1956). *The Times*, p. 6.

Enough is Enough (10 May 1968). *London Daily Mirror*, p. 1.

Feldstein, Jonathan. 'Walking in Jesus's Footsteps More Meaningful Than Walking on the Moon.' Townhall.com, 17 July 2018. Retrieved from https://townhall.com/columnists/jonathanfeldstein/2018/07/17/walking-in-jesuss-footsteps-more-meaningful-than-walking-on-the-moon-n2501123

Film Rocks, Rolls Today (19 December 1956). *Los Angeles Times*, p. 47.

From a royal family album (26 October 1965). *Detroit Free Press*, p. 40.

Former Foreign Office Officials (Disappearance). (7 November 1955). House of Commons Debate, Vol. 545, Columns 1496–1497.

Furness, Hannah. 'Prince Philip passes Outward Bound Trust patronage to Prince Andrew after interviewing him for the job.' *The Daily Telegraph*, 12 March 2019. Retrieved from https://www.telegraph.co.uk/royal-family/2019/03/12/prince-philip-passes-outward-bound-trust-patronage-prince-andrew/

Georgian. 'This is the Man.' *Woman's Journal*, June 1953, p. 34.

GFM 35: German War Documents Project: German Foreign Ministry and other related Archives: Selection of Documents made by the German War Documents Project: Microfilms and files. The UK National Archives, 2019. Retrieved from https://discovery.nationalarchives.gov.uk/details/r/C8595

Ghana's 'National Welcome' to Duchess of Kent (5 March 1957). *The Guardian*, p. 1.

Gilbreath, Edward. 'Level Ground at the Cross.' *Christianity Today* Billy Graham Commemorative Issue, April 2018, pp. 80–81.

Gilliam, Terry. 'Tributes to The Goon Show & Spike Milligan.' The Goon Show Site, 2019. Retrieved from http://www.thegoonshow.net/tributes/terry_gilliam.asp

Gladwell, Malcolm. 'Trust No One: Kim Philby and the hazards of mistrust.' *The New Yorker*, 20 July 2014. Retrieved from https://www.newyorker.com/magazine/2014/07/28/philby

Graham, Joan. 'London rumors of rift in Royal Family growing.' *The Baltimore Sun*, 8 February 1957, p. 1.

Greenslade, Roy. 'Aberfan: a reporter's letter home reveals the true horror of the tragedy.' *The Guardian*, 20 October 2016. Retrieved from https://www.theguardian.com/media/greenslade/2016/oct/20/aberfan-a-reporters-letter-home-reveals-the-true-horror-of-the-tragedy

Grice, Elizabeth. 'Lord Snowdon: "Taking photographs is a very nasty thing to do".' *The Daily Telegraph*, 5 May 2010. Retrieved from https://www.telegraph.co.uk/culture/photography/7368664/Lord-Snowdon-Taking-photographs-is-a-very-nasty-thing-to-do.html

Grigg, John. 'A Second Opinion.' *The Manchester Guardian*, 13 October 1966, p. 18.

—. '"Look" & the Kennedys.' *The Manchester Guardian*, 20 October 1966, p. 16.

—. 'Punched, Abused, Challenged.' *The Spectator*, 16 August 1997, p. 13. Retrieved from http://archive.spectator.co.uk/article/16th-august-1997/13/punched-abused-challenged

Gwilym. 'Today We Mourn As a Nation. The victims of the Aberfan disaster will NEVER be forgotten in our country.' *Ein Gwlad News*, 21 October 2018. Retrieved from https://eingwlad.wales/NewsPortal/index.php/2018/10/21/today-we-mourn-as-a-nation-the-victims-of-the-aberfan-disaster-will-never-be-forgotten-in-our-country/

Hahn, Kurt. 'Prince Philip Was My Pupil.' *Maclean's*, 15 August 1947. Retrieved from https://archive.macleans.ca/article/1947/8/15/prince-philip-was-my-pupil

Hanford, Emily. 'Kurt Hahn and the roots of Expeditionary Learning.' American RadioWorks, 10 September 2015. Retrieved from http://www.americanradioworks.org/segments/kurt-hahn-expeditionary-learning/

Hardy, John. 'Prince Philip spotted driving without a seatbelt just days after crash – prompting police warning on road safety.' *The Daily Telegraph*, 19 January 2019. Retrieved from https://www.telegraph.co.uk/news/2019/01/19/prince-philip-spotted-behind-wheel-just-two-days-crash-apparently/

Hattenstone, Simon. '"Try working for Vogue. Yah ... no money at all" – Lord Snowdon on life as a "snapper".' *Guardian*, 30 May 2005. Retrieved from https://www.theguardian.com/artanddesign/2005/may/30/photography

Hauptfuhrer, Fred. 'Much of Britain Is Not Amused by Poet John Betjeman's Tribute to the Queen.' *PEOPLE*, 21 February 1977. Retrieved from https://people.com/archive/much-of-britain-is-not-amused-by-poet-john-betjemans-tribute-to-the-queen-vol-7-no-7/

Heald, Tim. 'Blue movies and casual flings – the amazing truth about Princess Margaret's marriage.' *London Evening Standard*, 3 July 2007. Retrieved from https://www.dailymail.co.uk/femail/article-465725/Blue-movies-casual-flings--amazing-truth-Princess-Margarets-marriage.html

Helliker, Adam and Jane Slade. 'Friends recall happy times with their Princess of laughter.' *The Daily Telegraph*, 10 February 2002. Retrieved from https://www.telegraph.co.uk/news/uknews/1384378/Friends-recall-happy-times-with-their-Princess-of-laughter.html

His Royal Highness Prince Philip, Duke of Edinburgh: A Portrait from the Life by Stephen Ward (24 June 1963). *Illustrated London News*, p. 1.

BIBLIOGRAPHY

Hoggart, Simon. 'Tories set sail for early poll.' *The Guardian*, 22 June 1974, p.1.

How a Prince was saved (21 March 1923). *Launceston Daily Telegraph*, p. 8. Retrieved from https://trove.nla.gov.au/newspaper/article/153394827

Howe, Caroline. 'Sammy Davis Jr. endured being called "boy", "c**n" and the N-word. But his greatest humiliation came when JFK refused to let star perform at the inauguration after he married a white woman, says his daughter.' *Daily Mail*, 18 April 2014. Retrieved from https://www.dailymail.co.uk/news/article-2607068/He-endured-called-boy-c-n-N-word-Sammy-Davis-Jr-s-greatest-humiliation-came-JFK-refused-let-perform-inauguration-married-white-woman.html

'If' by Rudyard Kipling. Poetry Foundation, 2019. Retrieved from https://www.poetryfoundation.org/poems/46473/if---

Interview with Prince Philip (July 2003). Alliance of Religions and Conservation (ARC). Retrieved from http://www.arcworld.org/news.asp?pageID=1

Jackson, Ceri. 'The mistake that cost Aberfan its children.' BBC, 21 October 2016. Retrieved from https://www.bbc.co.uk/news/resources/idt-150d11df-c541-44a9-9332-560a19828c47 http://www.minesandcommunities.org/article.php?a=13542

Jackson, Harold. 'David Blee: CIA chief who rescued the agency from paranoia.' *The Guardian*, 21 August 2000. Retrieved from https://www.theguardian.com/news/2000/aug/22/guardianobituaries.haroldjackson

Jenkins, Peter. 'The Unflappable Old Magician.' *The New York Times*, 5 March 1989. Retrieved from https://www.nytimes.com/1989/03/05/books/the-unflappable-old-magician.html

Jobson, Robert. 'Duke of Edinburgh car crash: Prince Philip, 97, involved in serious accident at Sandringham Estate.' *London Evening Standard*, 17 January 2019. Retrieved from https://www.standard.co.uk/news/uk/duke-of-edinburgh-in-car-crash-near-sandringham-estate-a4042131.html

Johnston, Jenny. 'Mothers bound by grief: 50 years on from Aberfan, the haunting stories of survivors and how parents of the 116 schoolchildren crushed by a coal tip found solace by meeting every week since.' *Daily Mail*, 11 October 2016. Retrieved from https://www.dailymail.co.uk/news/article-3833303/The-mothers-bound-grief-50-years-Aberfan-haunting-stories-survivors-mothers-116-children-engulfed-coal-tip-solace-meeting-week-half-century.html

Jones, Patrick. 'My Schooldays with Prince Charles.' *Sydney Morning Herald*, 30 June 1963, p. 35.

Jones, Tony. 'Lord Snowdon dead: Princess Margaret's husband and royal photographer dies aged 86.' *Independent*, 13 January 2017. Retrieved from https://www.independent.co.uk/news/uk/home-news/lord-snowdon-dead-dies-died-princess-margaret-husband-celebrity-photographer-antony-armstrong-jones-a7526156.html

Kelly, John. 'The 10 most scandalous euphemisms.' *BBC News Magazine*, 15 May 2013. Retrieved from https://www.bbc.com/news/magazine-22470691

King Paul Gained Wide Popularity (7 March 1964). *The New York Times*, p. 2. Retrieved from https://www.nytimes.com/1964/03/07/archives/king-paul-gained-wide-popularity-monarchy-was-in-disfavor-when-he.html

Kington, Miles. 'Innocent days at the Thursday Club.' *The Independent*, 16 January 1996. Retrieved from https://www.independent.co.uk/voices/innocent-days-at-the-thursday-club-1324245.html

Kocsak, Stephanie. 'The Secret History of *The Crown*.' The 18th-Century Common, 10 January 2018. Retrieved from https://www.18thcenturycommon.org/the-secret-history-of-the-crown/

Laguerre, Andre. 'The Queen who loves the sport of kings.' *Sports Illustrated*, 18 October 1954. Retrieved from https://www.si.com/vault/1954/10/18/546755/the-queen-who-loves-the-sport-of-kings#

Lambert, Bruce. 'Lord Zuckerman, 88, a Scientist of Scope Who Guided Churchill.' *The New York Times*, 2 April 1993. Retrieved from https://www.nytimes.com/1993/04/02/obituaries/lord-zuckerman-88-a-scientist-of-scope-who-guided-churchill.html

Lehmann-Haupt, Christopher. 'Michael Straight, Who Wrote of Connection to Spy Ring, Is Dead at 87.' *The New York Times*, 5 January 2004. Retrieved from https://www.nytimes.com/2004/01/05/nyregion/michael-straight-who-wrote-of-connection-to-spy-ring-is-dead-at-87.html

Leslie Arthur Julien 'Hutch' Hutchinson: From Harlem to Hampstead, 1900–1969. (28 September 2017). *Harlem World Magazine*. Retrieved from https://www.harlemworldmagazine.com/leslie-arthur-julien-hutch-hutchinson-harlem-hampstead-1900-1969/

Levin, Bernard. 'Lord Mountbatten and the Suez Fiasco: how the truth was nearly suppressed.' *The Times*, 5 November 1980.

Levy, Geoffrey. 'Did Lord Snowdon have a fling with the Queen Mother's page Backstairs Billy?' *London Daily Mail*, 20 September 2009. Retrieved from https://www.dailymail.co.uk/femail/article-1214901/Did-Lord-Snowdon-fling-Backstairs-Billy.html

Logevall, Fredrik. 'Vietnam '67: Why Lyndon Johnson Dropped Out.' *The New York Times*, 24 March 2018. Retrieved from https://www.nytimes.com/2018/03/24/opinion/lyndon-johnson-vietnam.html

Lord Altrincham Hits Back: Stands by his views on Monarchy. (1957, August 31). *The Manchester Guardian*, p. 1.

Lord Altrincham's Assailant Fined. (1957, August 8). *London Times*, p. 3.

Lord George Brown is dead at 70; Candid British Foreign Secretary (4 June 1985). *The New York Times*, p. 5.

Macintyre, Ben. 'Operation Labour: how Soviet spooks infiltrated the left.' *The Times*, 24 February 2018. Retrieved from https://www.thetimes.co.uk/article/operation-labour-how-soviets-plotted-to-infiltrate-the-left-harold-wilson-jeremy-corbyn-3rkblqr97

Macintyre, Donald. 'The 1963 Cabinet Papers / The Leadership Crisis: The Queen sent 'reviver' to sick Macmillan.' *The Independent*, 1 January 1994. Retrieved from https://www.independent.co.uk/news/uk/the-1963-cabinet-papers-the-leadership-crisis-the-queen-sent-reviver-to-sick-macmillan-1404060.html

Macleod, Iain. 'Tory Leadership.' *The Spectator*, 17 January 1954, p. 5.

McLean, Ian. 'Aberfan: no end of a lesson.' *History & Policy*, 5 February 2007. Retrieved from http://www.historyandpolicy.org/policy-papers/papers/aberfan-no-end-of-a-lesson

Middle East War Threat Eases (9 August 1956). *Edmonton Journal*, p. 4.

Midgely, Dominic. 'EXPOSED: The full scale of the negligence that led to Aberfan disaster.' *Daily Express*, 20 June 2016. Retrieved from https://www.express.co.uk/life-style/life/723226/Aberfan-mining-disaster-south-wales-exposed-full-scale-negligence-50th-anniversary

Montgomery, Paul. 'Margaret Unperturbed by Boycott at U.N.' *The New York Times*, 20 November 1965, p. 29.

Moore, Charles. 'How Harold Macmillan supervised our decline: A review of The Macmillan Diaries Volume II (Macmillan).' *The Daily Telegraph*, 8 May 2011. Retrieved from https://www.telegraph.co.uk/comment/columnists/charlesmoore/8501657/How-Harold-Macmillan-supervised-our-decline.html

Mr Anthony Blunt (21 November 1979). House of Commons Debate, Vol. 974, Columns 405–407.

Mr Harold Philby (1 July 1963). House of Commons Debate, Vol. 680, Column 35.

Muggeridge, Malcolm. 'The Royal Soap Opera.' *New Statesman*, 22 October 1955. Retrieved from https://www.newstatesman.com/lifestyle/lifestyle/2012/05/royal-soap-opera

Myers, Frank. 'Harold Macmillan's "Winds of Change" Speech: A Case Study in the Rhetoric of Policy Change.' *Rhetoric and Public Affairs*, Vol. 3, Number. 4, 2000, pp. 555–75. *JSTOR*. Retrieved from www.jstor.org/stable/41939631

'NC-bloody-B': The National Coal Board in South Wales. National Museum Wales, 25 February 2008. Retrieved from https://museum.wales/articles/2008-02-25/NC-bloody-B-The-National-Coal-Board-in-south-Wales/

Nevin, Charles. 'Obituary: Princess Margaret.' *The Guardian*, 10 February 2002. Retrieved from https://www.theguardian.com/news/2002/feb/11/guardianobituaries.princessmargaret

New king starts empire wondering (22 January 1936). *The Baltimore Sun*, p. 6.

New World Encyclopedia contributors, 'Bill Haley,' *New World Encyclopedia*, //www.newworldencyclopedia.org/p/index.php?title=Bill_Haley&oldid=1001990 (accessed 27 January 2019).

Norton-Taylor, Richard. 'Michael Straight.' *The Guardian*, 8 January 2004. Retrieved from https://www.theguardian.com/news/2004/jan/09/guardianobituaries.usa

Not the Truth, Says Duke (1 August 1957). *Manchester Guardian*, p. 1.

Obituary: Michael Straight (17 January 2004). *Daily Telegraph*. Retrieved from https://www.telegraph.co.uk/news/obituaries/1451875/Michael-Straight.html

O'Gara, Eilish. 'Prince Philip: Married to the Monarchy.' *Newsweek*, 12 June 2015. Retrieved from https://www.newsweek.com/prince-philip-married-monarchy-328397

Olden, Mark. 'White riot: The week Notting Hill exploded.' *The Independent*, 29 August 2008. Retrieved from https://www.independent.co.uk/news/uk/home-news/white-riot-the-week-notting-hill-exploded-912105.html

On this day (20 July 1957). *BBC News*, 2008. Retrieved from http://news.bbc.co.uk/onthisday/hi/dates/stories/july/20/newsid_3728000/3728225.stm

Our London Correspondence: Fleet Street, Tuesday Night, Photographer (26 June 1957). *The Guardian*, p. 6.

Palace rumours 'are untrue' (11 February 1957). *Daily Herald*, p. 1.

Parker, John. 'Prince Harming.' *Chicago Tribune*, 25 August 1991. Retrieved from https://www.chicagotribune.com/news/ct-xpm-1991-08-25-9103030536-story.html

Pear, Robert. 'U.S. Says 1939 German-Soviet Treaties Are Real.' *The New York Times*, 5 June 1989. Retrieved from https://www.nytimes.com/1989/06/05/world/us-says-1939-german-soviet-treaties-are-real.html

Peerage Act of 1963. UK Parliament, Parliamentary Archives, Catalogue Number HL/PO/PU/1/1963/c48, 2019. Retrieved from https://www.parliament.uk/about/living-heritage/evolutionofparliament/houseoflords/house-of-lords-reform/from-the-collections/from-the-parliamentary-collections-lords-reform/lords-reform-1963-1999/peerage-act-1963/

Press Criticizes Royal House for Silence over Margaret (21 October 1955). *San Francisco Examiner*, p. 4.

Pressly, Linda. 'The 'Forgotten' Race Riot.' *BBC News*, 21 May 2007. Retrieved from http://news.bbc.co.uk/2/hi/uk_news/6675793.stm

Profile – Ulanova (7 October 1956). *The Observer*, p. 3.

Prince Philip and the Profumo Scandal (24 June 1963). *Daily Mirror*, p. 1.

Purdy, Ken. 'Prince Philip: England's Most Misunderstood Man.' *LOOK*, 7 April 1964, p. 35.

Queen mobbed by Ghanaians (20 November 1961). *Canberra Times*, 1961. Retrieved from https://trove.nla.gov.au/newspaper/article/105852759?searchTerm=Nkrumah%2C%20queen%2C%20dance&searchLimits=l-format=Article|||l-category=Article

Queen Sees Ulanova 'Giselle' Ballet (26 October 1956). *Manchester Guardian*, p. 20.

Queen's awards? (2 November 1957). *Birmingham Daily Post*, p. 18.

Rather, Dan. '1964 Election.' The Dolph Briscoe Center for American History at the University of Texas at Austin, 2019. Retrieved from https://www.danratherjournalist.org/political-analyst/election-coverage/1964-election

Renegade British Diplomats Deny Being Communist Agents (13 February 1956). *Ottawa Journal*, p. 17.

Restraint Order On Ex-Footman (11 November 1960). *The Manchester Guardian*, p. 5.

Robertson, Nan. 'A Life in Pictures: Lord Snowdon's 30 Years as a Photojournalist.' *The New York Times*, 10 November 1979. Retrieved from https://www.nytimes.com/1979/11/10/archives/a-life-in-pictures-lord-snowdons-30-years-as-a-photojournalist-not.html

Rocco, Fiammetta. 'A Strange Life: Profile of Prince Philip.' *The Independent*, 13 December 1992. Retrieved from https://www.independent.co.uk/arts-entertainment/a-strange-life-profile-of-prince-philip-1563268.html

Royal Family: An intimate look at the monarchy (23 August 1969). Annapolis Maryland: *The Capital* newspaper, p. 20.

Sir Antony Jay, co-author of Yes Minister – Obituary (23 August 2016). *The Daily Telegraph*. Retrieved from https://www.telegraph.co.uk/obituaries/2016/08/23/sir-antony-jay-co-author-of-yes-minister--obituary/

Smith, J. Y. 'Harold Macmillan, 92, Former British Prime Minister, Dies.' *The Washington Post*, 30 December 1986. Retrieved from https://www.washingtonpost.com/archive/local/1986/12/30/harold-macmillan-92-former-british-prime-ministerdies/362648e9-c114-4264-8fde-4d0395c7ef1d/?utm_term=.ed608a16c72b

Socialite Rolls Himself 'Out' (25 September 1956). *Palm Beach Post*, p. 5.

Statement by Princess (1 November 1955). *The Times*, p. 8.

Sweet, Paul. 'The Windsor File.' *The Historian*, Vol. 59, Number 2, Winter 1997, p. 279.

Taylor, Paul. 'The (Teddy) Boys are back in town.' *Manchester Evening News*, 6 April 2013. Retrieved from https://www.manchestereveningnews.co.uk/news/nostalgia/teddy-boys-back-town-2522273

Teddy Boys. Brighton Museum, 26 February 2015. Retrieved from https://brightonmuseums.org.uk/discover/2015/02/26/teddy-boys/

The Coal Industry Act 1994 (Commencement No. 7) and Dissolution of the British Coal Corporation Order 2004, No. 144 (C.6). 22 May 2004. UK National Archives, 2019. Retrieved from http://www.legislation.gov.uk/uksi/2004/144/made

The Greek War In Asia Minor: Prince Andrew's History (1 July 1930). *The Times*, p. 10.

The International Year of Disabled People (14 January 1981). House of Lords Debate, Vol. 416, Column 79.

The Last Debutantes (17 July 2008). *Country Life*. Retrieved from https://www.countrylife.co.uk/out-and-about/theatre-film-music/the-last-debutantes-33059

The Monarchy Today (August 1957). *The National and English Review*, Vol. 149, No. 894, front cover.

BIBLIOGRAPHY

The Queen at 90: Memories from people around Wales (21 April 2016). BBC. Retrieved from https://www.bbc.com/news/uk-wales-36082650

The Queen at Accra Ball (20 November 1961). *The Times*, p. 8.

The Queen's dance with Dr. Nkrumah: S. African criticism (26 November 1961). *The Times*, p. 6.

The Righteous Among the Nations: Princess Alice, Greece (2019). Yad Vashem. Retrieved from https://www.yadvashem.org/righteous/stories/princess-alice.html

The Spiritual Side of Apollo 11 (2017). St Peter's Episcopal Church, Port Royal, Virginia. Retrieved from https://www.churchsp.org/spiritualsideapollo11/

Thornton, Michael. 'The royal gigolo: Edwina Mountbatten sued over claims of an affair with black singer Paul Robeson. But the truth was even more outrageous ...' *Daily Mail*, 14 November 2008. Retrieved from https://www.dailymail.co.uk/femail/article-1085883/The-royal-gigolo-Edwina-Mountbatten-sued-claims-affair-black-singer-Paul-Robeson-But-truth-outrageous-.html

—. 'David Cameron should look to Harold Macmillan for political guidance.' *The Spectator*, 21 October 2013. Retrieved from https://blogs.spectator.co.uk/2013/10/cameron-should-look-to-harold-macmillan-for-guidance/

Tingle, Rory. 'When Edward VIII went to see Hitler: Never-before-seen photos emerge for sale of Duke of Windsor's infamous trip to Nazi Germany in 1937.' *Daily Mail*, 8 October 2018. Retrieved from https://www.dailymail.co.uk/news/article-6251937/Never-seen-photos-Edward-VIII-visiting-Mercedes-Benz-factory.html

Travis, Alan. 'After 44 years secret papers reveal truth about five nights of violence in Notting Hill.' *The Guardian*, 24 August 2002. Retrieved from https://www.theguardian.com/uk/2002/aug/24/artsandhumanities.nottinghillcarnival2002

Trayner, David. 'Does this prove Jack the Ripper was member of Royal Family?' *Daily Star*, 26 February 2016. Retrieved from https://www.dailystar.co.uk/news/latest-news/497089/jack-the-ripper-prince-albert-victor-Duke-Clarence-Avondale-evidence-letters-gonorrhoea

UK inflation rate in 1973: 9.10%. Official Data Foundation, 2019. Retrieved from http://www.in2013dollars.com/UK-inflation-rate-in-1973

U.K. Ponders Moves As Suez Canal Seized (27 July 1957). *Edmonton Journal*, p. 19.

United Kingdom Marks 50th Anniversary of Death Penalty Abolition. Death Penalty Information Center, 2015. Retrieved from https://deathpenaltyinfo.org/node/6296

Wales backs Charles for king (25 June 1999). *BBC News*. Retrieved from http://news.bbc.co.uk/2/hi/uk_news/377976.stm

War Situation (4 June 1940). House of Commons Debate, Vol, 361, Columns 795–796.

Watch for bombers at Tubes, Yard says (28 December 1973). *The Times*, p. 3.

Whelan, Zara. 'Netflix's The Crown, Caernarfon and a look back to the 1969 Investiture.' *North Wales Live*, 18 November 2018. Retrieved from https://www.dailypost.co.uk/whats-on/film-news/netflixs-crown-caernarfon-look-back-15422075

Whitehall, 22 February 1957 (22 February 1957). *London Gazette*, Issue 41009, p. 1209.

Why 492 West Indians Came to Britain (23 June 1948). *The Manchester Guardian*, p. 3.

Why Margaret's Smile Is Rare These Days (24 April 1960). *Des Moines Register*, p. 1.

Williams, Janice. 'Meghan Markle will change royal views on race relations, according to Princess Diana's biographer.' *Newsweek*, 20 April 2018. Retrieved from https://www.newsweek.com/meghan-markle-race-relations-royals-894823

Wilson 'had Alzheimer's when PM' (10 November 2008). *BBC News*, 2019. Retrieved from http://news.bbc.co.uk/2/hi/health/7720200.stm

'Wilson, (James) Harold, Baron Wilson of Rievaulx (1916–1995)' by Roy Jenkins, *Oxford Dictionary of National Biography*, 7 January 2016. Retrieved from https://www.oxforddnb.com/view/10.1093/ref:odnb/9780198614128.001.0001/odnb-9780198614128-e-58000

Wilsworth, David. 'Behind the Pomp with the Royal Family: The Queen prepares salad while Anne grills steak.' *The Times*, 20 June 1969, p. 8.

Woods, Audrey. 'Princess Margaret, "one hip chick," dies.' *Everett [Washington] Herald*, 9 February 2002. Retrieved from https://www.heraldnet.com/news/princess-margaret-one-hip-chick-dies/

Wrath at the helm? (26 May 1957). *The Times*, p. 7.

Young, B. A. 'Foundation-Stones and Things.' *The National and English Review*, Vol. 149, No. 894, August 1957, p. 73.

Ziegler, Philip. 'Prime Ministers in the Post-War World: Harold Wilson.' Gresham College, 21 February 2006. Retrieved from https://www.gresham.ac.uk/lecture/transcript/print/leadership-and-change-prime-ministers-in-the-post-war-world-harold-wilson/

SCRIPTS

Aberfan: The Untold Story. BBC, 2006, 00:43. Retrieved from https://en.wikipedia.org/wiki/Aberfan_Disaster_Tribunal#cite_note-25

Elizabeth II, Queen. *Christmas Broadcast 1961*. Royal, 2019. Retrieved from https://www.royal.uk/christmas-broadcast-1961

—. *Christmas Broadcast 2004*. Royal, 2019. Retrieved from https://www.royal.uk/christmas-broadcast-2004

Epstein, Rafael. *Queen's 80th Birthday Marked by Popularity*. The World Today, 19 April 2006, 12:34:00. Retrieved from http://www.abc.net.au/worldtoday/content/2006/s1619027.htm

Milligan, Spike. *Goon Show* Script: *The Whistling Spy Enigma, Series 5, Episode 1*. The Goon Show Site, 28 September 1954. Retrieved from http://www.thegoonshow.net/scripts_show.asp?title=s05e01_the_whistling_spy_enigma

Millward, Edward. *The Real Prince Charles*. 2001.

Morgan, Peter. *The Crown,* Post Production Scripts, Episodes 201–210. Copyright NETFLIX, 2017.

—. *The Crown,* Post Production Scripts, Episodes 301–310. Copyright NETFLIX, 2019.

Osborne, John. *The Entertainer: A Full-length Play*. Woodstock: The Dramatic Publishing Company, 1957.

—. *Look Back in Anger*. New York: Penguin Books, 1982.

LECTURES

Thorpe, D. R. 'Leadership and Change: Prime Ministers in the Post-War World – Macmillan.' Lecture. Gresham College, 30 November 2005. Retrieved from http://www.gresham.ac.uk/lectures-and-events/leadership-and-change-prime-ministers-in-the-post-war-world-macmillan

Winthrop-Young, Jocelin. 'Kurt Hahn and the Pursuit of Genius.' Lecture. Round Square Conference, 28 September 2001, St Philip's College, Alice Springs, Australia. Retrieved from https://ulange.beepworld.de/files/internatesalemhahnpersnlichkeitsdefizite.pdf

ACKNOWLEDGEMENTS

T*HE CROWN* IS A PULSATING TEAM EFFORT, AND THIS BOOK has been a part of that – with its own very lively pulsations. These start at the top with Peter Morgan, our showrunner, captain of the team and inspiration for the entire project. At Left Bank Pictures, I am grateful to Andy Harries for his on-going support – along with the soothing hand-on-the-brow of Suzanne Mackie at moments of special excitement. I have greatly enjoyed the creative sparks ignited by Georgina Brown – and particularly by Annie Sulzberger, whom I must thank for her superb research. Thumbs up to Michael Foster and Jonathan Pegg for keeping the sparks to a minimum.

At Bonnier Publishing it has been a pleasure to run my words past the wry and sophisticated scrutiny of Richard Collins, under the supportive eye of managing editor Oli Holden-Rea. Thank you to Matt Inman for his transatlantic perspective

– and also to Vivien Hamley for the brilliantly researched photographs that have brought such visual life on the page to the years 1956-1977.

The back-of-the-book source notes set out the outstanding historians and biographers on whose work I have relied – a number of them personal friends – and I have been able to supplement their perspectives with first-hand contributions from the late Joe Haines, Commander Michael Parker, as well as from Francis Wyndham and other *ST Colour Mag* colleagues of our royal house photographer in the 1960s.

More recently I am grateful for the personal insights of Robert Armstrong, Lady Anne Glenconner, Andrew Lownie, and Dr. Yvonne Ward – and thank you in America to Katherine Graber and Amber Thomas, Archivist and Proxy Researcher at the Billy Graham Centre Archives, as well as to Dr. Bruce Camp for his help with the biblical references. Susan Link Camp has, as ever, been a tower of strength, particularly following our decision to display source note evidence for the book in full.

Chapter after chapter benefitted from the keen scrutiny of my friend Ben Dyal and his sharp-eyed colleague Mrs. Norris – and none of the words could have existed in the first place without the input of my warm and wise 'J.C', Jane Corrin.

The love and advice of my daughter Scarlett has been beyond price. And then there is always – and unfailingly – the love, support and inspiration of my darling Jane, the Queen of *my* life.

Robert Lacey, October 2019.

INDEX

PICTURE CREDITS